FOURTH EDITION

Communication and Gender

Lea P. Stewart
Rutgers University

Pamela J. Cooper
Northwestern University

Alan D. Stewart
Rutgers University

with

Sheryl A. Friedley
George Mason University

Boston New York San Francisco
Mexico City Montreal Toronto London Madrid Munich Paris
Hong Kong Singapore Tokyo Cape Town Sydney

Editor in Chief: *Karen Hanson*
Senior Editor: *Karon Bowers*
Editorial Assistant: *Jennifer Trebby*
Marketing Manager: *Mandee Eckersley*
Editorial Production Administrator: *Anna Socrates*
Editorial–Production Service: *Matrix Productions Inc.*
Composition and Prepress Buyer: *Linda Cox*
Manufacturing Buyer: *JoAnne Sweeney*
Cover Administrator: *Kristina Mose-Libon*
Electronic Composition: *Modern Graphics*

For related titles and support materials, visit our online catalog at www.ablongman.com.

Library of Congress Cataloging-in-Publication Data

Communication and gender/Lea P. Stewart . . . [et al.].—4th ed.
     p.   cm.
   Includes bibliographical references and index.
   ISBN 0-205-31720-0
   1. Sex role—United States.   2. Interpersonal communication—United States.
3. Stereotype (Psychology)—United States. I. Stewart, Lea.

HQ1075.5.U6 C63   2003
305.3'0973—dc21

                                                                                    2001053711

Printed in the United States of America
10 9 8 7 6 5 4 3 2 1   06 05 04 03 02

CONTENTS

PREFACE

Welcome to the fourth edition of this book, which is designed to introduce students to major concepts in communication and gender. The text surveys the literature in gender as it is affected by and affects communication behavior. In-depth coverage is given to issues of gender in language and nonverbal behavior, as well as communication and gender in friendship, courtship, marriage, family, education, media, and organizations. Students will gain a better understanding of the process of communication and how it affects the social construction of gender. Strategies for change are offered for students who wish to further explore their own communication behavior as it relates to gender.

The study of communication and gender has become a significant part of the research in the field of communication. In 1967, less than 1 percent of the articles published in major communication journals dealt with these issues. By 1986, the number of articles had increased to 7.5 percent (Cooper, Stewart & Friedley, 1989). (Although we have not conducted a formal study since then, our perception is that this number is even higher today.) Both women and men are investigating these topics; in fact, over one-fourth of the articles in this area are written solely by men. This field of research appears to be an area of study in which men and women are more likely to work *together* than in other fields. Only 12 percent of the total number of articles published in major communication journals in the 1970s and 1980s were co-written by males and females, while more than 25 percent of the articles on communication and gender were co-written by males and females. The fourth edition of this book was prepared to reflect this growing body of scholarly work.

Research on various aspects of gender continues to be a strong area of interest to scholars in the communication field. Using computer-aided techniques that were not available to Cooper, Stewart, and Friedley in 1989, Stephen (2000) examined 70 communication journals from 1962 to 1997 and found 1,136 articles dealing with the role of gender, feminism, or women's studies–related research. Although much of this work can be found in the journal *Women's Studies in Communication*, articles dealing with gender appear throughout the communication literature in journals including *Communication Education, Journal of Communication, Quarterly Journal of Speech, Public Relations Review*, and *Critical Studies in Mass Communication*.

You will see a number of important changes in this edition. Our world is constantly evolving and perhaps the most significant changes have occurred in our views of women and men. As recently as the mid-1970s, job ads in newspapers were divided by sex (jobs for men and jobs for women); it was difficult for women to obtain credit cards in their own names; organizations that offered maternity leave for new mothers did not offer comparable leave for new fathers; and the female detective was an almost unknown entity in fiction. Major changes have now occurred in each of these areas and in many more, which is a reflection of our evolving views of communication between males and females.

We have revised this book to reflect these changing views of communication and gender. In addition to updating the research presented in each chapter, we have added material on cultural, racial, and ethnic diversity, or noted the necessity for more research.

In each chapter you will encounter the feature "Consider This!" These selections reflect diverse viewpoints to challenge readers and to encourage class discussion. We believe these ideas present important points of view that are often missing from textbooks.

Each chapter closes with a set of suggested activities we call "Finding Your Voice." Students will find these hands-on activities thought-provoking.

We have annotated the "Further Reading" suggestions at the end of each chapter to give readers additional information on topics of interest.

Many people helped in the preparation of this edition. A number of students in the Department of Communication at Rutgers University helped in various stages of manuscript preparation for this edition. Emily Wexler did a wonderful job on tasks ranging from the mundane to the thoughtful. Jane-Anne Mennella contributed a paper she wrote for a senior-level communication course.

Many people provided their help when we needed it most. Tamara Conklin, of the Bahá'í World Centre in Haifa, Israel, responded to an Internet inquiry and kindly sent us the original source for some material we were seeking. Marlene Matarese is owed very special thanks for her excellent work as a research assistant who did an amazing job finding materials both quickly and competently. We extend our very special thanks to Karon Bowers from Allyn and Bacon, who inspired and motivated us to complete this edition. Our continuing thanks go to Ralph Webb, who showed us how to be scholars, taught us a deep respect for learning, and enabled us to see beyond the stereotypes.

In preparing for the fourth edition, we would like to thank the following reviewers for their helpful critiques: Victoria DeFrancisco, University of Northern Iowa; Kathryn Dindia, University of Wisconsin, Milwaukee; and Larry Lance, University of North Carolina, Charlotte.

Finally, thanks to our families and friends who loved and supported us during this project, and served as continuing reminders of the positive qualities in all of us.

1   Perspectives

In our daily lives, we encounter an ever-changing variety of communication situations. From walking down the street to speaking with a friend to asking a question or delivering a presentation in a classroom, we face an almost uncountable number of opportunities to communicate with others. These situations involve messages we communicate intentionally (such as asking a question in class) as well as messages we communicate unintentionally (such as being perceived in a particular way because of how we look). As you probably have observed, men and women may communicate differently, whether intentionally or not, and sometimes people communicate differently to women and men.

Have you ever experienced any of the following situations?

You are jogging down the street on a bright spring day. The birds are chirping and all seems right with the world. You've completed half a mile and the knee that had been bothering you feels pretty good. You start to get a little nervous, though, because you're coming up on that park. You really don't like to run past there, but there's no other way to get from your apartment to the gym without passing it. As you start to run by, it happens again. One of the people in the park starts yelling: "Hey there, cutie. Nice shorts! Whatsa matter—too stuck up to talk to us? Wanna come home with me, babe?" Your mood turns sour, and you continue your run, dreading the run back. Maybe tomorrow that guy will be someplace else when you go by. Maybe you should run at a different time.

Remember when you went to see your math T. A. because you weren't doing very well in the class? You felt pretty stupid and frustrated, but you decided you'd better see him before your grades got even worse. You couldn't make it during his office hours so you asked him after class for an appointment. He seemed a little rushed, but told you to come Tuesday at 3:00. On Tuesday, you walked over to his office with copies of all your tests so he could look at them. When you got there, a male student was talking to the T. A. about his exam. The T. A. looked up and said, "Oh, right, we had an appointment. Well, I don't have time to talk to you right now. Come back during my office hours."

What about the time you were working on that group project? Remember the first meeting? You decided to make some popcorn because you wanted the group to be friends, not just people who got stuck together and had to do a project. Everybody seemed to like the popcorn, but no one seemed to like your ideas. It was difficult to pin down, but something was wrong. Every time you said something, Brian interrupted and then Mark told Steve what a great idea he had. You really didn't want to do the typing, but everybody voted on the idea so fast that you couldn't say no. Now that you think about it, the guys kept leaning forward and blocking your view. And, of course, whenever Mark had a point to make, his voice just got louder and louder until everyone else stopped to listen to him.

Do any of these situations sound familiar to you? Can you remember similar situations happening in your life? If you are a woman, you are probably nodding in agreement. Although you may not have experienced these exact situations, you may remember some that are similar—situations in which you were hassled on the street, ignored in favor of a man, or subtly discouraged from participating in a group. If you are a man, you may not be able to identify as strongly with these situations. You may never have been a victim of street harassment. If you are interested in math, you probably were encouraged to pursue that interest. Groups usually listen to your ideas and give you credit for them.

Now imagine the following situations:

You are involved in a relationship with someone you really like, but you can't figure out what's going wrong. Something seems to be the matter, but no matter what you try, you can't seem to make the other person happy. You go out to nice places, bring flowers, offer compliments, but the other person is just not satisfied and always wants to talk about "your relationship." You're happy in this relationship so you just don't see the point of always talking about it.

Remember the last time you were with a group of your friends talking about music? You disagreed on some topic. Everyone had an opinion. You were just getting into a lively discussion when someone walked in and told you to quiet down. You couldn't figure out what the problem was because you were just having a friendly discussion.

The person you are dating is always telling you to be more sensitive. You're not sure exactly what is wanted, but you try. One day, you learn that your best friend has been in a very bad car accident and may not survive. You just lose it. You can't stop crying. You're really upset and can't get yourself together. Another of your friends is at first sympathetic, but after a while, becomes uncomfortable and wants you to pull yourself together. But you can't. You wonder, isn't this what being sensitive is all about?

Do any of these situations sound familiar to you? Can you remember similar situations happening in your life? If you are a man, you are probably nodding in agreement. Although you may not have experienced these exact situations, you probably remember situations that are similar: situations in which you wanted to have a relationship and not analyze it, situations in which you raised your voice in a discussion without intending to signal that you were angry, or situations in which people felt uncomfortable when you lost control even though you thought that was what they wanted. If you are a woman, it may seem natural to you to talk about relationships. You may only raise your voice when you are very upset about something. And no one gets uncomfortable when you cry a lot.

When we were first writing this book, a very perceptive reviewer suggested that we begin this chapter in an unexpected way for a gender textbook, that is, with the male examples first. We thought about this suggestion for a long time, but decided against it. But we wanted to share with you our thinking on this issue because it brings up important points for you to think about while reading. First, this book is about gender and communication, which means that we are concerned with how both men *and* women communicate. We want men as well as women to learn something about themselves as they read this book. Nevertheless, we are mindful of the fact that in the past the woman's point of view has often been minimized or even ignored in many textbooks. So we decided to open this chapter with situations we thought women were more likely to identify with, followed by situations men were more likely to identify with.

Of course, since women and men share many of the same experiences in our society, you may have identified with both sets of examples. One of the objectives in writing this book is to help you explore why you may or may not be able to identify with these situations and others like them: the hundreds of communicative experiences each day that shape our identities as men and women.

Working Definitions

As human beings, we are born with certain biological characteristics that are considered in society to be male or female. With rare exceptions, people are labeled according to their biological sex at birth, or even before birth. We will use the term *sex* when referring to the biological and physiological characteristics that make us male or female (Ivy & Backlund, 1994). **Sex differences** can be defined as *"biological differences in genetic composition and reproductive anatomy and function"* (Unger & Crawford, 1992, p. 17). Although biological sex is certainly important, current theory contends that relatively few attributes of human behavior or communication are innate, that is, determined by our biological sex. For example, men generally have lower voices than women, but some women have very low voices, and physical conditions such as a cold or special training can change vocal range.

The vast majority of our communication behavior is learned. We are all born into a culture, and that culture has a significant effect on our communication. Culture helps shape the rules and norms for our communication behavior. Through the socialization process we learn culturally defined guidelines for our behavior, including the overall communication behavior our culture defines as appropriate for men or for women.

Of course, in most cultures many individual communicative behaviors are appropriate for both men and women. For example, speakers of the English language raise their voices at the end of a sentence to signal that they are asking a question. Both men and women use this rising intonation to express a question.

While the term *sex* can be used to divide male and female animals from any species, *gender* "is a distinction that is specific and unique to human beings" (Lott, 2000, p. 112). **Gender** refers to *the social construction of masculinity and femininity within a culture*. As Unger and Crawford (1992) note, "gender is what culture makes out of the 'raw material' of biological sex" (p. 18). Communication behaviors that are socially constructed as appropriate for women and men are labeled *feminine* and *masculine*. All cultures have a gender system that functions to construct what it means to be feminine or masculine. As Rakow (1986) notes:

> Gender . . . is usefully conceptualized as a culturally constructed organization of biology and social life into particular ways of doing, thinking, and experiencing the world. . . . It is in communication that this gender system is accomplished. Gender has meaning, is organized and structured, and takes place as interaction and social practice, all of which are communication processes. That is, communication creates genders who create communication. (p. 23)

Thus gender is a socially constructed phenomenon.

Lott (2000) notes that theorists have examined gender from three perspectives: "(1) as a system of social relationships in which gender interacts with, and influences, institutional structures; (2) as what people 'do' in social interactions in accord with norms about what is appropriate for them; and (3) as an attribute used by individuals for self-identification within their culture" (p. 112). In addition, feminist theorists would contend that gender emerges from a social system of inequality in which some people are permitted to have more power than others.

Another important concept to consider is gender identity. **Gender identity** *"includes psychosexual development, learning social roles, and shaping sexual preferences"* (Lorber & Farrell, 1991, p. 7). Thorne (1993) reminds us that children do not merely learn their gender identities; they are active participants in creating them in a social context. Thorne contends that instead of asking "Are girls and boys different?" the more significant question is, "How do children actively come together to help create, and sometimes challenge, gender structures and meanings?" (p. 4).

Gendered Communication

As children develop their gender identities, they come to communicate in culturally defined feminine and masculine ways. These communication behaviors continue during adulthood. In North American culture, for example, some women find it acceptable and enjoyable to talk about their relationships; men can find it socially safe in a gathering of male strangers to talk about sports or politics. But both male and female parents often talk about their children. In other cultures, men may be encouraged to display public signs of emotion in particular circumstances or women may be expected to cover their faces in public.

Analyzing gendered communication as socially constructed does not mean that all women or all men behave similarly or that there is no similarity between women and men. We are all members of multiple cultural groups that influence our behavior and the behavior of others toward us. Societal changes that affect one group to which we belong may have no impact on us because of our membership in some other group. For example, many of the recent changes in the U.S. socioeconomic system have affected a comparatively small portion of the population. While large numbers of Euroamerican, middle-class women and many Asian Indian women are pursuing job opportunities outside the home, other groups of women continue to define their primary responsibilities as centered in their homes.

As noted earlier, there are many similarities in the communication behaviors of men and women; in fact, some researchers argue that men and women overlap in their communication actions 99 percent of the time (Canary & Hause, 1993). For example, individual women and men may be assertive or soft-spoken. Men frequently talk about their families, and women may talk about sports. The degree of similarity between men and women in gendered behavior varies from culture to culture. In some cultures, women and men dress very differently and have vastly different social responsibilities. At the opposite end of the continuum, an anthropologist has discovered a gender-egalitarian society of people on a South Pacific island in which women and men live and work as virtual equals in all aspects of the society (Wilford, 1994).

Because gendered communication behavior is socially constructed, it may change over time as our conceptions of gender change (Ivy & Backlund, 1994). For example, the role of women in our society has changed tremendously over the years. In the early 1800s it was thought inappropriate for women in the United States to speak at public gatherings. And until recently, women were expected to be the primary caretakers of young children. Now more and more women are pursuing careers outside the home, and men, who were once seen primarily as the sole source of financial support for their families, are taking a more active role in day-to-day parenting. These changing social roles are accompanied by changes in communication behavior. It is no longer unusual to see women anchoring network television newscasts or to hear men discussing the paternity leave policies of the companies where they work. Read "Consider This: Genders in Transition" for a demonstration of some of these changes.

In any gendered system, however, some communicative behaviors are associated with males or with females, although such associations are not necessarily accurate reflections of individual behavior. For example, women may be viewed as having less mechanical aptitude than men. We all know women who are more adept with tools and machinery than some men, but the stereotype still exists. In the United States, it is seen as masculine to be interested in sports, but many men have neither the desire nor the ability to participate in or even to talk about these activities.

Stereotypes *exist when a large portion of a society agrees that certain traits or behaviors are commonly associated with a given group of people* (Harriman, 1985). Stereotypes may have some basis in reality and may help us to understand our social world better,

CONSIDER THIS!
Genders in Transition

For every woman who is tired of acting weak when she knows she is strong, there is a man who is tired of appearing strong when he feels vulnerable.

For every woman who is tired of acting dumb, there is a man who is burdened with the constant expectation of "knowing everything."

For every woman who is tired of being called "an emotional female," there is a man who is denied the right to weep and to be gentle.

For every woman who is called unfeminine when she competes, there is a man for whom competition is the only way to prove his masculinity.

For every woman who feels "tied down" by her children, there is a man who is denied the full pleasure of shared parenthood.

For every woman who is denied meaningful employment or equal pay, there is a man who must bear full financial responsibility for another human being.

For every woman who was not taught the intricacies of an automobile, there is a man who was not taught the satisfaction of cooking.

For every woman who takes a step toward her own liberation, there is a man who finds the way to freedom has been made easier.

Smith, 1994

but they may not be accurate descriptions of particular individuals. Nevertheless, stereotypes persist and gender stereotypes affect our perceptions and, consequently, our communication with others. For example, a male nurse is employed in a profession traditionally occupied by women and, therefore, may be seen as violating a gender stereotype. He is filling a nurturing, caretaking role that is seen as inappropriate for men, according to traditional gender ideology. Nursing continues to be a female-dominated profession in part because many men are unwilling to violate this gender stereotype.

Some authors prefer to use the term **ideology** to describe the *"collection of related beliefs about women and men" in society* (Lott, 2000, p. 113). These beliefs about gender influence individuals' behavior. In the United States, for example, our gender ideology includes the belief that men and women have different attitudes toward domestic responsibilities. The relationship between gender ideology and behavior is not a simple one, however. Behavior may be influenced by what we believe about women and men but can also be influenced by what we think will be the consequences of "our actions in light of a prevailing set of gender beliefs and further, in which beliefs are influenced by the actions we observe ourselves and others engaged in" (Lott, 2000, p. 114). In other words, our personal experience is mediated by our beliefs about gender.

You may be asking yourself how gender influences communication behavior, or how does gender ideology affect interactions. Although these concepts will be explained in more detail in Chapter 2, three critical questions should be remembered when examining communication:

1. Which aspects of gender ideology are important factors affecting our communication?
2. What are the implications and consequences of gender ideology in our everyday interactions?
3. What can be done to change gendered communicative behaviors that have negative consequences for individuals?

Throughout this book we will examine what researchers have learned about gender ideology in communication, and we will attempt to answer these questions. One way to begin finding answers is to examine some of the settings in which communication occurs. But before we do that we need to clarify our definition of communication.

Approaches to Studying Communication

The word *communication* is abstract and, like many words, has multiple meanings. It is not our purpose to argue the advantages and disadvantages of various definitions, but merely to note their complexity. In this book, we will use **communication** to mean *the creation of meaning through messages or symbolic cues, both verbal and nonverbal.* In our view, verbal communication is linguistic, or language-centered, including both the spoken word and sign language. Nonverbal communication is nonlinguistic, consisting of cues that are not words. Nonverbal symbolic cues include proxemics (the use of space), physical characteristics (such as height, weight, facial features), artifacts (such as jewelry, makeup, clothing), body movement, touching behavior, and paralanguage (such as voice qualities and characteristics).

Social interaction, created through communication, allows us to convey our own identity and to convey our expectations for others' identities. Because all identities are based in part on how people communicate with us, and because people communicate differently to males and females in some contexts, as noted earlier, communication plays a key role in the development of our gender identity.

In a process-centered view, each person in a communication event defines the other person and the relationship between them. They communicate how they view one another and the relationship between them. For example, if Michelle smiles when she meets David and says, "Hi, how are you?" and David answers, "Fine, thanks," but frowns and moves hurriedly on, David defines the relationship at that point in time. His words imply a greeting, yet his expression and his actions define the relationship (at least for the moment) in a negative way: he does not want to talk to Michelle. This interaction may affect Michelle's gender identity. Her friendly greeting and smile are not reciprocated by the male she is addressing. She may feel rejected and decide to be less friendly in future encounters with males. Or she may label David "a jerk" and avoid speaking to him again.

People with different social experiences may construct different meanings in the same situation. One possible interpretation of the above situation is that Michelle has a traditionally feminine gender identity and expected David to react to her friendly greeting in a positive way. When this reaction did not occur, Michelle assumed her greeting was somehow inadequate and decided to be even friendlier in future encounters with David. David, on the other hand, may have a traditionally masculine gender identity and did not realize that his greeting was abrupt or dismissive of Michelle. The next time he sees her, he will be surprised if she is angry with him.

Perceptions of a relationship message and the communication event as a whole on the part of the people involved in the event will affect subsequent communication between them. Events may have multiple interpretations. Michelle may not perceive the preceding transaction as one in which David did not want to talk to her. She may perceive that David thought she was someone else or that he was just in a hurry to get to class. But if Michelle interprets the relationship as negative and thinks, for example, that David is angry with her, this perception will affect the way Michelle interacts with David on subsequent occasions. Perception is affected by a number of variables including values, beliefs, self-concept, communication skill, and knowledge. For example, as we will see in Chapter 7, adolescent girls' low self-concept of their mathematical abilities may affect their perception of a teacher's communication with them as well as their achievement in math, while teachers' expectations of male students may affect the amount of discipline they receive in the classroom.

Scholars who study the communication process contend that perceptions can be affected by the context in which the communication occurs. Context includes such variables as the physical setting in which the interaction occurs, the people involved in the interaction, the time of the interaction, and cultural influences. For example, it is not uncommon for couples in two-career marriages to have many disagreements concerning responsibility for household duties such as making dinner or shopping for groceries. A husband who believes that housework is primarily a woman's job probably will not be overly eager to help with household chores, and will be in conflict with a wife who believes that household duties should be shared because she has a job outside the home, too. In this case, the couple views household tasks as gendered.

Settings for Social Interaction

Gender is an important influence in many settings in which social interaction or communication occurs. Being female or male places us in one of the most important social groups to which each of us belongs. Men and women may communicate differently in intimate relationships such as friendship and marriage. For example, many women share a number of intimate details of their personal lives with each other, such as how they feel about relationships. When talking to men, women may be more likely to provide conversational support by asking questions and generally keeping the conversation going. Men are more likely to try to change the subject when they feel the conversation has become too personal too quickly.

When we categorize others according to what we believe is masculine or feminine, this social grouping is based on ideological perceptions of qualities that are thought to belong to males and females. For example, a teacher may criticize a male child more harshly than a female child because "he needs the discipline." The teacher is grouping male and female students into masculine or feminine categories and modifying communication behavior toward the students based on this grouping.

Lott (2000) refers to these differential responses as an ideology of difference. She argues that "gender is the imposition of cultural meaning onto reproductive distinctiveness," and "an ideology of difference serves inequality and power differentials through its proscriptions and prescriptions, by limiting our vision and restricting our possibilities" (p. 118). In addition, relying on gender ideology may lead to confusion since people often do not behave according to our gendered beliefs. Throughout this book, we will be presenting often contradictory research results that will confirm this contention.

Categorizations based on gender occur in many aspects of our lives. Our first experience with social categorization occurs in the family. The degree to which your parents modified their communication behavior toward you based on your gender influenced your developing gender identity. As a child, were you encouraged to do the dishes, play with toy soldiers, wear pretty dresses, or learn to defend yourself? Were you told how pretty you were or how tough you were? If adults interacted with you based on their perceptions of appropriate behavior for your gender, this behavior affected your gender identity and, consequently, your communication behavior. We will discuss these issues in Chapter 6.

The educational setting, discussed in Chapter 7, provides another situation in which people react to others on the basis of gender. Teachers sometimes treat boys and girls differently. Some textbooks still portray boys and girls or men and women differently (Sadker & Sadker, 1994). Perhaps you remember elementary schoolbooks that depicted Mom staying home and Dad going to work. These early experiences helped to shape your view of appropriate communication behavior for men and women. In many ways these stereotypes continue across all educational levels, including college.

The media, discussed in Chapter 8, can also portray men and women according to stereotypical images. Some advertisers still try to make women feel guilty about their weight and to make men feel that the only way to have a good time is by choosing the right beer. While it is now common, until recently it was difficult to find a television situation comedy in which a woman worked outside the home. Many people watch reruns of *The Brady Bunch* and other television shows that depict men and women in gender-stereotypic roles. And a number of men on television still spend most of their time hitting people with their fists or driving expensive cars very fast. Even the music we hear every day often reinforces these stereotypic images.

The occupational setting, discussed in Chapter 9, is another area in which gender issues in communication are important. In general, large numbers of women are employed in organizations, but traditionally men have run the organizations and establish the norms for effective communication behavior. Women may find it difficult to gain access to certain occupations. Some employees communicate differently with male and female supervisors, and some supervisors use a different communicative style with male and female employees. In corporate settings, men and women may face additional challenges. Some women bump their heads against the glass ceiling of corporate success, while some men are hesitant to take advantage of parental-leave policies.

Thus we believe that gender affects and is affected by communication in different contexts. Five of the important settings in which gender has a major impact on our communication are friendship, marriage, educational settings, the media, and organizations. By examining some of the various settings in which communication occurs, we can determine how gender affects our communication and how our gender identity is developed through communication. In addition, after examining the implications and consequences of these effects, we may be able to change some of the gender ideologies that have negative consequences for people interacting in these settings.

Our Perspective

As you can see from this discussion, we are concerned with how gender identity is constructed and with how gender affects communication in various contexts. You probably can think of a great deal of evidence from your own experience that suggests how men and women have learned to communicate or how their communication is perceived in various situations. Many of your observations are supported by evidence from research. In the chapters that follow, we analyze, discuss, and synthesize the results of much of this research.

Given our experiences and the research we have examined, we believe that there are three important areas to consider when discussing gender ideologies that affect communication in various contexts. First, to understand communication more fully, we need to know *what behavior exists* (that is, the ways in which men and women communicate) and *what types of gender ideology occur* (that is, how people communicate differently based on their expectations of stereotypically masculine or feminine communication behavior).

In addition to knowing how gender ideologies affect communication, we need to know the *implications* and *consequences* of these behaviors. In other words, how are men and women affected by the actual or perceived differences in their communication behaviors? We know, for example, that women who use more stereotypically feminine speech (such as starting sentences with "I think" or "perhaps") are perceived as less certain of their ideas, while men who use these same speech forms are often considered polite. In the workplace, employees report that they are more satisfied with supervisors who use more gender-stereotypic communication patterns. Male supervisors generally are expected to be assertive, and female supervisors are expected to be more friendly. Employees report that they are not as willing to respect friendly male supervisors or assertive female supervisors. Thus, gender ideologies have certain consequences that need to be understood. "Consider This: The Changing Role of Fathers" illustrates one of the consequences of gender stereotyping.

Finally, although gender ideologies may affect our communication in particular ways, these behaviors can be changed. We need to explore *strategies* that can be used

CONSIDER THIS!

The Changing Role of Fathers

Yes—it's true: mothers change lots of diapers. But in today's world, fathers are changing their infants' diapers, too. And, given the predictable nature of infants' needs, some of this diaper changing occurs in public places like shopping malls, restaurants, parks, and zoos. But are these accommodations ready for the father who has to diaper a baby? Apparently not, according to several sources ("Dads Change Diapers," 1989) and some personal observation. Although there has been some progress in this area, most baby-changing facilities in public places are located in or near women's rest rooms making it difficult for fathers on their own to find a suitable place to diaper their children.

to improve our communication environment. For example, sexist language that perpetuates gender inequities can be eliminated. Teachers should encourage participation from all students in their classes. Men and women can learn to appreciate each other's communication in intimate relationships.

Throughout this book we include commentaries regarding communication and gender. Called "Consider This!" these readings will challenge your thinking about gender and communication in our world.

We hope that after reading this book you have a clearer understanding of the nature of the issues involved in gender ideologies in various communication settings. We hope you will be able to use some of the strategies we suggest to become more aware of your own communication behavior and how it can influence others.

FINDING YOUR VOICE

1. In a group of four to five people, list as many differences between men and women and between boys and girls as you can in 30 minutes. List any differences that come to mind. You can include differences in communication behavior (for example, males talk louder than females) and differences in other areas (for example, women earn less money than men; boys are more aggressive than girls). After 30 minutes, each group should write its list on the chalkboard under the headings *Males* and *Females*. After these lists are compiled, discuss each item individually. Decide whether the item is based on biological differences between males and females (for example, on average, men are taller than women), on culturally constructed gender roles (for example, men tend to talk about sports more than women do), or on gender stereotypes (for example, women gossip more than men do; men are less sensitive than women are). What are the implications of each of the items on your list for communication and gender?

2. Take the list you compiled in Activity 1 and categorize each item in terms of communication setting: Does the behavior occur primarily in friendships, marriage, educational

environments, the media, or organizations? Do gender stereotypes occur in a particular setting or across all settings? What types of gender stereotyping occur most frequently in each setting? What are the implications of your observations for communication between females and males in these settings?

3. Make a list of the communication settings you encounter each day. How do gender stereotypes influence your communication in each of these settings? Do others communicate with you differently in particular settings based on gender stereotypes? In which settings do gender stereotypes seem to have the greatest effect? Why?

4. Have a male and a female in your class role-play a married couple buying a car together. Have another student play the role of salesperson. Observe their behavior and list those individual behaviors that are based on gender stereotypes. Have the same students reenact the situation with the male playing the wife's role and the female playing the husband's role. Which behaviors do you feel are based on gender stereotypes? How did the car salesperson react to the couple in each situation? How do gender and gender stereotypes affect our communication in this type of situation?

5. Reread the examples of uncomfortable situations discussed at the beginning of this chapter. Describe situations in which you feel uncomfortable because you are male or female. Describe situations you think make students of the other sex uncomfortable. In what types of communication settings are men and women more likely to feel uncomfortable? Why? Would these situations make you feel uncomfortable if you had a different gender identity? What steps can be taken by each person involved to make these situations more comfortable?

FURTHER READING

Arliss, L. P., & Borisoff, D. J. (Eds.). (2001). *Women and men communicating: Challenges and changes*, 2nd ed. Prospect Heights, IL: Waveland.
This book contains a group of readings examining changing communication contexts as women become more involved in the public sphere of society and as men work to become more nurturing and vulnerable in their relationships.

hooks, b. (1984). *Feminist theory: From margin to center*. Boston, MA: South End Press.
Noted feminist theorist bell hooks proposes new directions for feminist theory that include the experiences of African American women and men.

Kramarae, C., & Spender, D. (Eds.). (1992). *The knowledge explosion: Generations of feminist scholarship*. New York: Teachers College Press.
This group of essays chronicles the changes in academic disciplines (including journalism and mass communication) since the development of the women's studies field. The book includes a discussion of the major debates in feminist scholarship today.

Segal, L. (1990). *Slow motion: Changing masculinities, changing men*. New Brunswick, NJ: Rutgers University Press.
Segal traces the changing roles of men beginning in the 1950s, examining such issues as looking back in anger and looking beyond the gender hierarchy. The author poses, and answers, the question: Can men change?

CHAPTER

2 Gender Identity

When people learn that they are parents-to-be, they begin to impart an identity to the unborn child. The importance of that identity may differ from one parent to another, but it most likely will include masculine or feminine characteristics. With modern medical technology, a parent-to-be may know the sex of a child several months before its birth and begin thinking about the child as a boy or girl. In most cultures, children are given a name at birth that usually indicates their sex, thus beginning the distinction between males and females in our society (Smith, 1985).

This distinction can lead to a polarization in which "men and women are placed at opposite ends of the humanity pole" (Canary & Hause, 1993, p. 136). In recent years, however, research has sought to explain why people communicate the way they do by searching beyond the idea of gender differences and traditional masculine and feminine roles. Researchers have focused on the social constructs of gender rather than on biological distinctions. This research has begun to lead us away from the rigid definitions of feminine and masculine that often result in sexism and gender ideology detrimental to everyone. Instead, this research is exploring new horizons in the study of gender identity. By studying gender identity and its development, we have been able to provide more accurate descriptions and explanations of human rather than simply *male* and *female* communication behavior.

In this chapter, we examine various theoretical explanations for the development of gender identity. We then discuss the influence of gender ideology on communication and propose several strategies for changing traditional gendered behaviors. You will see how earlier polarized explanations have given way to theories that attempt to bring together instead of divide women and men.

Theoretical Explanations for Gender Development

As discussed in Chapter 1, gender *is the social construction of masculinity and femininity within a culture*. Gender refers to a person's psychological, social, and interactive characteristics (Pearson & Davilla, 1993). Scholars in many academic fields have explored the nature of gender and how it develops. Generally, three major theoretical explanations have been posited: biological, psychological, and social. The next few sections will discuss each of these theoretical perspectives providing a review of historical background followed by a look at current theories.

Theories help us describe and explain phenomena that we observe in our everyday life. Lugones and Spelman (1983) propose the following criteria for judging good theories:

1. The theory or account can be helpful if it enables one to see how parts of one's life fit together, for example, to see connections among parts of one's life one hasn't seen before.
2. A useful theory will help one locate oneself concretely in the world, rather than add to the mystification of the world and one's location in it.
3. A theory or account not only ought to accurately locate one in the world but also enable one to think about the extent to which one is responsible or not for being in that location. . . . A useful theory will help people sort out just what is and is not due to themselves and their own activities as opposed to those who have power over them. (p. 578)

Try to use Lugones and Spelman's criteria to judge the usefulness of each of the following theories to your understanding of the development of your own gender identity.

Most psychological and behavioral differences between women and men are socially constructed. For example, almost every culture has a gendered division of labor (Kon, 1975). Although some of these divisions can be explained by physical differences (men may do tasks that demand greater physical strength), other divisions are not so easily explained. Historically, in some societies men have been the wood carvers while women were the grain millers. Although some jobs are segregated by sex within many societies, the variations among societies can be great. Thus, different conceptions of gender have developed in various societies through the communication process.

Although we agree that gender is socially constructed, it is important to review biological theories for historical perspective.

Biological Theories

Traditional Perspective

In early and now-rejected theories, gender was viewed as based on a biological dichotomy of male versus female. Theorists who held this view believed that women and men differed substantially on a wide variety of personality traits, attitudes, and interests that, to a large degree, were biologically based and, therefore, believed to be innate. These theorists believed that males and females had a psychological *need* to develop either masculine or feminine traits, including different communication behaviors. Individuals who did not develop the so-called appropriate characteristics were seen as having profound difficulties in their personality and life adjustment. According to this traditional perspective, psychological differences between the men and women as well as the individual's psychological need to develop and maintain a normal identity simultaneously accounted for and justified traditional divisions of work and family responsibilities by gender (Pleck, 1977, pp. 183–184). For example, men became mechanics because they were inherently mechanical while women were primary caregivers because they were innately nurturing.

Obviously, relying on this traditional perspective of gender leads to gender stereotyping that encourages people to view others as members of rigid categories

CONSIDER THIS!

Jane-Anne Mennella Reminds Us That "I Can Fix Cars, Too"

I took auto shop in high school and although I don't know everything about cars, I know enough so that I won't get ripped off by mechanics, and if I got stuck somewhere I could help myself. . . . My older sister likes fixing cars and is so skilled that she got offered a scholarship to one of the best automotive schools in the nation. My brother tends to be good at anything that involves technology, but he occasionally asks my sister or me what we think. I am not handy with tools or anything like that; I just know how an engine works and sometimes why it doesn't.

My mother loves to tell the story about when my track coach's truck wouldn't start and he was waiting for me to come out of the locker room to look at it. My sister, who had come to pick me up, got to it first and by the time I had changed my clothes, his truck was running—much to the admiration of the guys standing around it.

When I got to college though and people found out I knew something about cars, I began to receive weird reactions. As a freshman, I was sitting out on the front steps of my dorm with a group of friends when we noticed an elderly man's car wouldn't start. I took a look, saw it was a loose cable, and hooked it back up. The man thanked me and drove away, ending what I thought was a trivial incident. A couple of days later, I learned that the story had gotten around and people were asking, "Does she look like a guy?" and "Is she a lesbian?" I was shocked that other students thought I would look a certain way or made assumptions about my sexual orientation just because I knew how a battery should be connected.

Another time I was telling someone in class how I had suggested that my brother prime a new fuel pump with a turkey baster. A female student sitting in front of us (a stranger to me) turned around and said, "Aren't you afraid guys won't want to date you if you know more about cars than they do?" I have two replies to that question. The first is that a secure person wouldn't care if I knew more about something than he or she did, especially cars, and the second is, who decided that cars are a "guy thing"?

It bothers and fascinates me that people question that I know something about cars. I took auto shop so I wouldn't have to rely on a stranger if I got stuck one day. I didn't learn about cars because I want to intimidate men, and I don't believe that because I'm a female I can't understand cars. What I can't understand is why people don't realize it is logical for me to have knowledge that saves me a lot of time and money and also helps protect my safety. Why isn't this logical to everyone else?

Mennella, 1994

rather than as individuals with unique human qualities. Gender ideology assigns individuals inflexible role prescriptions that dictate communication behavior.

When gender ideology leads to **sexism**—*discrimination against people on the basis of their sex*—the result is detrimental to everyone. For example, companies are required by law (the 1993 Family and Medical Leave Act—see DiMona & Herndon, 1994) to grant employees unpaid, job-protected leave for family care (such as the birth, adoption, or serious illness of a child), but many men are still hesitant to take advantage of their company's family-leave policy for fear of negative perceptions on the part of management and the impact such perceptions could have on their careers.

From your own experience you may have noticed that, in most situations, rigid differences between individuals' behavior are not the norm. For example, some men are very nurturing, and some women have powerful leadership qualities. In reality, there is a greater overlap of behaviors between men and women than is predicted by the traditional perspective.

Newer Perspective

A newer perspective on gender development has evolved from studies that focus on the social construction of gender. This perspective recognizes the existence of some biologically based differences, but also emphasizes the importance of the social environment in shaping behavior and deemphasizes the idea that behavior is biologically determined.

Nevertheless, some research concerning the structure of the brain and its effect on female and male hormonal differences supports the claim that males and females are physiologically different in some ways. Obvious biological differences include physical size, anatomy, and sexual organs. Recent research on the brain has discovered several differences between males and females.

Kimura (2000) notes that researchers have found that the right cortex is thicker in males' brains than the left cortex, leading researchers to conclude that "the two hemispheres are more asymmetrically organized for speech and spatial functions in men than in women" (p. 72). Parts of the corpus callosum (connecting the two hemispheres) are thought to be more extensive in women. Nevertheless, as Kimura points out, the evidence that these anatomical differences lead directly to behavior differences is "meager and conflicting." In other words, we cannot conclude that any difference in brain structure is responsible for communication differences between women and men.

A difference that may have significance for communication is the variation in maturation rates between males and females. In general, beginning before birth, female physical development advances more quickly than that of males. As Tibbetts (1976) notes, "this acceleration in the rate of growth is maintained by the female . . . to the age of 17 1/2 years" (p. 31). Remember how many girls were taller than the boys in elementary school? Differences in maturation rates may affect development of skills to a greater or lesser degree in males and females. For example, Firester and Firester (1974) describe the impact of maturation differences on the physiological capability of manual dexterity:

The female superiority in wrist movement, fine finger movement, and manual dexterity continues throughout childhood. At age two the girl is biologically six months older than the boy. This difference continues to increase until, by the age of thirteen, the girl is biologically two years older than the boy. (p. 31)

A variety of social consequences may result from a simple physiological difference such as manual dexterity. For example, girls may be rewarded in school for displaying neatness in such tasks as coloring, drawing, and handwriting. Boys, on the other hand, may be labeled messy, clumsy, or even inept simply because they do not possess the same level of motor-skill development (Simmons & Whitfield, 1979).

Because the potential impact of labeling such as this by peers and adults can be significant, the development of gender identity is not simply a consequence of nature or biologically based differences, but results from culturally based interactions. The socialization process that enhances the development of a child's gender identity is inherently tied to the communication process; communication is the medium through which this socialization occurs. We will examine this concept more fully in the next section when we discuss psychological theories of gender development. It is important to remember that although biology influences the threshold at which given behaviors appear, these thresholds can be and often are altered by social influences.

Psychological Theories

Freudian Identification Theory

The earliest psychological theory of gender development that we will discuss is *identification theory*, which has its origins in Freudian psychoanalytic theory. Freud postulated that identification with a same-sex parent–model was "the means by which each child acquires the behaviors which society would require of her or him as an adult" (Frieze, Parsons, Johnson, Ruble, & Zellman, 1978, p. 97). Freud believed that the type of identification experienced by a child was determined by whether the child was male or female. According to this theory, male development was controlled by defensive identification (fear of retaliation from a powerful figure) while female development resulted from anaclitic identification (fear of loss of love). According to Freud, identification with the same-sex parent was the mechanism that explained how children acquired appropriate gender behaviors (Kessler & McKenna, 1978). As Frieze and colleagues (1978) note, "sex differences in behavior were seen [by Freud] as the direct, irreversible consequence of perceived and actual anatomical differences" (p. 97).

Freud's theory has been widely criticized among other things for its assumption that women are biologically inferior to men. Frieze and colleagues (1978) conclude that:

Freud's theories provide us with an instructive example of masculine bias. The essence of this bias is that the female is seen as an inadequate male. There are a number of problems with this approach, the main one being that a woman is not a man. Males and females exist with certain inherent and socially conditioned differences. Assigning one sex a higher value than the other seems a useless exercise. (pp. 33–34)

Social Interaction Theories

Many psychological theorists reject identification theory and believe instead that gender is shaped through our interactions with others in society. According to these theories, systematic attempts to influence the behaviors of females and males begin at birth. **Socialization**—*the process by which children acquire the values and behaviors seen as appropriate for their gender*—has been examined by many researchers. According to Bandura (1969):

> Sex-role differentiation usually commences immediately after birth, when the baby is named and both the infant and the nursery are given the blue or pink treatment, depending upon the sex of the child. Thereafter, indoctrination into masculinity and femininity is diligently promulgated by adorning children with distinctive clothes and hair styles, selecting sex-appropriate play materials and recreational activities, promotion [of] associations with same-sex playmates, and through non-permissive parental reactions to deviant sex-role behavior. (p. 215)

Scholars interested in the impact of socialization on gender have focused their attention on the mechanism by which individuals acquire a gender identity. The two major theories that attempt to explain gender from this perspective are social learning theory and cognitive developmental theory. Proponents of these theories believe that same-sex modeling observed through communication with others is crucial to the process of gender development.

Social Learning Theory

According to **social learning theory,** *information provided by same-sex models both at home and in the media, along with reinforcement for gender-appropriate behaviors from significant others, serves as the foundation for acquiring gender.* This theory is that "boy-like" and "girl-like" behaviors are shaped by significant others during the preschool years. For example, this theory emphasizes the important modeling a mother provides her daughter when she buys the groceries, prepares the meals, or works outside the home. Likewise, when a father repairs the car, leaves home to go to work, or runs the vacuum cleaner he provides his son modeling behavior for masculinity. Children adopt gendered behaviors when they are rewarded for performing culturally appropriate behaviors and punished for culturally inappropriate behaviors (Frieze et al., 1978). For example, a little girl playing dress-up may be admired while a little boy who puts on makeup and tries on a pair of his mother's high heels may be scolded. (See "Consider This: The Risky Business of Raising Sons" for an example.) According to Kessler and McKenna (1978):

> Eventually, through differential reinforcements from parents, teachers, peers, and others, children begin to know what they can and cannot do. They begin to anticipate

CONSIDER THIS!

The Risky Business of Raising Sons

One day Djasi wanted to wear a skirt. A woman had given it to me as a gift while I was pregnant, and I never got rid of it. It was in a drawer. He found it and said, "Oh, this is a skirt and it's for me and I want to wear it." And he tried it on in the house, but then I had to explain to him that he couldn't wear it outside. I said that most of the time men didn't wear dresses and so it wasn't a common thing for people to do and I thought we should give the skirt to the little girl who was a friend of his. And he said fine and we did that. I really didn't know what to do. There is no right answer.

Aria, 1993

the consequences of various behaviors, and they begin to value gender "appropriate" behaviors because they are rewarded and to devalue gender "inappropriate" behaviors because they are punished or ignored. The child learns the label ("boy" or "girl") appropriate to the rewarded behaviors, and learns to apply that label to her/himself. (p. 92)

Reinforcement for so-called "gender-appropriate" behavior begins at birth. For example, male and female adults in a research study were asked to respond to a nine-month-old infant (on videotape) who was reacting to an emotional stimulus. Half the adults were told that they were observing a female infant and half were told that they were observing a male infant. The adults consistently reported that the "boy" showed more pleasure and less fear than the "girl." Generally, negative emotions displayed by the infant were more likely to be labeled *anger* when the infant was thought to be a boy; the same emotions were labeled *fear* when the infant was thought to be a girl (Condry & Condry, 1976). Another study of perceived knowledge of an infant's sex indicated that female infants tend to be perceived as more angry, fearful, or distressed if adults are told that they are boys, while male infants tend to be perceived as more joyful or interested if adults are told that they are girls (Haviland, 1977). If infant girls are seen as more pleasant and passive, and infant boys as more distressed and aggressive, the impact of these labels on parents' behavior is apparent. An infant perceived as angry may be treated differently than an infant thought to be afraid. A frightened infant is usually held and cuddled by parents; an angry infant may be reprimanded or ignored. The more frequent attribution of the characteristic of fear to infant girls than to boys may explain why girls tend to be held and cuddled more than boys.

Perhaps as a result of this differential treatment, female infants tend to be more socially oriented than male infants (Beckwith, 1972). Observations of infants at six, nine, and twelve months of age indicate that girls tend to be more responsive than boys when their mothers speak to them and girls initiate more interaction with their mothers than boys do (Gunnar & Donahue, 1980). By twelve months of age, girls also demonstrate a greater social competence, directing more positive communication behaviors and more proximity-seeking responses to their mothers than boys do (Klein & Durfee, 1978). Tests designed to measure levels of positive involvement during interactions between seventeen-month-old infants and their mothers indicate that girls demonstrate a higher level of positive involvement (Clarke-Stewart, 1973). Another study reports that parents hold longer conversations with nineteen-month-old daughters than sons of the same age (Golinkoff & Ames, 1979). At various stages throughout infancy girls are perceived to be more socially oriented than boys. This characteristic is attributed to girls during infancy because of their perceived ability to initiate more interaction, to demonstrate more positive involvement behaviors, and to direct more proximity-seeking responses toward mothers than boys do.

As children grow, these differences continue to develop. Conversational interaction observed between two-year-olds and their mothers indicates that compared to mothers of boys, mothers of girls talk more, ask more questions, repeat their daughters' utterances more often, and use longer utterances. Thus, mothers may be more actively engaged in verbal interaction with their daughters than they are with their sons. This differential treatment of boys and girls may be attributable to two basic gender stereotypes: (1) a general expectation that girls should be more verbal than boys and (2) a general expectation that boys should be encouraged to move away from their mothers. By encouraging physical independence in boys, verbal interaction with them becomes more difficult (Cherry & Lewis, 1978).

Children as young as two years possess the ability to identify males and females, even when they see pictures of females with stereotypically masculine characteristics such as having short hair or wearing pants (Thompson, 1975). At 30 months of age, toddlers are able to identify males and females and to use the pronouns *he* and *she* correctly when identifying a specific person. In addition, toddlers are able to place their own picture into the correct sex-based classification and, while they do not express a preference for same-sex or other-sex labels, toddlers identify objects such as household articles and clothing using gendered labels. For example, the broom belongs to a woman and the hammer belongs to a man.

Three-year-olds are quite confident of another person's biological sex and are able to identify their own sex. Unlike their younger counterparts, however, three-year-olds consistently select the adjective *good* as an appropriate descriptor for objects stereotypically associated with their own gender (e.g., girls describe baby dolls as "good"). By three years of age, toddlers both accept and prefer to be referred to by the appropriate pronoun for their sex (*he* or *she*).

Although parents are often the primary communicators of gender roles to their very young children, once these roles are learned they are reinforced by other children. Preschoolers take advantage of opportunities to shape each other's behavior. From about three years of age, children both reinforce their peers for gender-appropriate behaviors and punish them for gender-inappropriate ones (Lamb & Roopnarine, 1979). Boys are more likely than girls to administer both positive and negative reinforcements for gendered behaviors. Positive reinforcements for gender-appropriate behaviors are more common than punishment for inappropriate ones. Male toddlers are more likely to be positively reinforced by their peers for masculine behaviors such as playing football, while female toddlers are more likely to be positively reinforced by their peers for feminine behaviors such as cheerleading (Fagot, 1978). Because a clear sense of gender is established by three years of age, positive reinforcement for stereotypically masculine activities is more effective for boys, while positive reinforcement for stereotypically feminine activities is more effective for girls.

Cognitive Developmental Theory

Representing a slightly different perspective, **cognitive developmental theory,** based on the work of Jean Piaget and expanded by Lawrence Kohlberg, *claims that a child's concept of gender—what is masculine and feminine—develops in stages until five or six years of age.* At three, children can accurately label themselves ("I am a girl"), but this is not a stable construct. For example, they do not yet understand that a person's biological sex does not change (Kessler & McKenna, 1978). By the age of six, proponents of this theory suggest, the child recognizes that biological sex is a stable variable that remains constant regardless of changes in external characteristics such as clothing or hairstyle. A six-year-old knows that he is a boy and that he will always be a boy. At that point, according to Kohlberg, a child has a stable gender identity (Kessler & McKenna, 1978). Ruble, Balaban, and Cooper (1981) explain the importance of this construct when they write that "this stage of gender constancy is thought to be critical; specifically, it is assumed that children become interested in same-sex models and perceive sex-appropriate behaviors as reinforcing because of the newly acquired sense of inevitability of their gender rather than the reverse" (pp. 667–668). According to Kessler and McKenna (1978), "once children develop stable gender identities, they begin to prefer gender-typed activities and objects. This is because children value and wish to be like things that they perceive as similar to themselves" (p. 97).

Unlike social learning theory, cognitive developmental theory posits that gender constancy is attained at a specific point during development; when this occurs, the child's role shifts from one of passive receiver of gender reinforcement to one of active seeker of reinforcement. According to this theory, as children develop stable gender identities they identify with their same-sex parent; children understand that they are similar to same-sex children and adults (Kessler & McKenna, 1978). In this view, little girls want to be like their mothers and little boys want to be like their fathers. Once a sense of gender constancy is established the child begins to seek out behavior to imitate. Thus, cognitive developmental theorists believe that children play an active role in their own development, and seek information that they think will improve their interaction with the world. Of course, this interaction is limited by their stage of development (Frieze et al., 1978).

In general, the cognitive developmental perspective suggests that children first make a cognitive judgment—"I am a girl" or "I am a boy"—after which they begin to value and enact behaviors that are considered masculine or feminine. This sequence is different from that of social learning theory: A girl desires rewards; she is rewarded by her parents and peers for feminine actions; therefore, she wants to do more feminine things. In the cognitive developmental view, a girl asserts that she is a girl, then wants to do feminine things and, therefore, the opportunity to do feminine things is rewarding; the process works in the same manner for boys.

Table 2.1 reviews the major differences among the psychological theories discussed in this section.

Regardless of the timing of the gender development process and regardless of whether it is viewed as primarily passive or active, the acquisition of gender has

TABLE 2.1   Comparison of the Three Psychological Theories on Learning Gender Identity

Freudian Identification	Social Learning	Cognitive Developmental
Role of Innate Characteristics large role: anatomy is destiny; body structure determines personality	no role	small role: cognitive maturation; structuring of experience; development of gender identity
Role of Child active	passive	active
Motive internal: reduce fear and anxiety	external: reinforcements internal: expected reinforcement	internal: desire for competence
Permanence very permanent and irreversible	permanent only if external reinforcements or self-reinforcements maintain behavior; difficulty in changing comes from internalized self-reinforcements and conditioned emotional responses	semi-permanent once schemata are stabilized; change depends on presentation of discrepant information and on the child's cognitive maturity
Sources parents or parent surrogates	parents as well as the larger social system	parents and the larger social system in interaction with the child's cognitive system
Age by 4 or 5	throughout life, but early years are very important	throughout life, but years 3–20 are most important; years between 6–8 and 16–18 are crucial for change in stereotypic beliefs

Frieze et al., 1978

much of its basis in the communication process. Significant others who provide gender modeling or who are actively sought as role models act through the process of communication.

Before we go on to discuss social role theories, we should note that most of the research we have discussed so far applies solely to people from North American cultures. In fact, as the American Association of University Women report *How Schools Shortchange Girls* (1992) reminds us:

> It is important to recognize that the research [on the development of gender identity] consists primarily of studies on white middle-class girls and boys. The effects of race, ethnicity, and socioeconomic class on gender development have not been studied adequately. (p. 10)

West and Fenstermaker (1995) state: "no person can experience gender without simultaneously experiencing race and class" (p. 13). As you continue reading this chapter, keep in mind the important influences of race, ethnicity, and socioeconomic status on your gender identity.

Social Role Theories

Some scholars have described the development of gender identity in terms of the learning of gender roles and role-related behavior rather than the learning of individual or discrete behaviors, such as aggression or verbal ability. **Social roles** *are a set of behavior patterns that define the expected behavior for individuals in a given position or status.* Many roles have a complementary role associated with them. For example, one must have a child to be a parent, a student to be a teacher, an employer to be an employee.

Two strands of thought are distinguishable in the social-roles perspective of gender development. One is derived from Talcott Parsons and deals with the learning of gender roles in early life. The other, symbolic interaction, is based on the work of George Herbert Mead and analyzes the learning of gender roles throughout the life cycle.

Parsons (1964), a somewhat traditional theorist, suggests that males and females first develop their social roles through interaction in the family. Parsons explains the development of gender roles in early childhood as an identification with or rejection of the mother. For girls, the process of gender development is a process of identifying with the mother. For boys, it is one of rejection of the mother's female role. According to this theory, as a male child grows older he realizes that he cannot be like his mother because he is a male, not a female. He must deny his early identification with his mother in order to develop his male identity. This theory was developed at a time when mothers were assumed to be the primary socializing force for their children. More recent social-role theories note the importance of the role of the father in developing gender roles in children. Current theorists argue that it is important for boys to have male role models in their lives, too. (These studies will be discussed in more detail in Chapter 6.)

Symbolic interaction suggests that *individuals develop their view of self from their perceptions of the expectations of significant others* (Blumer, 1969; Mead, 1934). In terms of gender development, expectations of appropriate behavior for males and females are communicated by other people. Boys may be told, "Don't run like a girl," "Big boys don't cry," and "Don't act like a sissy." Girls may be told, "Act like a lady," "Don't be so bossy," and "Good girls don't hit people." As children perceive the expectations of others, they interpret and evaluate these expectations and act in accordance with them.

In sum, social learning theory suggests that the development of gender is the result of reinforcement or encouragement of appropriate behaviors. Cognitive developmental theory suggests that children decide which behaviors are appropriate for their gender and adopt those behaviors. Social-role theory focuses on the learning of gender roles, sets of behavior patterns that define expected behavior.

Critical of these theories for their assumption that all males and females are socialized into a "laundry list of behavioral characteristics," Kimmel (1987) contends that this assumption makes the roles of men and women seem static. In reality, masculine and feminine roles are enacted in a dynamic relationship with each other in everyday life. "The paradigm ignores the extent to which our conceptions of masculinity and femininity . . . is relational; that is, the product of gender relations that are historically and socially conditioned. Masculinity and femininity are relational constructs, the definition of either depends upon the definition of the other" (p. 12). A more useful perspective on gender, Kimmel says, posits that both genders are socially constructed.

Kimmel and Messner (1998) adopt a social constructionist perspective in which they argue that "the meaning of masculinity is neither transhistorical nor culturally universal, but rather varies from culture to culture and within any one culture over time. . . . Men's lives also vary within any one culture over time. The experience of masculinity in the contemporary United States is very different from that experience 150 years ago" (p. xx). This observation obviously applies to femininity as well. This historical and comparative perspective allows us to understand that masculinity and femininity also vary within a society and are constructed differently by class, race, ethnicity, age, and other relevant societal factors. Kimmel and Messner envision these factors as "axes" that modify each other. For example, they contend that "black masculinity differs from white masculinity, yet each of them is also further modified by class and age" (p. xxi).

Moral Voices Theory

In her landmark book *In a Different Voice*, Carol Gilligan (1982) expanded the understanding of human development with a consideration of women that was missing from many previous theories, especially those proposed by Kohlberg (1981). Gilligan believes that the early social environment is experienced differently by male and female children and that this experience leads to basic differences in personality development. She argues "given that for both sexes the primary caretaker in the first three years of life is typically female, the interpersonal dynamics of gender identity formation are different for boys and girls" (p. 7). Her argument is based on Chodorow's (1974) observation that females' identity formation takes place in the context of an ongoing relationship with their mothers while males must separate psychologically from their mothers in order to define themselves as masculine. For Chodorow (1978), male development entails a "more emphatic individuation and a more defensive firming of experienced ego boundaries" (p. 167). According to this theory, females experience themselves more like their mothers and fuse the experience of attachment with the process of gender development.

Gilligan (1982) concludes that "since masculinity is defined through separation while femininity is defined through attachment, male gender identity is threatened by intimacy while female gender identity is threatened by separation. Thus males tend to have difficulty with relationships, while females tend to have problems with individuation" (p. 8). As an example, Gilligan notes that little boys are much more likely to argue about the rules when playing games. Little girls will stop playing a game if an argument about the rules appears to threaten their relationship. To boys, arguing about rules is part of the game; to girls, the continuation of the game is subordinated to the continuation of the relationship.

This concern for relationships continues into women's adulthood, says Surrey (1991), contending that a "conception of self-in-relation involves the recognition that, for women, the primary experience of self is relational, that is, the self is organized and developed in the context of important relationships" (p. 52).

Gilligan (1982) says that "women not only define themselves in a context of human relationships but also judge themselves in terms of their ability to care" (p. 17). She sees the ability of women to care for others as a great strength, noting that:

> Women's construction of the moral problem as a problem of care and responsibility in relationships rather than as one of rights and rules ties the development of their moral thinking to changes in their understanding of responsibility and relationships, just as the conception of morality as justice ties development to the logic of equality and reciprocity. Thus the logic underlying an ethic of care is a psychological logic of relationships, which contrasts with the formal logic of fairness that informs the justice approach. (p. 73)

According to this theory, women are more likely to see problems in terms of conflicting responsibilities and their impact on their relationships with others, while men are more likely to base their judgments on a hierarchical set of principles determining what is right and wrong. Table 2.2 summarizes this theory.

Gilligan's theory (1982) is important from a communication perspective because it is based on the assumption "that the way people talk about their lives is significant, that the language they use and the connections they make reveal the world that they see and in which they act" (p. 2). Yet Gilligan has been severely criticized for advocating a polarized approach to gender: males follow an ethic of justice and females follow an ethic of care. According to Gould (1988),

TABLE 2.2   Gender Differences in Developmental Patterns

Developmental Issue	Female Tendencies	Male Tendencies
basis of identity	■ identity develops in and through relationships with others ■ permeable ego boundaries	■ identity develops by differentiating self from others ■ firm ego boundaries
basic interpersonal stance	■ connections with others are necessary to personal security ■ separate is unsafe ■ interdependence is natural and good	■ connections with others can threaten autonomy ■ separation is preferred ■ independence is natural and good
orientation toward others	■ meet the needs of others with whom one is connected	■ honor others' rights when they don't conflict with one's own rights
moral / ethical principles invoked	■ show CARE ■ be responsive and understanding to others	■ be FAIR ■ be impartial in respecting others' rights
source of moral response	■ judge each person and relationship in its own context and terms ■ what is "right" in one case may not be in another because needs differ among people	■ generally accepted rules apply to relationships and to various individuals ■ altering the rules for each situation is acting in an ad hoc manner

Wood and Lenze, 1991

while it is true that women's experiences differ from men's, a strictly psychological explanation cannot do justice to the political context within which the male and female voices develop. Moreover, a vision of society modeled solely upon the private sphere is primarily hypothetical because it gives no explicit recognition to the institutional, structural barriers or the roles of power and wealth in maintaining sexual stratification. (p. 414)

Gilligan, however, has maintained that the association between the ethic of care and women is not absolute. More recent theorists contend that both men and women can demonstrate an ethic of care in their everyday lives (Pritchard, 1991).

Aspect Theory

In response to the somewhat rigid categories offered by Gilligan, Ferguson (1989) proposed a theory of gender that views conscious selfhood as an ongoing process in which individual priorities and social constraints limit and define a person's identity. According to Ferguson, the self has many aspects that are developed by participating in social practices, including communication, that call for certain skills or values. For example, Ferguson claims that women who participate in business enterprises with men may share what Gilligan calls the masculine voice of moral reasoning (ethic of justice). In the same way, men who actively participate in coparenting may develop a feminine voice of moral reasoning (ethic of care) based on this experience.

Ferguson (1989) says that

> if the self is seen as having many aspects, then it cannot be determined universally which are prior, more fundamental, or more or less authentic. . . . Furthermore, the *contents* of masculinity or femininity vary with the social practices they are connected to. A woman defending her child against attack . . . is supposed to be showing her feminine protective maternal instinct. But a similar aggressive, perhaps violent act against a man who has made deprecating sexist remarks is not considered feminine. (pp. 101–102)

According to this theory, difficulties may arise when a person is faced with the "psychological incongruity of having to operate with conflicting values" (p. 102). Thus, social workers whose jobs encourage caring may find themselves in a complex government bureaucracy that requires a masculine ethic characterized by rights and justice. Or lawyers who want to share housework and child care with their spouses may experience pressure from their colleagues at work to spend more time in the office.

Overall, this theory is a "rejection of the essentialist idea that all women [or men] have the same inner and authentic self that can only be empowered by the same choices" (Ferguson, 1989, p. 105). Polarization is avoided by recognizing that males *and* females may exhibit responsibility-oriented (caring) or rights-oriented feelings and behaviors depending on the situation (Gould, 1988).

Perspectives on Gender Identity

Throughout this book, we have been referring to males and females, women and men, and boys and girls. Our discussion of these terms reflects what Epstein (1988) has called the "sex division of society" (p. 25). As we have seen, two theoretical perspectives attempt to explain the division of the contemporary world into males and females who exhibit socially constructed masculine and feminine behaviors. One perspective (such as identification theory) is a dichotomous model that argues that there are basic differences between the males and females. Some supporters of this position (such as Freud) believe that differences between men and women are biologically determined; others (such as social learning theorists) believe that these differences are the result of social conditioning in early life. They are "lodged in the differing psyches of the sexes by the psychoanalytic processes that create identity," says Epstein. Others support a combination of these factors. The second perspective

> insists that the two sexes are essentially similar and that the differences linked to sexual functions are not related to psychological traits or social roles. . . . This perspective suggests that most gender differences are not as deeply rooted or immutable as has been believed, that they are relatively superficial, and that they are socially constructed (and elaborated in the culture through myths, law, and folkways) and kept in place by the way each sex is positioned in the social structure. . . . This view ascribes observed differences in behavior to a social control system that prescribes and proscribes specific behaviors for women and men. (Epstein, 1988, p. 25)

Respected scholars have argued from each of these theoretical perspectives.

One of the most comprehensive attempts to summarize the research on the dichotomous approach to psychological sex differences is *The Psychology of Sex Differences* by Maccoby and Jacklin (1974). Despite the varying quality of the research reviewed and the many methodological problems with the 1,400 studies reviewed in this volume (this research is reviewed in Clarke-Stewart, Friedman, & Koch, 1985), the general conclusions of Jacklin and Maccoby (1978) provide a useful overview of the study of gender differences. They divide the studies they review into three categories: (1) fairly well established gender differences, (2) unfounded beliefs about gender differences, and (3) gender differences still open to question.

Well-Established Differences

Jacklin and Maccoby (1978) discuss two general categories in which they believe that fairly well established gender differences exist: (1) verbal versus visual–spacial abilities and (2) aggression.

According to this research, girls have greater *verbal ability* than boys. In infancy, girls are more responsive to tones, speech patterns, and vocal cues (Gunnar & Donahue, 1980). Girls begin to speak and read earlier than boys.

In terms of *visual–spacial abilities*, male infants seem to attend to different cues than female infants. As boys grow and develop their motor ability they are more likely to manipulate objects. In preschool, boys are better at manipulations in two-or three-dimensional space, such as folding paper or building things with blocks. From about age 10, boys excel in visual–spatial ability. Beginning at ages 12 or 13, boys gain mathematical skills faster than girls, but the difference is not as great as in spatial ability. This research seems to indicate that when problems can be solved by either a verbal or a spatial process, girls and boys may be equal, but that girls excel when a problem requires a verbal solution, and boys excel when it requires a spatial solution (Clarke-Stewart, Friedman, & Koch, 1985).

Kimura (2000) notes that, on average, men perform better on certain spatial tasks such as tests that call for imagining how an object rotates. In addition, men score higher than women on tests of mathematical reasoning or tests of "target-directed motor skills." Men also do better in navigating their way through a specified route. Women, in Kimura's research, are faster at a task called "perceptual speed" that involves identifying matching items. In addition, they have greater verbal fluency (such as finding words that begin with a specific letter) and are faster in arithmetic calculation. Women also do slightly better at "precision manual tasks," such as placing pegs in holes on a board. It is important to note, however, that these studies show average differences. There is a great deal of overlap in cognitive abilities between men and women. In addition, sometimes changing the instructions can change the results of a study. For example, Sharps, Price, and Williams (1994) did not find differences in spatial abilities when the object to be rotated was a familiar one and the instructions did not emphasize the spatial nature of the task.

These differences in verbal and visual abilities of males and females, although fairly well established, should not be overemphasized. Some studies have not found these differences. In addition, statistically significant differences may not be very large in real terms and may apply only on average, not to any particular individual (Baenninger & Newcombe, 2000). In recent years Maccoby has suggested that since boys score as high as girls on the verbal part of the SAT, she is no longer convinced that girls have greater verbal abilities than boys (Hall, 1987).

Reviewing 32 observational studies of children six years old and younger, Maccoby and Jacklin (1980) note that 24 of the studies report that boys exhibited more aggression than girls and eight indicated no differences in level of aggression between boys and girls. None of the studies found greater female aggression. Longitudinal studies suggest that aggression in girls is more likely to be verbal than physical. Girls are more likely to express their aggression in verbal slights and antisocial acts than with physical force (Clarke-Stewart, Friedman, & Koch, 1985). Boys may be more apt to fight than to talk out their differences.

Unfounded Beliefs About Differences

Maccoby and Jacklin (1974) discuss four areas of unfounded beliefs about gender differences. Contrary to these beliefs, research indicates that (1) girls do not have less self-esteem than boys, (2) girls are not more suggestible than boys, (3) girls are not better at rote learning and simple repetitive tasks, and boys are not more analytical or better at tasks that require higher-level thinking, and (4) boys are not more motivated to achieve.

The domains from which girls and boys derive their *self-esteem* do differ, however. When asked to describe themselves, boys point to qualities such as ambition, energy, power, initiative, instrumentality, and control over external events (Gunnar-Von Gnechten, 1978). They talk about their success with sports or with girls. Girls, in contrast, describe themselves as generous, sensitive, considerate, and concerned for others (Block, 1983). Thus, boys take pride in being powerful and masterful. Girls take pride in human relationships and expressiveness.

While there is no difference in being *suggestible*, girls are somewhat more likely to adapt their judgments to the standards of their peer group, and boys are more likely to accept peer-group values even when these values conflict with their own.

Girls and boys are equally proficient at all types of *learning*. Girls are not better at rote learning and simple repetitive tasks. Boys are not better at complex cognitive tasks, and they do not excel at disembedding information, except when the task is visual–spatial, such as arranging blocks in a pattern or fitting puzzle pieces together.

Although boys do not have more *achievement motivation* than girls, levels of achievement motivation and behavior vary with the type of task and the conditions involved. Under neutral conditions, girls are often more achievement-oriented than boys.

Questionable Differences

Jacklin and Maccoby (1978) cite three areas in which there is still a question about the existence of gender differences: (1) whether girls are more compliant and passive than boys, (2) whether boys are more active than girls, and (3) whether girls are more sociable and nurturing than boys.

Dominance is the opposite of *compliance*. Boys make more attempts to dominate one another and adults than girls do, but girls and boys are equally willing to explore novel surroundings. Girls are no more likely than boys to withdraw from social interaction or to withdraw in the face of aggression, thus demonstrating a tendency against being *passive*.

Infant girls and boys do not differ in overall *activity* levels; however, preschool boys are more active than preschool girls in certain situations, such as when other boys are present. Boys and men consistently describe themselves as daring and adventuresome more than do girls and women (Longstreth, 1970), and researchers find them to be so (Block, 1983).

Jacklin and Maccoby (1978) suggest that boys and girls are equally *sociable*. They base this conclusion on research findings that indicate boys and girls are equally likely to imitate another person, to depend on adults and to seek their help, and to stay alone in a room. Girls, however, tend to prefer to have one other companion with them, while boys prefer large peer groups.

One survey of empathy research notes that girls are more likely than boys to respond vicariously to another's feelings. Their words of sympathy, facial expressions, and posture are more likely to reflect the distress of the person they watch (Clarke-Stewart, Friedman, & Koch, 1985).

Thus, although most of this research was based on a dichotomous or polarized conception of gender, much of it supports the contention that innate gender differences are relatively superficial. A more useful approach to the examination of gender differences focuses on how human behavior is socially constructed and how these social constructions affect males and females.

Strategies for Change

It is important to avoid what Steele (1996) called the "stereotype of limitation" (cited in Lott, 2000, p. 117). Eagly (2000) contends that the stereotype of women is generally more positive than men, but notes that "the favorability of the female stereotype may be a mixed blessing because the particular kinds of positive characteristics most often ascribed to women, primarily 'niceness-nurturance' qualities, probably contribute to the exclusion of women from certain kinds of high-status roles (e.g., those that are thought to require toughness and aggressiveness)" (p. 109).

One alternative conceptualization that has been proposed to the bipolar gender division in society is the concept of androgyny. Morse and Eman (1980) argue that the dichotomous biological classification of male and female offers little explanation about why people think and behave the way they do. As we discussed earlier, gender stereotypes describe males as aggressive, assertive, active, and independent, and females as passive, subjective, noncompetitive, and dependent. These labels often do not accurately reflect individual behavior.

Sandra Bem (1974) popularized the concept of *psychology androgyny*, maintaining that individuals can blend both masculine and feminine psychological identities. Bem identifies four psychological orientations: (1) *androgynous* (high association with both stereotypically masculine and feminine traits, for example, someone who has leadership qualities and is sensitive to the needs of others); (2) *masculine* (high association with stereotypically masculine traits and low association with stereotypically feminine traits, someone who has a strong personality and is not compassionate); (3) *feminine* (high association with stereotypically feminine traits and low association with stereotypically masculine traits, someone who is helpful but not independent); and (4) *undifferentiated* (low association with both sets of traits, someone who is neither dominant nor warm). A number of studies based primarily on a dichotomous perspective have used Bem's measure of psychological orientation and found it to be more appropriate than biological sex when measuring communication similarities and differences.

Bem (1974) used the term *androgyny* (a combination of the Greek words *andros*, meaning male, and *gyne*, meaning female) to represent a person who is, for example, assertive and independent as well as gentle and warm. Bem argues that masculinity and femininity do not represent a bipolar construct. Rather, it is possible for a person to exhibit both stereotypically masculine and feminine traits. Three assumptions underlie Bem's theory of androgyny: (1) androgyny allows a person more behavioral flexibility, (2) this flexibility allows a person to adapt better in various social situations, and (3) both males and females may attain this situational flexibility.

Bem (1974) argues that this concept of androgyny offers a healthier orientation than a traditional polarized gender orientation because the androgynous individual has a wider range of traits and is, therefore, able to adapt more effectively to more situations. Some research supports this view. Androgyny has been positively correlated with self-esteem (Lamke, 1982) and psychological development (Waterman & Whitbourne, 1982), for example.

Most notably, a great deal of research on androgyny has examined the relationships among biological sex, gender, and social influence. These findings indicate that people with stereotypically feminine psychological traits are more likely to use tears, emotional alteration, and subtlety to influence others. Feminine females, masculine males, and androgynous individuals tend to have a higher need for approval than cross-sex-typed persons; in addition, androgynous and stereotypically masculine individuals receive more positive peer evaluations than stereotypically feminine individuals (Falbo, 1977). Androgyny and masculinity are more closely associated with self-esteem, body satisfaction, and sexual satisfaction than is femininity (Kimlicka, Cross, & Tarnai, 1983). Androgynous individuals report better personal adjustment, and others rate them higher in adjustment (Jackson, 1983; Major, Carnevale, & Deaux, 1981). Androgynous individuals also demonstrate high levels of communication competence (Wheeless & Duran, 1982) and are better able to adapt to communication situations (Wheeless, 1984).

In evaluating individuals' performances in interpersonal situations, the use of gender orientation has provided more insight than merely knowing the biological sex of the participants. Since complex interpersonal situations require the use of both traditionally masculine and feminine social skills, androgynous individuals are highly effective in interpersonal situations. For example, androgynous males are able to use warm, complementary social behaviors when these affective responses are necessary; androgynous females are able to use effective refusal social skills when faced with unreasonable requests from others (Kelly, O'Brien, & Hosford, 1981). The ability to blend traditionally masculine and feminine qualities when necessary in interpersonal situations maximizes interpersonal effectiveness.

Several communication variables have been studied in relationship to androgyny. For example, females and androgynous males tend to disclose more information about themselves than masculine males. In addition, androgynous females and males report less communication apprehension than feminine females (Greenblatt, Hasenauer, & Freimuth, 1980). Other communication variables that have been studied in relationship to androgyny include dominant and submissive nonverbal cues (Putnam & McCallister, 1980), persuadability (Montgomery & Burgoon, 1980), touching behavior (Eman, Dierks-Stewart, & Tucker, 1978), communication in small groups (Patton, Jasnoski, & Skerchock, 1977), and communication competence (Reiser & Troost, 1986).

Korabik (1990) speculates that androgynous women would be more favorably viewed as leaders since they would be perceived as both likeable and competent. Androgynous women may achieve higher levels of success in organizations, including higher pay, because they are better adapted to the demands of the workplace (Kirchmeyer & Bullin, 1997).

Brems and Johnson (1989) examine the concept of androgyny in relation to masculinity, femininity, maleness, and femaleness. They find that men and individuals who score high on masculinity have a more positive view of their problem-solving abilities, are more confident, and are more likely to approach problem-solving situations. The researchers also report that men are more likely than women to use denial as a strategy for coping with problems. This research does not measure actual ability to solve problems but focuses on individuals' feelings about problem-solving situations. As Brems and Johnson note, "men may not easily admit to themselves or others any potential problems or difficulties, whereas women may be more aware of and open to internal states" (p. 192).

Gender identity is influenced by culture and ethnicity. While there is little research examining androgyny across racial and cultural groups, a study of African

American women found that most of the respondents reported an androgynous gender identity but continued to hold traditional beliefs about the women's role in the family (Binion, 1990). As Binion notes, this finding supports the contention that African American women are socialized to be self-sufficient, independent, hardworking, and resourceful yet at the same time accept a traditional female gender ideology and "enjoy being mothers" (p. 499).

Androgyny research has been seriously criticized, however. Several authors maintain that it reflects considerable theoretical and methodological problems (see, for example, Gill, Stockard, Johnson, & Williams, 1987; Marsh & Myers, 1986). Weaknesses that have been cited in androgyny research include a lack of agreement on the definition of androgyny, reliability and validity problems in the scales used to measure androgyny, and an inability to generate clear statements concerning the relationship of androgyny to external criteria of social effectiveness and competency.

A major problem in androgyny research lies with the instruments used to measure the concept. During the 1970s several self-report scales were developed to measure androgyny. The first and most widely used scales are the Bem Sex Role Inventory (BSRI; Bem, 1974) and the Personal Attributes Questionnaire (PAQ; see Spence & Helmreich, 1978). Both instruments categorize a person as either masculine, feminine, undifferentiated (low in both masculinity and femininity), or androgynous (high in both masculinity and femininity). Feather (1984) argues that these measures of androgyny may be measuring not only descriptive beliefs about an individual's characteristic ways of behaving but also prescriptive beliefs about what modes of conduct individuals think they ought to prefer. For example, Feather finds that individuals who think people should be loving and helpful are more likely to describe themselves as loving and helpful.

After reviewing criticisms of the BSRI concerning its reliability and validity, Wheeless and Dierks-Stewart (1981) modified the scale. They identify 10 items for the masculine (or instrumental) dimension and 10 items for the feminine (or sensitivity) dimension rather than Bem's 20 items for each dimension. The revised BSRI addresses many of the problems associated with the earlier version. Wheeless and Wheeless (1982) present a new method for scoring the BSRI that conceptualizes androgyny as a continuous concept instead of discrete categories. (See the suggested activities at the end of this chapter to measure your own androgyny score on this scale.)

Whether you agree with the theoretical definition and instruments used in the measurement of androgyny, it is evident that having a wide range of communication skills and behaviors enables you to adapt your communication appropriately for various situations, thus becoming a more competent communicator.

Summary

Gender is an integral part of every individual's identity. Although gender may have some roots in biological differences that affect sensory processing, physical capabilities, and maturation rates, most of our psychological and social constructs and communication behaviors are learned through interactions with others and observations of their behavior. Gender reflects the psychological traits and social responsibilities traditionally labeled masculine and feminine in our culture. While biological, psychological, and social role theories have been put forth to explain the process by which we acquire our gender identity, the importance of communication in this process cannot be ignored. Communication plays a vital role in shaping and reinforcing both the acquisition and development of gender. In addition, we define our gender in relation to the other. Through the process of communication, we socially construct what it means to be masculine and feminine in our culture. As we noted at the beginning of this chapter, studying these similarities and differences helps us provide more accurate descriptions and explanations of *human* rather than simply *male* and *female* communication behavior.

FINDING YOUR VOICE

1. Examine the adjectives below from the revised Bem Sex Role Inventory (BSRI). (A complete list of items can be found in Bem, 1974, and Wheeless and Dierks-Stewart, 1981.) Mark how each item applies to you (1 = Never or almost never true; 7 = Always or almost always true).

   1. Helpful

      | 1 | 2 | 3 | 4 | 5 | 6 | 7 |

   2. Independent

      | 1 | 2 | 3 | 4 | 5 | 6 | 7 |

   3. Assertive

      | 1 | 2 | 3 | 4 | 5 | 6 | 7 |

   4. Has strong personality

      | 1 | 2 | 3 | 4 | 5 | 6 | 7 |

   5. Forceful

      | 1 | 2 | 3 | 4 | 5 | 6 | 7 |

   6. Has leadership qualities

      | 1 | 2 | 3 | 4 | 5 | 6 | 7 |

   7. Sensitive to others' needs

      | 1 | 2 | 3 | 4 | 5 | 6 | 7 |

   8. Understanding

      | 1 | 2 | 3 | 4 | 5 | 6 | 7 |

   9. Compassionate

      | 1 | 2 | 3 | 4 | 5 | 6 | 7 |

   10. Sincere

      | 1 | 2 | 3 | 4 | 5 | 6 | 7 |

   11. Eager to soothe hurt feelings

      | 1 | 2 | 3 | 4 | 5 | 6 | 7 |

   12. Dominant

      | 1 | 2 | 3 | 4 | 5 | 6 | 7 |

   13. Warm

      | 1 | 2 | 3 | 4 | 5 | 6 | 7 |

   14. Willing to take a stand

      | 1 | 2 | 3 | 4 | 5 | 6 | 7 |

   15. Tender

      | 1 | 2 | 3 | 4 | 5 | 6 | 7 |

16. Friendly

1	2	3	4	5	6	7

17. Aggressive

1	2	3	4	5	6	7

18. Acts as a leader

1	2	3	4	5	6	7

19. Competitive

1	2	3	4	5	6	7

20. Gentle

1	2	3	4	5	6	7

Check your responses against the following list.

Feminine	*Masculine*
helpful	has strong personality
sensitive to others' needs	willing to take a stand
understanding	dominant
compassionate	forceful
sincere	assertive
eager to soothe hurt feelings	competitive
warm	aggressive
tender	has leadership qualities
friendly	independent
gentle	acts as a leader

Total the ratings for the feminine items. Total the ratings for the masculine items. Calculate your androgyny score using the following formula: $2(M+F) + (F-M)$. (This scoring procedure is from Wheeless & Wheeless, 1982.) Compare your score with others in your class. The higher the score the more androgynous you are.

2. Find examples of three magazines directed at parents-to-be or parents of young children. What types of gender stereotyping occur in these magazines (for example, advertisements for trucks picturing only boys, articles on how to dress your little girl in pretty clothes, advice on what type of behavior parents can expect from boys and girls)? In general, what types of messages about gender ideology are being communicated to parents?

   Using the same magazines, look for examples of more balanced gender portrayals (for example, advertisements for computers picturing both boys and girls, pictures of fathers feeding their infants, articles on nonsexist child rearing). Overall, are there more ads and articles portraying gender stereotypes or portraying balanced roles for boys and girls? What implications does this finding have for raising children?

3. Visit a day-care center or elementary school. Keep a journal and record the activities in which young children participate. Code your observations in terms of the sex of the child you are observing. List as many activities as you can. For example, what types of toys do the children play with? How much time does each child spend interacting with others? How much time does each child spend in solitary play? What types of activities are conducted? How much running takes place? After you have completed your observations, summarize your findings, and draw some conclusions about differ-

ences and similarities between young girls and boys in play and interactive behavior. Do your findings agree with the research described in this chapter?

4. Historical changes affect how individuals develop their gender identity. To determine some of these historical influences, interview your oldest relative (for example, a grandparent) or someone approximately the same age, and a parent or someone approximately the same age. Try to get a picture of what life was like for these people as they were growing up. Ask questions such as:

    ■ What was your family like while you were growing up? How many brothers and sisters did you have? Were your parents strict? What types of things were you allowed to do, and what types of things were you forbidden to do? Why? What did your parents want you to grow up to be? How did you know this?

    ■ Where did you go to school (elementary school, junior high, high school, college)? Were the schools large or small? What was it like to be a student in school at that time? What sorts of things concerned students? Did you enjoy school? Why or why not?

    ■ When you were in school, what did you want to do after you graduated? Did you achieve this ambition? Why or why not?

    From the information you have gathered, draw some conclusions about what it was like growing up in your parents' and grandparents' generations. How were gender expectations communicated to them? For example, were they told what career to pursue or discouraged from pursuing a particular career? Were they encouraged to excel in school or in sports? Were they expected to marry and raise a family? In general, how have the gendered messages changed over the years? How are the gendered messages you receive different from those received by your grandparents and parents?

FURTHER READING

Brumberg, J. J. (1997). *The body project: An intimate history of American girls.* New York: Vintage Books. This book presents a fascinating history of young girls' perceptions of their bodies from the 1830s to the present. Numerous examples from the media, diaries, and popular culture trace the change in societal concerns with character to the modern focus on appearance.

Gilligan, C., Ward, J. V., & Taylor, J. M. (1988). *Mapping the moral domain: A contribution of women's thinking to psychological theory and education.* Cambridge, MA: Center for the Study of Gender, Education and Human Development, Harvard University Graduate School of Education. This book provides a collection of readings that offer a framework for the development of gender identity. The authors focus on early childhood and adolescent development.

Kimmel, M. S., & Messner, M. A. (1998). *Men's lives,* 4th ed. Boston: Allyn and Bacon. This edited collection of articles presents an excellent overview of the many roles for men in contemporary society. Chapters deal with issues of concern to men, including ethnicity, religion, sexual orientation, the family, and the future.

Thomas, J. C. (1990). *A gathering of flowers: Stories about being young in America.* New York: Harper-Collins. A collection of 11 short stories depicting what it is like to be young in America, exploring such diverse cultures as urban San Francisco, a Chippewa Indian reservation, and a Latino barrio in Chicago.

CHAPTER

3 Language

The language we use reflects and shapes our perceptions of the world as well as communicates our view of the world to others. We form lasting impressions of people based on the language they use. In addition, people may modify their behavior toward us based on our language use. Most important, our language also communicates the gender ideology prevalent in our culture.

Imagine the following conversation:

A: I've had a rotten day. My head's killing me.

B: I'm sorry. Do you want me get you an aspirin?

A: I flunked that stupid chemistry exam. I hate that course. We keep getting formulas we've never seen before. I'm sick of it.

B: What about . . .

A: Yeah, hate it.

B: Would you like to go to a movie tonight?

A: I told you, I'm tired. I'm going to crash and then maybe just get pizza.

B: That's okay with me.

What can you conclude about the people in this conversation? You may have concluded that Person A is a man and that Person B is a woman. If you did, how did you come to that conclusion? Are men usually interrupted? Do they reply calmly to a verbal assault? Of course they do sometimes, but according to gender stereotypes and some research evidence, women are more likely be the conciliatory ones in a conversation.

The short conversation above demonstrates some common gendered communication behaviors. In Chapter 2, we examined parents' communication with their children. In this chapter, we will discuss the impact of language on gender, several gender stereotypes perpetuated by our language, the implications and consequences of gendered language, and some strategies for change.

Children's Language Use

Before turning our attention to adult use of language, let's look at some gender differences in children's language and at some of the gender ideologies associated with these differences.

A common gender ideology you may have heard is that girls talk before they walk, and boys walk before they talk. This idea reflects the belief that girls demonstrate various levels of language competence earlier than boys. This stereotype may not be true, however, depending on the language function observed. To explore the emergence of specific language functions, uses, and strategies, Haslett (1983) observed preschoolers engaging in conversations. Her research emphasizes some interesting distinctions between boys' and girls' linguistic skills.

According to Haslett, language serves four functions for children: a *directive* function (concerned with directing actions and operations), an *interpretive* function (concerned with communicating the meaning of events and situations the child witnesses), a *projective* function (concerned with projecting and exploring situations that the child is not actually experiencing, through imagination and past experiences), and a *relational* function (concerned with establishing and maintaining relationships among people).

Three-year-old children primarily use language to fulfill an interpretive function. Through language, they master information about their environment. In addition, children at this age use language to serve the relational function of expressing their own ideas and needs. For three-year-olds, both of these functions tend to reflect an egocentric or self-centered view of the world. As children grow to four years of age, however, a developmental shift occurs and the projective function of language increases. Children start to use imagining strategies to create new roles and contexts for their play. In addition, they begin to use language that serves a relational function directed more toward others.

Girls tend to develop these strategies at an earlier age than boys. As a result, girls develop greater cognitive complexity and communicative adaptability in using these strategies during the toddler and preschool years. For example, at three years of age, boys may comment on imagined contexts of their play, but girls can hold up an object like a wooden block and imagine it is something else or imagine that they are a character from a story and speak appropriately for that character. According to Haslett (1983), boys alter the context and girls alter "their identity through enacting different roles in their play" (p. 125). When boys comment on the imagined contexts of play, inevitably this commentary is in the form of sounds (for example, growls associated with animals or crash noises associated with cars) that accompany their play activity. Girls, in contrast, use commentary concerning imagined contexts with greater complexity; they usually elaborate in detail on the imagined play context, its imaginary actions or problems. Overall, young girls are able to rename or reidentify people and objects in their play context, use language associated with specific roles in play, and extensively comment on the imagined context. This sequence of imagining strategies appears later in boys.

In addition to imagining strategies, three-year-old boys and girls use self-maintaining strategies, language used to identify their own needs and protect their own self-interests, such as "I'm hungry" or "leave my doll alone." Almost half of the self-maintaining strategies used by three-year-old girls emphasize "other" rather than "self." At approximately four years of age, there is a significant drop in the frequency of self-maintaining strategies. This reduction appears to reflect children's decreasing egocentricity as well as their growing social and communicative knowledge. By age four, children begin to realize the necessity of acknowledging the feelings and rights of others to achieve desired goals. Girls develop these linguistic strategies earlier than boys by using other-emphasizing strategies more than self-emphasizing strategies. According to Haslett, these strategies reflect traditional gender socialization patterns that reinforce females for being nurturing and other-directed and males for being aggressive and self-assertive.

This difference in aggression and self-assertiveness is also seen in mixed-age play groups. Boys use longer utterances than girls (Haas, 1978) and talk more in same-age dyads than in mixed-age dyads, while girls talk the same amount regardless of their play partner's age (Langlois, Gottfried, Barnes, & Hendricks, 1978). This difference may be accounted for by the nature of dyadic interaction. Older boys often use verbal instructions to direct younger boys, who obey and rarely respond verbally in the dyad. Girls are more likely to try to establish a reciprocal relationship that encourages more verbal interaction regardless of their play partner's age. This behavior reflects a gender ideology that encourages cooperative behaviors for girls and competitive behaviors for boys.

Children and adolescents ranging from five to fifteen years old learn the rules appropriate for friendly conversation primarily in same-sex peer groups (Maltz & Borker, 1982). Since boys' groups tend to be hierarchical in structure, with language used primarily to assert dominance as well as to attract or to maintain an audience, boys often follow different rules for friendly conversations. Boys view friendly conversation among their peer group as training for verbal aggression. Even boys who are friends may try to outdo each other in conversations. Girls tend to interact in same-sex groups in a more egalitarian manner. As a result, girls use friendly conversation as a training ground for cooperation. Their speech patterns tend to reflect a desire for cooperation and a desire to negotiate shifting alliances in the group. These patterns may be related to supportiveness goals of cooperating and signaling attention found later in adult women's speech (Sgan & Pickert, 1980). If these differing purposes for conversation exist between boys and girls, and are reinforced by peer groups during childhood and adolescence, they may help account for some of the aspects of adult male–female communication discussed later in this chapter. (See Chapter 5 for a more extensive discussion of communication in friendships.)

While this research suggests that boys develop more competitive communication patterns and girls develop more cooperative communication patterns, Sgan and Pickert (1980) note that girls use assertive behaviors just as often as boys do. They analyzed children's verbal indicators of assertiveness (for example, use of commands, instructions, and suggestions) in working together to complete a cooperative task. While kindergarten and first-grade boys use assertive verbal indicators more often than girls and direct those verbal indicators to boys more often than to girls, this behavioral trend is equalized by the time the children reach the third grade. By this age, girls use just as many assertive verbal indicators as boys and direct these verbal indicators toward both boys and girls. While assertive behaviors are not necessarily the same as the aggressive behaviors identified with competition, they are not the behaviors often identified with cooperation and compliance.

This discrepancy in findings may be explained by examining the definition of the tasks the children were asked to complete in these studies. Girls may have used as many assertive verbal indicators as boys because of how the boys reacted to the nature of the task. In a task that is defined for them as cooperative, boys may use fewer assertive verbal indicators than when they are interacting in all-male peer groups. Girls, on the other hand, may be reacting to the presence of boys in the task group. Although girls tend to be more egalitarian in all-girl play groups, they may use more assertive verbal indicators in play groups that include boys and girls.

In addition to gendered aspects of their own language use, children are aware of gender ideologies concerning male and female speech. Language characterized as *male* or *female* by adults is consistently identified and appropriately labeled *male* or *female* by children (Fillmer & Haswell, 1977). First-grade through fifth-grade children can identify statements that reflect gender-stereotyped language. Children from ages seven to twelve show an increasing ability to recognize certain language behavior as appropriate for males or females. Edelsky (1976) asked students to identify twelve language variables as more likely to be used by a man or by a woman and found that seven-year-olds consistently identified only two of the forms: *adorable* was seen as feminine and *Damn it!* was seen as masculine. By age twelve, however, children consistently identified all twelve variables. All commands were judged to be masculine, and forms such as *oh dear, so,* and *very* were consistently seen as feminine.

Weatherall (1998a) studied four-year-old children and found that they were aware of themselves as gendered. For example, during play the children would make spontaneous references to being a girl or boy (for example, "I only play with other boys" or "Girls play with the dolls"). In addition, the children used gender as a guide for enacting the interpretation of their play (for example, the blue doll dressed as a man was placed in the front of the train because "he" was the driver). Weatherall does note, however, the overall similarities between the speech of the boys and girls (for example, both girls and boys used the same linguistic devices to get attention). Weatherall (1998a) calls for researchers to move beyond merely looking at differences "to looking at how gender is constructed, enacted, maintained as well as challenged in linguistic interaction" (p. 8).

CONSIDER THIS!

In Japan . . .

From national magazine covers to signs fronting women's centers, a linguistic revolution is taking place all over [Japan]: the traditional character for woman, *fujin*—which is derived from an image of a person with a broom—is finally being replaced by the neutral term *josei.* And the Ministry of Labor announced recently that within a few years it will use *josei* in all official documents.

Ms., 1993

Communicative Competence

Our use of language is an important facet of our *communicative competence*. According to Milroy (1980), communicative competence involves "knowledge of when to speak or be silent; how to speak on each occasion; how to communicate (and interpret) meanings of respect, seriousness, humour, politeness or intimacy" (p. 85). We all strive to be competent communicators. Researchers who study language have concluded that the language used by men and women can differ in significant ways.

Coates (1988) points out that, "the fact that women and men differ in terms of their communicative behaviour is now established sociolinguistic fact. The problem remains of *explaining* such difference" (p. 65). There are two conflicting views of how and why women and men possess different communicative norms, based on two conflicting views of women's status in society. One view focuses on power differentials in society and sees women as a group that is oppressed and marginalized. The other view generally ignores issues of power and sees women as simply different from men. The two approaches to gender differences in communicative competence (dominance/deficit and difference) reflect these views (Coates, 1988; Weatherall, 1998a). The **dominance/deficit approach** *"interprets linguistic differences in women's and men's communicative competence as a reflection of men's dominance and women's subordination" in society*, whereas the **difference approach** *"emphasizes the idea that women and men belong to different subcultures:* the differences in women's and men's communicative competence are interpreted as reflecting these different subcultures" (Coates, 1988, pp. 65–66). These two views will be discussed in more detail below.

Dominance/Deficit Approach

Research based on the dominance/deficit approach to communicative competence is based on the idea that the hierarchical nature of gender relations is reflected in gender differences in language (Coates, 1988; Weatherall, 1998a). The most widely known example of the dominance/deficit approach is Robin Lakoff's *Language and Woman's Place* (1975). Lakoff's work supports a dominance/deficit model, claiming that women's language is a reflection of their inferior status in society. Lakoff has been strongly criticized for comparing the language used by women to a male standard (Spender, 1985). These critics accuse Lakoff of implying that any deviation from the male standard is a deficiency on the part of women that should be changed.

Although Lakoff's work on women's language is based more on casual observation and introspection than on empirical research (Cameron, McAlinden & O'Leary, 1988), it has been extremely influential and has made the study of women's language an important issue for researchers (Coates, 1988). Lakoff outlines three areas of gender differences in communicative competence: (1) lexical traits (word choice); (2) phonological traits; and (3) syntactic–pragmatic characteristics.

Lexical Traits.   One of Lakoff's most noted assertions is that women use a larger number of words than men to describe things that interest them and that have been relegated to them as women's work. For example, according to Lakoff women use more words to describe colors than men do. A woman might go shopping for a mauve dress or a taupe scarf. Men rarely use descriptions such as rust, lavender, or cranberry. Even children seem to follow this norm, as shown in the following conversation:

Two girls—6 years old at most—are engaged in singsong conversation [on a seesaw].

> Girl One, suspending her playmate in the air: Mr. Brown won't let you down till you say my favorite color.
> Girl Two: Sea green?
> Girl One: N-o-o-o-o.
> Girl Two: Turquoise?
> Girl One: N-o-o-o-o.
> Girl Two: Magenta? (Alexander, 1988, p. C2)

People have specific vocabularies for topic areas that concern them. Men who are interested in fishing, concerned with physical fitness, or involved in construction jobs use specific terms connected with these activities. It is usually seen as more acceptable for women to use vocabulary from these areas than for men to use specialized vocabularies developed by women. For example, you are more likely to hear women talk about bench pressing, needle-nosed pliers, or having the home-court advantage than to hear men talking about lilac sweaters or how flattering a particular color looks on one of their friends.

According to Lakoff, both men and women use neutral adjectives such as *great* and *terrific*. Women are more likely to use adjectives such as *adorable, charming, sweet,* and *lovely*. Men are more likely to use terms such as *nice, good,* or *pretty*. Although women may freely use more neutral words, men may be ostracized for using women-only words. A woman is in danger, however, if she chooses from the women-only list in an inappropriate situation. For example, a female business executive sounds young and inexperienced if she says, "That's a super idea!" Men are also limited by their inability to use some of the women-only words in appropriate circumstances. It is annoying to some women to ask their partners how they look and receive a one-word reply like "Fine" or "Nice." In this instance, a larger vocabulary for expressing admiration would be helpful.

Turner, Dindia, and Pearson (1995) conducted a study of college student task groups and found that women use more justifiers (giving evidence for a statement such as "I believe . . . because . . ."), intensifiers (words that create intensity such as *so, awfully,* and *quite*), and agreement (direct statements of agreement, such as "You're right" and "I agree"). Women use these behaviors more in conversation regardless of whether their conversational partner was male or female. Men use more vocalized pauses ("ah," "er," "um").

Phonological Traits.   According to Lakoff, more stereotypically feminine people speak "in italics" by emphasizing some words more than others. For example, a feminine speaker might say, "I really *think* you *should* consider staying in *school*." Although at first glance it might appear that italics strengthen an utterance, in actuality they diminish its strength by trying to give the listener directions on how to act.

According to the dominance/deficit model, when speakers are not sure they can convince listeners to do something, they may use double force to make sure their meaning is clear.

Lakoff also contends that women are more likely than men to end a statement with a rising intonation. For example, in response to a question such as "Do you want this report by Friday?" a woman who ends her sentences with a rising intonation would reply, "Yes, please?" Making a statement into a question this way can undercut the strength of the message. As more women move into positions of relative power in our society, differential use of this construction is disappearing, but some women still continue this linguistic habit.

Syntactic-Pragmatic Characteristics. As Lakoff (1975) notes, "Women are not supposed to talk rough" (p. 55). This difference appears in little boys who "drop their g's" in words like *runnin'* and *goin'*, whereas little girls are less apt to omit the final consonants in words. A common gender stereotype holds that women are expected to speak more grammatically than men. On the average, women's speech is closer to the norm of standard speech than men's, especially in formal situations (Smith, 1985). Conversely, there is clear pressure on men to use more nonstandard grammatical forms. Coates (1986) contends that male speakers signal their solidarity with each other by using nonstandard forms of speech. For example, think about the speech you hear on the basketball court or in the locker room. These are settings where grammatically precise speech would sound out of place.

In perhaps the most widely examined aspect of her book, Lakoff contends that women are more likely than men to end sentences with *tag questions* such as "It's really hot, isn't it?" As a dominance/deficit theorist, Lakoff views tag questions as inappropriate.

In addition to tag questions, Lakoff maintains that women's speech contains more hedges—such as *well, you know*, and *kinda*—than men's speech. These words convey the impression that the speaker is unsure of the accuracy of the statements. Of course, the use of hedges may be appropriate in situations where there really is doubt about a statement, but even in situations when they are stating facts, women are more likely than men to start sentences with *I think, I guess*, or *I wonder.* Lakoff argues that women use these linguistic devices more than men because they are conforming to the gender ideology that assertiveness is inappropriate for women.

Tag questions may signal uncertainty, but they also can facilitate conversation by eliciting further comment for the other interactant (Weatherall, 1998b). Research has shown that women use facilitating tag questions more than men (Holmes, 1984). Research evidence, however, does not support Lakoff's observations about tag questions and hedges. Men also use these linguistic devices. In one study, when taped conversations from a university workshop were analyzed, men used 33 tag questions while women used none (Dubois & Crouch, 1975). O'Barr and Atkins (1980) studied men's and women's speech in a courtroom and report that hedges and tag questions are neither typical of the speech of women nor solely confined to the speech of women. In some situations, no one uses tag questions: a study of college students' conversations found so few tag questions used that the researchers could not study them (Martin & Craig, 1983).

It is important to consider the gender composition of the dyad to fully understand the use of tag questions and hedges. Men and women use slightly different language patterns when talking to each other than when talking to people of the same sex. Females use more qualifying words such as *maybe* and *sort of* when talking to females than when talking to males (Martin & Craig, 1983). Males use more qualifying words (*maybe, guess, well, kind of*) when talking to males than to females (Sayers & Sherblom, 1987). In support of these differences, Mulac, Weimann, Widenmann, and Gibson (1988) find more gendered language use in same-sex than in mixed-sex dyads. Thus, some aspects of gendered language are more prominent when females are talking to females or when males are talking to males.

Perceptions of language can be influenced by gender, too. In a study of a small group situation, women who used tag questions and **disclaimers,** "*introductory expressions that excuse, explain, or request understanding or forbearance,*" were perceived less positively and were less influential than women who stated their views more directly (Bradley, 1981). In this setting, males were viewed as intelligent and well informed even if they failed to support their arguments or if they used verbal qualifiers (statements such as "Well, I'm no expert, but . . ."). In contrast, women who failed to support their arguments or used verbal qualifiers were perceived as less intelligent and knowledgeable. Thus, the same linguistic devices can be perceived differently depending on whether they are used by men or by women. Bradley (1981) concludes that qualifying phrases may be seen as indicators of uncertainty and nonassertiveness when used by women but as "tools of politeness and other-directedness" when used by men (p. 90).

Cameron, McAlinden, and O'Leary (1988) reassess the issue of tag questions and find that "use of tag questions in conversation between equals seems to correlate with conversational role rather than with gender" (Coates, 1988, p. 67). In conversations among people of different status, certain forms of tag questions are used by the more powerful participants. Thus, tag questions are indications of subordination based on a variety of factors including gender or class.

Support for the Dominance/Deficit Approach.   There is research support for the dominance/deficit model. For example, Woods (1988) concludes that in workplace groups, gender rather than organizational status determines who holds the floor. In her study, male speakers interrupted more and were interrupted less than female speakers. Males also spoke significantly longer than females in this situation. West (1984) reports similar results in a study of doctors.

Carli (1990) finds women more tentative than men in male-female dyads. Her study is based on **expectations states theory,** which contends that *inequalities in face-to-face interactions are a function of the relative status of the participants.* According to this theory, when people of different status interact, it is improper for the person of low status to communicate too aggressively because that behavior would be seen as an attempt to gain status at the expense of the other person.

Tentative speech may be effective for women in some circumstances. Carli (1990) reports that in mixed-sex groups, women who speak more tentatively are more influential with men but less influential with women. Thus, the use of tentative speech may enhance a woman's ability to influence a man but may reduce her ability to influence a woman. In this study, both male and female speakers judged a woman who spoke tentatively as less competent and knowledgeable than a woman who spoke assertively. Although Carli concludes that gender differences in the use of tag questions, disclaimers, and hedges are probably a function of status differences between men and women, "tentative language may be used [by women] as a subtle influence strategy" (Carli, 1990, p. 949).

Difference Approach

The difference approach to communicative competence holds that

> women and men talk differently, or behave differently in spoken interaction, because they are socialized in different sociolinguistic subcultures. . . . [This approach] reflects a growing political awareness among linguists that by labeling men's language as "strong" and women's language as "weak," we were adopting an androcentric viewpoint. The difference . . . approach attempts to investigate sex differences in communicative competence, and in particular women's language, from a positive standpoint. (Coates, 1988, p. 69)

One of the earliest conceptualizations of this approach is Maltz and Borker's (1982) list of women's and men's features of language (Crawford, 2000). Unlike Lakoff, they do not contend that these language differences reflect a power imbalance between men and women, but that women and men have internalized different norms for conversation. They argue that communicative competence is developed in same-sex play groups, and consequently communication problems may occur in mixed-sex interactions because women and men may have different expectations for interaction or may interpret specific facets of language differently (Coates, 1988; Crawford, 2000).

According to the difference approach (sometimes called the cultural approach), differences in speech style develop because of early communication patterns since boys and girls play in predominantly separate groups. This approach argues that

> a female subculture creates and maintains relationships of closeness and equality. Hence criticism is couched in socially acceptable ways and females can interpret accurately and sensitively the speech of others. Thus women develop a cooperative style of communication. Males on the other hand come from a culture where they have learnt to assert a position of dominance, attract and maintain an audience and where they must assert themselves by interrupting when another person has the floor. Thus their style of communication is predominantly competitive. (Weatherall, 1998a, pp. 2–3)

For example, a study of African American children in a Philadelphia neighborhood (Goodwin, 1988) reports that boys are more likely to use commands ("Gimme the pliers"; "Get off my step"), while girls are more likely to use modal auxiliaries such as "can" and "could" ("We *could* go around looking for more bottles"). Goodwin also finds that girls' groups are more likely to be nonhierarchically structured in a cooperative form. Boys' groups are usually hierarchically structured and based on competition. Girls, however, may organize themselves hierarchically depending on the context. For example, girls are able to exhibit leadership and issue commands in situations of urgency, such as when the safety of a group member is threatened. Girls also construct their play hierarchically in situations such as playing house, when someone takes on the role of a mother giving instructions to her children.

In general, these data support the conclusion that males are more likely to pursue a style of interaction based on *power* while females are more likely to use a style based on *solidarity and support* (Coates, 1986). These norms are effective when they are followed by all members of a group, but they can cause difficulties in male-female communication.

Coates (1986) examines several problem areas in conversations between males and females. For example, *questions* appear to have different meaning for males and females. Women use questions more than men, and they use them as a conversational maintenance strategy, that is, to keep the conversation going. Men are more likely to interpret a question as a simple request for information. They answer the question and feel that they have completed their task. Women then have to ask another question to continue the conversation. Both parties may feel frustrated because they do not understand the intent of the other person's behavior.

Links between speaker turns may also cause difficulties in male-female conversation. Women are more likely to start a speaking turn by directly acknowledging the contribution of the previous speaker and then talking about the previous topic ("I think Stephen is right. Let's all contribute five dollars for a gift."). Conversely, men are more likely not to acknowledge what has gone on before and to make their own point ("I'm going for pizza. What do you want on it?"). Because of these differing styles, women may feel that their comments are being ignored while men may feel that switching the topic implicitly expresses agreement ("If I disagreed, I would have said so").

Topic shifts may be very abrupt in all-male conversations. Women typically shift topics gradually. Men may be frustrated in a male-female interaction that they feel is dragging on too long or is not moving fast enough.

All-male groups can engage in *loud, aggressive arguments* that focus on seemingly trivial topics but are enjoyed for their own sake. They may include shouting, name-calling, and other insults. Conversely, many women try to avoid displays of verbal aggressiveness. They think these displays are unpleasant, and interpret them personally. As Coates (1986) explains, "for women, such displays represent a disruption of conversation, whereas for men they are part of the conventional structure of conversation" (p. 153).

Perhaps the most widely known advocate of the difference approach is Deborah Tannen. Tannen (1991) argues that women tend to organize their talk cooperatively while men are more likely to organize their talk competitively. She believes that "many women bond by talking about troubles, and many men bond by exchanging playful insults and put-downs, and other sorts of verbal sparring" (p. B1).

Using the Communication Styles Survey, Michaud and Warner (1997) found some support for Tannen's ideas concerning differences in "troubles talk" (when someone, usually a woman, recounts a problem in detail. They discovered that women are more likely to report that they would offer sympathy in response to troubles talk while men are more likely to change the subject or tell the person not to worry. In addition, men are more likely to report that they would feel hurt, put down or angry if someone gave them advice about their troubles, while women would be more likely to feel comforted, helped, or grateful if their close friends offered them advice. In general, the women in this study reported feeling more positive about receiving advice from a friend than the men did.

The difference approach has been criticized for failing to "theorize how power relations at the structural level are re-created and maintained at the interactional level" (Crawford, 2000, p. 99). For example, critics of Tannen argue that her theories help to maintain the privileged positions men hold in society without challenging them (Weatherall, 1998a). In this way, women are encouraged to adapt to the communicative style of men that could otherwise be interpreted as rude or insensitive. Another critique of this position contends that the difference approach fails to examine other categories that might affect language use such as race, ethnicity, class, age, or sexual orientation. As Crawford (2000) notes, "when sex is the only conceptual category, differences attributable to situations and power relationships are made invisible" (p. 100).

Recent work has begun to examine not only male-female and all-male speech events but all-female speech events, too. The following sections discuss several features of communication competence that have received a great deal of research attention: verbosity, interruptions, conversational initiation, and argumentativeness.

Verbosity.   Perhaps the idea of the talkative woman arises because women spend more time initiating and maintaining conversations than men do. A study of marital interaction found that to maintain a conversation, wives asked five times as many questions as their husbands did (Fishman, 1978). Wives' questions were used to engage their husbands in dialogue. Only 36 percent of the topics introduced by the wives in this study succeeded in engaging their husbands in conversation, while nearly all the topics (96 percent) the husbands introduced were discussed. (We will examine this idea in more detail later in this chapter.)

James and Drakich (1993) examined research studies on amount of talk and found that in 56 studies dealing with adult mixed-sex interaction, males talked more than females in 45 percent of the studies and talked more than females in some circumstances in another 18 percent of the studies. Only two studies found that females talked more than males.

Tannen (1990b) contends that men may talk more in public situations while women may talk more in private situations. She argues that men talk more when they feel the need to establish or maintain their status in a group. Women view talk as crucial in maintaining close relationships, and thus talk more in private settings.

Interruptions.   James and Clarke (1993) review 32 studies that have examined interruptions in male-female conversation and find no firm support for the belief that men interrupt women more than women interrupt men. Seventeen of these studies find no significant gender differences in interruptions. In ten studies, men produce more interruptions than women. A similar range of results is produced in studies of

CONSIDER THIS!

Who Does the Talking?

Developers of new technologies for the Internet are working on web pages that talk as well as other innovations like computers that give verbal directions to drivers and read people's e-mail. If you are wondering what these voices will sound like, Dr. Clifford Nass, a professor at Stanford University, has said, "Our studies show that directions from a female voice are perceived as less accurate than those from a male voice" and praise from a male voice is more valued (Eisenberg, 2000, p. G1). One company is planning to use a "friendly secretarial voice" for its e-mail reader and a male voice to deliver information on stocks since "a male voice is more credible in this context" (Eisenberg, 2000, p. G11). The question becomes: Should we limit ourselves to gender ideologies from the past that restrict both females and males or should we try to use these technologies to expand our awareness of the potential for all individuals to contribute to society?

same-sex interaction. Seventeen of the twenty-two studies in this category report no gender differences.

Marche and Peterson (1993) look at interruptions in conversations among children (grades 4 and 9) and college students, and find that males do not interrupt any more than females and that females are interrupted by their conversational partners just as frequently as males are interrupted by theirs. That is, males do not interrupt females any more than females interrupt males.

Interruptions can serve a control function or as conversational support. They can be used to communicate enthusiastic assent, elaboration of the other person's theme, and participation in the ongoing topic, or to take control of the speaking turn (Aleguire, 1978). It is unclear whether these interruptions are dominance related or rapport building. James and Clarke (1993) note that "no clear conclusions . . . can be drawn at this time from the existing research findings as to whether males' interruptions are more likely to constitute attempts to seize the floor than are those of females, or as to whether females are more likely than males to have dominance-related interruptions directed against them" (p. 258)

Interruption patterns do differ depending on the composition of the dyad, however. There are more other-sex interruptions (male-female or female-male) than same-sex (male-male or female-female) interruptions (Dindia, 1987; Turner, Dindia & Pearson, 1995). Thus, it is important to take into account whether the conversational partners are male or female when examining a variable such as interruptions.

Analyzing interruptions can be difficult because the function of interruptions varies. For examples, interruptions may be used as dominance indicators (taking the turn away from someone else on purpose), as confirming responses or signs of conversational involvement (a person may be so interested in what the other person is talking about that he or she is eager to contribute to the discussion), or as errors in turn taking (Turner, Dindia & Pearson, 1995).

Conversation Initiation. As discussed previously in this chapter, topics introduced by men tend to be noticed and carried on by their conversational partners while topics introduced by women may die a sudden death in spite of the fact that women tend to initiate more topics than men. Does the following example sound familiar to you?

Imagine that you are at a restaurant observing a couple having dinner. For a while, they read their menus and she asks him, "What are you going to order?" He responds, "The bacon and cheddar burger." She says, "That sounds good. I think I'll have the chicken Caesar salad." After the server takes their order, there is a moment of silence. Then she says, "I went to the mall today to look for a dress for my sister's wedding." He replies, "Yeah." She continues, "But I couldn't find anything I liked. I guess I'll have to keep looking around." He remains silent. She says, "Did you hear about what happened to Jennifer today? She had a big fight with Bob about spending so much money on a present for Allison's wedding." "Uh, huh," he responds. She tries again by asking, "Did you get the new tires for your car?" He says, "No, they didn't have time to balance them today so I have to go back tomorrow." Then she says, "Are they a good deal? Should I get some for my car?" He replies, "You don't really need new tires. Wait until they wear some more." She says, "Okay. I talked to your mother today. She wants us to come over for dinner on Tuesday." He looks over her shoulder and says, "Oh."

This example illustrates one way that men may inhibit conversations with women, by giving minimal responses such as "yeah" or "oh" to topics introduced by women. Men can control a conversation with little effort when they fail to respond to topics initiated by women, while having the topics they bring up accepted for discussion (Fishman, 1978). In a situation like this, women work harder in conversations because they initiate more topics, as well as respond to topics initiated by men (Parlee, 1979b).

As Smith (1985) notes, "there is considerable evidence that the norms of femininity and masculinity encourage women and men to construe communication situations and the goals of interaction somewhat differently" (p. 135). The traditional concept of masculinity is highly correlated with the *control dimension*, the extent to which a person can exert active control over the process and outcomes of an interaction. The *affiliative dimension*—the tendency to elicit warmth and approach—is associated with the traditional norms of femininity. Thus, men may be more concerned with aspects of control while women are more concerned with the goal of affiliation. These conflicting goals can be seen in the dialogue discussed previously. As a difference theorist, Smith (1985), contends, however, "Men are not 'dominant' and women 'muted': rather, men, who are encouraged to be masculine, manage and monitor the control-related aspects of interaction; while women, encouraged to be feminine, will tend to manage and monitor interaction in the pursuit of affiliative goals" (p. 136). This conclusion is supported by Mulac and colleagues (1988) who find that men are more likely to use direct control tactics such as directives ("you should write down your answers") and to maintain their speaking turns by using fillers to begin sentences ("and another thing . . . "), while women are more likely to use indirect control strategies such as questions ("what next") and to express interest in others through the use of personal pronouns such as *we*.

Argumentativeness.   Another behavior associated with communicative competence is argumentativeness. Considerable research has been conducted on this topic. Aggressive communication refers to two constructs: argumentativeness and verbal aggressiveness. **Argumentativeness** is defined as *a stable trait that predisposes an individual in communication situations to advocate positions on controversial issues and to attack verbally the positions that other people take on these issues* (Infante & Rancer, 1982). Thus, argumentativeness is seen as a subset of assertiveness: all arguing involves assertive behavior, but not all assertive behavior involves arguing. **Verbal aggressiveness** is seen as the negative side of aggressive communication. It is defined as *the predisposition to verbally attack the self-concepts of individuals instead of their positions on controversial issues* (Infante & Wigley, 1986). Skill in argumentative behavior is associated with communicative competence. Males have been found to score higher than females in both argumentativeness and verbal aggressiveness (Infante, 1985; Infante, Wall, Leap & Danielson, 1984). Nicotera and Rancer (1994) find that males score significantly higher than females on measures of both aggressive communication predispositions. In addition, both males and females perceive that males are more argumentative and verbally aggressive than females.

Women, however, are more likely to believe that arguing is a hostile, aggressive, and combative communication activity. They are more likely than men to believe that arguing is a strategy used for dominating and controlling another person (Nicotera & Rancer, 1994). Nevertheless, women are able to use this communication strategy when necessary. Infante (1989) finds that when an adversary uses verbal aggression, men are provoked to become more verbally aggressive themselves, while women respond by becoming more argumentative.

As we discussed earlier in this book, it is important to examine not only gender but also other factors such as race and ethnicity when considering communication behavior. Although a considerable amount of research has not been conducted in this area, we do know that argumentativeness and verbal aggressiveness are positively related for both Causasian and African American adolescents (Anderson, Raptis, Lin & Clark, 2000).

Gender and African American Speech

Most of the research on gender and language has been conducted with white, middle-class samples (Houston Stanback, 1985). This lack of diversity does not adequately describe the rich variety of language used by people throughout the United States and the world. Houston Stanback (1985) views communication as socially and culturally situated action and argues that research on black women's language has been particularly lacking. Reviewing the research in this area, she notes that in contrast to the idea of deferential speech, there is an absence of black male dominance in male-female encounters. She describes this phenomenon as black women's tendency to verbally "contend" with black men (p. 182). According to Houston Stanback (1985), "there is a fundamental tendency toward male-female communicative parity in black culture which starkly contrasts to the tendency toward communicative asymmetry which scholars emphasize for white women and men" (p. 182). She views this difference as a result of black women's continuing participation in both the domestic realm of the home and the public sphere of work.

Scott (1995) intensely studied black women's talk and found several prominent linguistic markers. For example, the women in her sample often used the word *girl* as a way of including others in their conversation. She notes: "Their use of 'girl' with another Black woman who is not necessarily one of their 'girls' but does share their same identity appears to demonstrate the solidarity use of this word" (p. 8). In addition, these women used the word *look* as a way to signal to white women that they refused to remain silent particularly in classroom situations. For example, one woman recounted saying, "Look, let me tell you something," while another said "Look, I don't agree, it's wrong" (p. 8).

In reviewing the speech of black men, Orbe (1994) finds six essential themes:

1. The importance of communicating with other African Americans—because of a feeling that non-African Americans had difficulty identifying and understanding the problems and situations faced by African Americans.
2. Learning how to interact with non-African Americans—through direct talks with others, observation, and trial and error.
3. Playing the part (SNAP!)—the ability to abandon the communication styles of the African American community and adopt the norms of European-American culture in situations such as business meetings.
4. Keeping a safe distance—conscious efforts to avoid interaction with non-African Americans.
5. Testing the sincerity of non-African Americans—strategies to identify people who were genuinely sensitive to issues of importance to the African American community.
6. An intense social responsibility—to help other African Americans and to make non-African Americans aware of different life experiences.

This section demonstrates the importance of considering various aspects of a person when drawing conclusions about communication behavior in any context. The information presented above demonstrates that race and ethnicity are important factors influencing communication and are closely related to gender in a variety of situations.

Implications and Consequences of Gendered Language

A great deal of research on language has examined sexism in vocabulary and the structure of language itself (Rakow, 1986). **Sexism** is *discrimination against individuals or groups on the basis of their gender.* Sexist language perpetuates negative gender stereotypes. Shear (1985) considers sexist language to be "toxic"; Ayim (1993) points out that, "our language fosters and perpetuates racist and classist bigotry as well" as sexism (p. 3).

Sexism

As a dominance/deficit theorist, Colwill (1993) contends that the status differential between men and women continues to be maintained by sexist language. She claims that language negatively affects our communication in four ways, through

1. using masculine words to refer to females and males (for example, *chairman*)
2. using titles of different levels for women and men (a woman is greeted as Betty while a man is called Mr. Smith)
3. using different words to describe women and men doing the same thing (nurse versus male nurse, writer versus female writer)
4. reinforcing gender stereotypes ("When a manager hires a secretary, he should choose her with care.") (p. 4)

In an innovative study, Turner (1992) followed a procedure suggested by Pearson (1985) and asked her students to make up genlets—words for situations that males and females believe are uniquely experienced by their gender and for which no current word exists. Turner found that the words developed by her students reflected a power differential between women and men. Women created words illustrating experiences that rendered them passive and anxious (such as *perchaphonic*, waiting for someone to call you on the phone and *herdastudaphobia*, feeling fear when passing a group of strange men on the street). Men were more likely to coin words that reflected a sense of power (such as *gearheaditis*, making your car the best one on the road and *beer muscles*, an alcohol-induced feeling of strength and toughness that may result in fighting). While both men and women in this study developed words dealing with food, women created words reflecting a concern with what their relationship partner thinks about their eating habits (*piglabelphobia*) and men portrayed eating as a competitive event (*scarfaholic*). In terms of physical appearance, women spoke of *brinkley-mirror*, indicating the insecurity they felt at being compared to a glamorous figure. Men saw *schwarzenegger-syndrome* as a challenge to work out more to develop bigger muscles than other men. Thus, where women indicate concern about pleasing others and insecurity over measuring up to others, men may see the same situations as arenas for competition.

Gendered Perceptions

Many gender stereotypes exist concerning men's and women's language use. For example, college students in one study were able to correctly identify the gender of cartoon characters from the captions alone (Kramer, 1974). Students assigned the logical, concise, businesslike, and controlling captions to male speakers, and the stupid, vague, emotional, confused, and wordy captions to female speakers—and in 75 percent of the cases they were right. Moving from cartoons to actual speech, these students characterized male speech as more attention seeking, dominating, authoritarian, aggressive, and frank. Female speech was characterized as friendly, gentle, enthusiastic, grammatically correct, but sometimes trivial (Kramer, 1978).

Research to determine the effects of these perceptions in interactions has focused on the use of deferential language. **Deferential language** is characterized by *the use of tag questions, qualifiers, hedges, and other forms of speech stereotypically associated with "women's language."* To determine whether these characteristics affect perceptions of speakers, Liska, Mechling and Stathas (1981) asked students to evaluate a transcript of a group discussion involving speakers who used deferential and nondeferential language. The raters evaluated the speakers who used deferential language as more submissive, less assertive, and less willing to take a stand than speakers who used nondeferential language. In addition, deferential language users were more likely to be perceived as feminine. In general, raters were more likely to perceive users of deferential language as having less power, but more personal warmth.

Communication Accommodation Theory (CAT) posits that speakers accommodate their speech to the speech of those with whom they interact most frequently (Yaeger-Dror, 1998). In most cases, this is an unconscious process in which individuals try "to talk more like those they interact with" (p. 41). Wheeless (1984) tested this theory by asking men and women to respond to several conversational situations, and found that all people use both stereotypical feminine and masculine language forms. Yet respondents who identified themselves in terms of the traditionally masculine or feminine gender roles discussed in Chapter 2 differed in the amount of conversational accommodation they used. Traditionally feminine individuals were more accommodating than traditionally masculine individuals. In other words, people who conform to a stereotypically feminine gender identity tend to use speech that is more considerate, cooperative, helpful, sensitive, sincere, submissive, and sympathetic.

Man-Made Language

According to Spender (1995), men have controlled the development of language, provided themselves with more positive words to describe themselves, and given themselves more opportunities to use those words. Throughout history the predominant holders of power have been men (government leaders, warriors, scholars, clergy), and powerful people set the standards for language. Of course, women have had some influence and will presumably have more as they assume positions of greater public power, but historically men have set the standards for language use outside the home.

How does this "man-made language," as Spender (1995) terms it, treat women? To begin with, the masculine form of a word is often taken as the standard while the feminine form of a word is derived from it. For example, men are authors, poets, princes and actors. Women are -esses. *Authoress* and *poetess* passed out of use as more women became successful in these professions, but we still use *princess* and *actress*. Even when we use different words to describe the masculine and feminine role, the masculine form comes first in the usual word order (Smith, 1985). Consider the following examples: husband and wife, man and woman, brother and sister, boy and girl, king and queen. Would it sound strange to you to say "wife and husband?"

Another indication of the tendency of the English language to omit women is the occurrence of **gender markers** (Pincus & Pincus, 1980). These are *words that indicate the biological sex of the person who is being described.* This is sometimes indicated explicitly or implicitly.

Occupational titles (like surgeon and mayor) can be gender marked in four ways (Pincus & Pincus, 1980). First, some terms have *male* and *female analogs* (for example, *barber/beautician, janitor/matron, tailor/dressmaker*). These are usually occupations that are or were segregated by sex: tailors made clothes for men; dressmakers made clothes for women. Second, some terms show *gender by inflection* (adding an ending, such as *actor/actress, executor/executrix*). These terms usually describe occupations that were initially male dominated, but that women have gradually entered. In Shakespeare's time, for example, all people who acted on the stage were male. Now, both males and females perform in theatrical roles. Third, some terms carry *male or female or neutral inflections* such as *chairman/chairwoman/chairperson; businessman/businesswoman/businessperson*. As more women enter these occupations, these words are changing to neutral forms—for example, *police officer* and *mail carrier*. Fourth, some terms *do not have overt gender markers* but are still considered as describing one sex or the other (*doctor, nurse, lawyer, secretary*). When we hear the word *nurse*, we may still picture a woman in a white uniform. The term *construction worker* still conjures up a large man in a hard hat.

Words used to describe men and women may have different connotations. Moely and Kriecker (1984) surveyed undergraduate students and others who indicated that *gentleman* and *lady* connote similar images of gentility and virtue. Nevertheless, *gentleman* was seen as warmer and more competent than *man*, whereas *lady* was seen as colder and less competent than *woman*. It appears that women prefer both women and men to think of them as *ladies*, while men prefer women to think of them as *gentlemen*, but want to be perceived as *men* by other men (Slama & Slowey, 1988).

The debate about the use of the term *Ms.* is a good example of differential treatment. The popular form of address for a man is *Mr.* which gives no indication of marital status. At one time the same was true for women: *Mrs.* was the courtesy title used by all adult women, while *Miss* designated female children. It has only been since the early 19th century that women have been identified as *Miss* or *Mrs.*, clearly indicating their marital status (Smith, 1985). Beginning in the 1970s, many women chose to eliminate marital status as a form of identifier, and adopted the term *Ms.* as the female courtesy title.

Even though *Ms.* was proposed as a marital status–neutral term equivalent to *Mr.*, it is often interpreted as a synonym for *Miss* (Baron, 1989). In addition, several stereotypes are associated with the term *Ms.* For example, women referred to as *Ms.* are perceived to be more achievement-oriented, more socially assertive, more dynamic, and less interpersonally warm than other women (Dion, 1987). In an interesting study, Rubin (1986) found that teachers who used the title *Ms.* were perceived as teaching more interesting courses than teachers who preferred *Mrs.* or *Miss.* Thus, a woman's choice of a title may influence how people perceive her and consequently affect their communication toward her.

Language and naming have enormous power over our perceptions and our behavior (Ayim, 1993; Weatherall, 1998b). Even male and female nicknames are not equivalent. Males both give and receive more nicknames (Phillips, 1990). While male nicknames tend to connote strength, hardness, and maturity (often ending in -o: Jocko, Bucko, Dude), female nicknames tend to connote beauty, kindness, and pleasantness (often ending in *-ie* or *-y:* cutie, sweetie, honey). Female children may be given versions of male names (Jamie, Johnny, Sidney), but male children rarely receive versions of female names.

Thus, language used to describe men and women reflects our gender ideology. Since language use is a reflection of the society in which we live, as long as society defines men and women in terms of gender stereotypes, gendered language use will persist.

Strategies for Change

Webb (1986) contends that using nonsexist language is a communication skill that should be learned in order to overcome problematic aspects of our language. Sexist language is particularly destructive because it allows us to operate with blind spots regarding gender stereotypes and bias (Wilcoxon, 1989). For example, Kitto (1989) finds that people perceive females labeled as *girls* to be more appropriate candidates for low-level jobs, while females labeled as *women* are seen as more appropriate for higher-level jobs. Kitto argues that gender ideologies associated with language have a powerful ability to influence our perceptions. If we eliminate sexist language, we can more easily see our own biases and learn to eliminate them.

Although language will not totally cease to reflect separate gender ideology

---

CONSIDER THIS!

Queer

Queer, a word long bandied in schoolyards and bars as a taunt, has acquired a new meaning: it has been adopted, proudly and defiantly, by a new generation of young militants. . . .

Those who define themselves as "queer" say they are reclaiming the term from bigots who use it as a slur, and turning it into an ironic badge of honor, not unlike the pink triangle that homosexuals were compelled to wear in Nazi Germany, which is now proudly worn by gay marchers and demonstrators. . . .

To Richard Goldstein, the executive editor of *The Village Voice*, who has begun using the word in his column, *queer* covers all sexual minorities, but also carries another nuance. "It's also a word that connotes militance: activists who are fervent or outrageous. It means the assertive homosexual."

Mr. Goldstein also thought it suggested youth. "I'm 47, too old to be queer—I'm gay."

And there are those who call themselves queer, yet do not relish the prospect of having the word spread beyond their community. "I am not for any straight writer using the word 'queer' in a mainstream publication," said Donna Mindowits, a writer for *The Village Voice*. "This is our word," she explained. "I can say it, but you can't."

Stanley, 1991

until society ceases to believe these ideas, some people advocate that language change can be used as a means to change society. The following sections describe some of the ways that have been suggested to change language to reflect a less rigid gender ideology. One of the communication skills that is worth developing is the avoidance of he-man language.

Avoiding He-Man Language

Using he-man language affects our perceptions of men and women. Complete the following sentences:

- As the construction worker surveyed the building site, . . .
- The nurse who works on the fifth floor is very helpful. In fact, yesterday . . .
- When a person wins the lottery, . . .
- After a judge instructs the jury, . . .

Was your choice of pronoun determined by traditional gender stereotypes or did you avoid them? People are more likely to use *he* when considering traditional male roles such as *judge* and *construction worker,* and *she* when considering traditional female roles such as *nurse* and *secretary* (Wheeless, Berryman-Fink, & Sarafini, 1982). Neutral roles (such as winning the lottery) are identified as either *he* or *they.* This exercise is an example of how traditional gender stereotypes affect our language choice.

Language also affects our perceptions of the world. When people read or hear sentences containing *generic pronouns* such as *he* (for example, "Everyone deserves his right to a fair trial"), some of them are more likely to believe that the sentences refer to men than to women. There are no feminine generics, that is, feminine words used to represent both the feminine and the masculine forms of a word (Smith, 1985). According to Ayim (1993), the term *woman* is not even generic for all females, since it usually focuses on white women, excluding black women, Native American women, and other women of color. Man-linked words (such as *chairman* or *spokesman*) are problematic because they are more likely to be perceived as referring to men than to women. Non-man-linked words (such as *chairperson* or *spokesperson*) are not (Todd-Mancillas, 1981).

Man-linked words also affect children's perceptions. Gelb (1989) reports that the ratio of male to female pronouns during story time in elementary school classrooms is three to one. When children who had heard these stories were asked to compose their own stories, boys made the central character male 97 percent of the time and girls made the central character male 81 percent of the time.

To include everyone in our language use, Todd-Mancillas (1981) and others suggest several alternatives to conventional man-linked and third-person singular masculine pronoun generics. First, existing language options can be used instead. For example, sentences can be pluralized ("Students are expected to type their papers" instead of "A student is expected to type his paper") or words such as *people* or *human beings* can be substituted for *man* or *mankind.* Second, constructions that call specific attention to both males and females can be used, such as *he or she, women and men,* or *his or her.* In addition, neutral words such as *server* (instead of *waiter* and *waitress*) or *worker* (instead of *workman*) can be used.

Shear (1985) contends that avoiding he-man language may actually improve one's writing style. For example, she notes that "you cut the verbiage in half when you change "a tenant needs a roof over his head" to "a tenant needs shelter." Similarly, you lessen the tedium in "his employees, his guests, or members of his family" when you substitute "his or her employees, guests, or family members" (p. 106). She suggests 14 ways to avoid sexist pronoun use:

1. *Add the female:* she or he, hers or his, he or she, his or hers.
2. *Use the first person:* I, me, my, mine, we, our, ours.
3. *Use the second person:* you, your, yours.
4. *Move the noun.*
5. *Repeat the noun.*
6. *Use a new noun instead of a pronoun or as a synonym for an old noun.*
7. *Use the plural*—one of the easiest, handiest methods.
8. *Delete the pronoun.*
9. *Use a new pronoun:* it, its, this, that.
10. *Use an article or conjunction:* a, an, the, but, and.
11. *Use who with or without a noun:* who, anyone who, someone who, whoever, no one who, one who, any (noun) who, a (noun) who, the (noun) who—helps emphasize a single individual.
12. *Rewrite*—the most work and the least often needed.
13. *Use the passive*—be cautious; the incompetent use it verbosely, the cunning use it evasively.
14. *Use they, their, them*—the simplest, most sensible method of all. (p. 108)

Far from considering *they* to be ungrammatical, when referring to a singular noun or pronoun, Shear (1985) notes that *they* was widely accepted in this usage in written English until the end of the 18th century when grammarians began attacking it. So writing sentences like "Everyone should return their course request forms to the department office" is actually a return to a former usage.

You may be asking yourself why it is important to use inclusive language even if it is more awkward than using the word *he.* Khosroshahi (1989) reports that using *he or she* gives rise to the greatest number of images of women, while using *he* elicits the least. *They* is somewhere in between. Schau and Scott (1984) also find that language referring specifically to males and females results in more gender-balanced associations than language that does not directly specify gender. Using *he* results almost exclusively in images associated with males.

Guidelines for Nonsexist Language

More people are becoming aware of the negative effects of sexist language. In one study, 42 percent of newspaper editors and 52 percent of magazine editors indicated that they preferred to use *he or she* instead of the generic *he* (Kingsolver & Cordry, 1987).

In addition, people with positive attitudes toward women are more likely to use language that is not male-biased (Jacobson & Insko, 1985). Students who typically have liberal attitudes toward women are more likely to report that sexism in language is an important issue (Murdock & Forsyth, 1985).

Sorrels (1983) offers eight guidelines for nonsexist communication:

1. Commit yourself to remove sexism from all your communication.
2. Practice and reinforce nonsexist communication patterns until they become habitual. The ultimate test is your ability to carry on a nonsexist private conversation and to think in nonsexist terms.
3. Set a nonsexist communication example and direct or persuade others to adopt your example.
4. Use familiar idioms whenever possible, but if you must choose between sexism and the unfamiliar, use the unfamiliar until it becomes familiar.
5. Take care not to arouse negativism in the receiver by using awkward, cumbersome, highly repetitious, or glaring revisions. A sufficient variety of graceful, controlled, sex-positive [words that value both sexes], dynamic revisions exist so that you can avoid entirely bland or offensive constructions.
6. Use the full range of techniques for correction of sexist communication, including reconstruction, substitution, and omission.
7. Check roots and meanings of words to be sure that the words need to be changed before changing them.
8. Check every outgoing message—whether written, oral, or nonverbal—for sexism before sending it. (p. 17)

Hellinger (1984) proposes two strategies for countering the linguistic invisibility of women. The first, the generic strategy, is to choose words that avoid reference to gender, such as *camera operator* or *newscaster*. This strategy helps to create truly generic occupations over time. The second, the visibility strategy, is to specifically include references to gender to highlight the visibility of women, for example, *businesswomen, congresswomen*.

Following these various suggested guidelines gives the nonsexist communicator a variety of means to avoid gender stereotypes. For example, simple changes such as using *workers* instead of *workmen*, *firefighter* instead of *fireman*, and *flight attendant* instead of *stewardess* include all people. Avoiding labels such as *woman doctor, boy genius,* or *male hairdresser* diminishes stereotyping. The U.S. government revised its *Dictionary of Occupational Titles* in 1975 with a 363-page guide that replaced such terms as *bellboy* with *bellhop*, *salesman* with *sales agent*, and *mailman* with *mail carrier* (Nilsen, 1979).

Table 3.1 gives some examples of less stereotyped language use for you to consider.

Unfortunately, studies have shown that lecturing on nonsexist language has virtually no effect on students' language habits. Even replacing a lecture with a more student-involved format such as computer-assisted instruction does not lead to any

TABLE 3.1   Alternatives to Stereotyped Language

Examples of Stereotyped Language	Possible Alternatives
cavemen	cave dwellers, prehistoric people
coed	student
freshman	first-year student
Dear Sir or Madam (in a letter)	Dear Title (e.g., Director of Admissions)
mailman	mail carrier, postal worker
mankind	humanity, society, women and men, the general public
manpower	personnel, staff
newsman	reporter, journalist
right-hand man/girl Friday	assistant, aide, helper
weatherman	meteorologist, weather forecaster
Marie Curie made a discovery that few people—men or women—could have made.	Marie Curie made a discovery that few people could have made.
Tricia Smith Wells is a highly successful woman in advertising.	Tricia Smith Wells is a highly successful advertising executive.
A farmer and his family . . .	Farmers and their children . . .
A truck driver spends long hours in his truck.	Truck drivers spend long hours in their trucks.
The librarian must catalog her books promptly.	Librarians must catalog books promptly.
A doctor and his dentist wife . . .	A doctor and dentist, who are married . . .
The tenant must not damage his apartment himself or let anyone else do so. The owner and his employees may enter the apartment to make emergency repairs to protect his property. He does not have to notify the tenant that he is coming.	The tenant must not damage this apartment or let anyone else do so. The owner or the owner's employees may enter the apartment to make emergency repairs to protect the property.
Hold the cat in your lap so that the dog can sniff his future friend. The cat will probably arch her back and hiss, ready to defend herself.	Hold the cat in your lap so that the dog can sniff a future friend. The cat will probably arch its back to defend itself.

Jenkins, Gappa, and Pearce, 1983; Miller and Swift, 1988; Shear, 1985; Sorrels, 1983 improvement (McMinn, Troyer, Hannum, & Foster, 1991). Changing language habits is difficult work. We hope that this chapter will motivate you to examine your language habits and change those that are not inclusive. Look carefully at your language even if you do not think there is any reason to change it. As Baron (1989) notes, language can be sexist in spite of good intentions.

Summary

In this chapter we have discussed gender and language use. Gender differences in language appear in young children. As preschoolers, girls comment on the imagined contexts of play with greater complexity than boys. As we might expect from traditional gender ideologies, girls use more other-emphasizing strategies than boys. As children and adolescents, boys view friendly conversation among their peers as training for verbal aggression. Girls tend to establish more egalitarian same-sex groups. Girls use friendly groups as a training ground for cooperation.

Although the traditional gender ideology holds that women talk more than men, in fact, men talk more than women. In general, males demonstrate more control in interactions. They may control conversations, in part, by failing to respond to topics initiated by women, which makes women search for new topics to initiate.

According to the dominance/deficit model, the different languages spoken by men and women are a product of their relative status in society. Differences occur in lexical traits, phonological traits, and syntactic–pragmatic characteristics. Although there is disagreement over the existence of many of these differences, speakers who use more deferential language are evaluated as more submissive, less assertive, and less willing to take a stand than speakers who use nondeferential language.

In addition to the gender ideology reflected by language use, women may be excluded by use of the generic pronoun *he*. Generic pronouns and man-linked words such as *chairman* are more likely to be perceived as indicating men than women. To correct this omission, writers and speakers are encouraged to use inclusive forms such as *worker* and *chairperson*, cast sentences in the plural to avoid the necessity of using a singular pronoun such as *he*, and, in general, avoid gender exclusion in their communication whenever possible.

FINDING YOUR VOICE

1. Role-play a situation in which a student is asking a teacher for an extension on the due date for a paper. Repeat the role play four times so that you observe a male student/female teacher, male student/male teacher, female student/female teacher, and female student/male teacher. Analyze the language behavior used by the participants in these interactions. Who talked more? When did interruptions occur? What effect did power have on these interactions? In general, how does the language behavior of males and females differ in dyadic interactions?

2. Review the characteristics of deferential language discussed in this chapter. If you are

a man, choose a situation in which you normally talk a great deal (for example, a discussion group, at dinner, or with your family) and try to use deferential language. For example, use hedges, tag questions, and more polite language than usual. How did people react to you? Did you feel comfortable in the situation? Why or why not? If you are a woman, identify a situation in which you tend to use deferential language (for example, a classroom, on a date, or with a professor), and try to use nondeferential language (for example, avoid tag questions and hesitations, directly state your opinions and support them). How did people react to you? Were you comfortable in the situation? Why or why not?

3. Ask ten males and ten females to complete the following sentences adapted from Wheeless, Berryman-Fink, and Serafini (1982):
   - When an artist becomes famous, . . .
   - Before a judge can give a final ruling, . . .
   - After a nurse has completed training, . . .
   - After a college athlete graduates, . . .
   - When a person loses money, . . .
   - When an elementary schoolteacher has a problem child in class, . . .
   - When the weather is rainy, . . .
   - When a construction worker completes a job, . . .
   - After a secretary has taken dictation, . . .
   - When a person wins a prize, . . .

   Count the number and type of pronouns your respondents used to start the second part of these sentences. Were your respondents more likely to use masculine pronouns with occupations that are traditionally masculine (for example, construction worker, judge)? Were your respondents more likely to use feminine pronouns with occupations that are traditionally feminine (for example, nurse, secretary)? What alternatives, if any, did they use? What are the implications of your results for gender stereotyping in language use?

4. Examine the language used in comic strips for signs of gender stereotyping. Look at traditional comics like *Beetle Bailey*, *Mary Worth*, or *Blondie* and compare the language with contemporary comics such as *Doonesbury*, *Sally Forth*, or *Luann*. What type of gender stereotypes do you find in the language used by men and women in these comic strips?

FURTHER READING

Ivy, D. K., & Backlund, P. (1994). *Exploring genderspeak: Personal effectiveness in gender communication.* New York: McGraw-Hill.
These authors provide a comprehensive overview of issues of gendered language use and an interesting discussion of conversational roadblocks in interpersonal relationships.

Kramarae, C., & Treichler, P. A. (1992). *Amazons, bluestockings and crones: A feminist dictionary.* London: Pandora.
This book documents words that illustrate women's contributions to the English language and expands the feminist lexicon. Definitions range from *Abbess* to *Zugassent* (a nineteenth-century utopian community in Oneida, New York based on visions of sex and class equality).

Penfield, J. (Ed.). (1987). *Women and language in transition.* Albany: State University of New York.

This collection of essays includes provocative writings on liberating language and identity creation. In addition, three essays discuss gender and language from the perspectives of women of color, including American Indian, Puerto Rican, and African American women.

Roman, C., Juhasz, S., & Miller, C. (Eds.). (1994). *The women and language debate: A sourcebook.* New Brunswick, NJ: Rutgers University Press.
This is a collection of essays examining subjectivity in language, women's use of language, and who says what to whom. It is a good introduction to major writers on gender and language use.

Tannen, D. (1994). *Gender and discourse.* New York: Oxford University Press.
This book contains five of Tannen's essays on language and gender and other research-based summaries. The essays cover a wide range of topics. Of particular interest is the essay on ethnic style in male–female communication.

4 Nonverbal Communication

Social psychologist Albert Mehrabian (1981) estimates that no more than 7 percent of social meaning in face-to-face communication is carried through the verbal message; the remaining 93 percent of social meaning is carried through nonverbal communication channels. A more conservative and perhaps more accurate estimate is that nonverbal cues convey 65 percent of the meaning in our conversations (Birdwhistell, 1970). Nonverbal communication most often reveals our emotions, our attitudes, our personalities, and the nature of our relationships with others. At the core of these messages, however, nonverbal communication reflects our gender and gender stereotypes. By understanding how nonverbal communication influences men and women, we can become more sensitive and responsive in our communication.

Think about this scene:

> Walking briskly, a department head enters the room where a weekly staff meeting is about to begin and slams the door. Chris is a middle-aged, corporate vice-president with short, silver–gray hair and penetrating blue eyes. The executive approaches the large, rectangular table where six staff members are seated. Standing erect at the head of the table, Chris places a brown leather briefcase on the table, slowly opens the briefcase, removes several folders, slowly closes the briefcase, and places it on the floor. Laying the folders in several carefully arranged stacks, the vice-president pauses and looks intently at the staff members seated around the table. Frowning, Chris nervously taps all five fingers on the tabletop and slowly sits down in the large chair at the head of the table. With a quick glance at the clock on the wall, Chris coughs once and begins to speak.

This scene was described through the use of words, but the executive has not yet uttered a single word; there was no dialogue. Although Chris has not yet communicated verbally, there is no doubt that the vice-president has communicated to those staff members in the room. Researchers have used a variety of frameworks to examine nonverbal communication. Perhaps the simplest definition is that **nonverbal communication** *includes all communication except that which is coded through words.* This includes facial expression, eye contact, gestures, posture, physical appearance, and clothing.

Nonverbal cues typically serve several functions because they can be used independently or in conjunction with the verbal message. According to Knapp and Hall (1996), nonverbal cues serve six primary functions. First, nonverbal cues may simply *repeat* the verbal message. If you give someone directions to a nearby grocery store, for example, you may use nonverbal gestures, pointing in the direction of the store, to accompany the verbal instructions; thus, your nonverbal gestures simply repeat the verbal message. Second, nonverbal cues may *contradict* the verbal message. A child who falls down and skins a knee may say she's "all right," but her sobs indicate pain and distress. Researchers report that when adults receive contradictory verbal and nonverbal cues, we tend to believe the nonverbal cues. Since most of us consider nonverbal communication more spontaneous than verbal communication and less likely to be contrived, we consider nonverbal cues more accurate reflections of meaning. Third, nonverbal cues may *substitute* for the verbal message altogether. A yawn signals a person is tired or bored, or a hand gesture may be used to let someone know everything is OK; the nonverbal messages are clear and no verbal message is necessary for communication to occur. Fourth, nonverbal cues may *complement* the verbal message. For instance, a hug enhances the meaning of the words "I love you" while a downward glance intensifies the meaning of the words "I'm disappointed in you." Fifth, nonverbal cues may *accent* parts of the verbal message, much as italics accent parts of a written message. Pointing a finger on the word *you* in the phrase "I hate you" or clenching a fist on the word *angry* in the phrase "I'm angry" emphasizes the importance of those specific parts of the verbal message. Finally, nonverbal cues may *regulate* the back and forth flow of communication between persons. Nonverbal cues that signal the initiation, maintenance, yielding, and termination of conversation are vital cues that regulate communication flow. All of these communication functions, used independently or in conjunction with the verbal message, are vital in understanding the importance of nonverbal cues in communication between people.

In this chapter, we will explore gender as it relates to nonverbal (nonlanguage) cues, discuss the implications and consequences of gender ideology in nonverbal communication, and suggest strategies for managing nonverbal cues that have negative consequences. Specifically, this chapter focuses on gendered behavior as it is manifested in nonverbal messages, and examines specific nonverbal cues including physical appearance, facial expression and eye behavior, body movement and posture, personal space and touching behavior, and the use of physical objects or artifacts.

Encoding and Decoding Ability

In terms of nonverbal communication, **encoding** is the *formation of messages that are communicated through nonverbal channels*; **decoding** is the *translation of nonverbal behaviors into meaningful messages*. In many instances, females are more proficient than males at both forming and interpreting nonverbal messages—a difference that emerges in childhood.

By and large, encoding and decoding are invisible processes. In other words, individuals perceive and interpret (attach meanings) to nonverbal cues almost instantaneously. While some research indicates that females are more proficient than males at forming and interpreting nonverbal messages (a difference that emerges in childhood), more recent research has failed to confirm these differences, especially for college-age adults.

Young girls at all stages of development tend to be better interpreters of emotional expression than boys (Trotter, 1983). One reason for this may be that mothers are far more restrictive in the range of emotions they display to and encourage from boys, as compared with girls. According to a variety of research studies, male infants are typically not exposed to as many emotional displays as females; as a result, girls who are exposed to these emotions throughout their development may develop a broader base of experience for interpreting emotional displays and greater latitude in the emotions they feel free to display. For example, women are better encoders of emotions such as pleasantness, disgust, fear, and anger, while men are slightly better encoders of guilt (Wagner, Buck, & Winterbotham, 1993). These researchers note that it is not that men do not feel these emotions, but that they have learned to mask the expression of them even in private settings.

One example of this behavior in U.S. culture is that it is traditionally considered feminine and acceptable for a female to cry, while in many circumstances it is still considered unmasculine and unacceptable for a male to cry openly. Consequently, women report crying (both privately and publicly) far more often than men (Lombardo, Cretser, Lombardo, & Mathis, 1983).

The **Profile of Nonverbal Sensitivity (PONS),** developed by Robert Rosenthal, is a *test commonly given to assess nonverbal decoding ability; it provides 220 two-second segments of a woman's face, body, and voice (content-free, but retaining vocal tone) in various combinations.* From a choice of two scenarios, the observer is asked to select the one enacted by the woman. Research using this test demonstrates that women are better at selecting the correct situation than men are (Rosenthal, Hall, DiMatteo, Rogers, & Archer, 1979). Some researchers have criticized the PONS test because the encoder in the scenarios is female and they believe the test may merely show that females are better decoders of nonverbal messages communicated by other females. Nevertheless, the PONS test continues to be a primary measure of nonverbal sensitivity. A review of 75 studies on differences in the ability to assess another person's feelings using vocal or facial cues indicates that in 84 percent of these studies, females were better nonverbal decoders than males (Hall, 1978). While this statistic alone is not conclusive, it strongly suggests that women tend to be more proficient than men at nonverbal decoding. In fact, women rate themselves higher than men on decoding abilities and both men and women perceive women as a group to be better encoders and decoders of nonverbal cues (Graham, Unruh, & Jennings, 1991).

Although some women may be more proficient at nonverbal encoding and decoding than men (Rotter & Rotter, 1988), we still have no definitive explanation for this proficiency. Hall (1979) uses a dominance theory and argues that greater nonverbal sensitivity is required of the oppressed in a society—in this instance, women. This theory, called the *oppression hypothesis,* argues that to survive social, political, and physical oppression, women must become better interpreters of the nonverbal messages around them. This message-interpreting capability then provides women the information necessary to predict accurately the behavior of the more dominant members of the society (men) and to adjust accordingly. The oppression hypothesis also asserts that since men are the dominant members of society, they are not nearly as motivated as women to be proficient in nonverbal encoding and decoding; men simply do not have the survival need to develop such proficiency.

Recent research regarding nonverbal expressiveness has questioned the oppression hypothesis and its impact on women's encoding abilities. For example, while some women may react to a sociopolitical climate of oppression by developing a passive, facilitating style of nonverbal expressiveness, other women do not. In fact, some women "may react to oppression by developing a dominant, almost aggressive expressive style, while at the same time being charismatic" (Tucker & Friedman, 1993, p. 115). Interestingly, these highly expressive and charismatic females usually appear extremely friendly in initial encounters and do not appear hostile or aggressive in situations where presenting a positive image is important. Perhaps in today's society it is advantageous for high-achieving women to appear friendly and facilitative yet capable and competent.

A second explanation for the perceived female encoding/decoding advantage may be that women know the social rules governing communication (especially in relationships) better than men; in essence, women rely more on symbolic communication while men rely more on direct perception (Noller, 1986). If this reliance on symbolism and social rules governing communication gives women an advantage in most communication situations, it may also explain why women lose their decoding advantage when they must interpret the idiosyncratic cues of a known encoder (the wink of an eye by a close friend), deception cues not typically governed by social rules (the foot-tap of a nervous liar), or nonverbal cues sent through less controllable channels that are also not governed by symbolic social rules (the sweaty palms of a first-time job applicant). These cues are decoded with equal success (or failure) by both women and men.

A third explanation for the perceived female encoding/decoding advantage may be that women are given more opportunity to practice nonverbal sensitivity in occupations traditionally considered feminine. Specifically, Buck (1976) finds that fine-arts majors and business majors are relatively proficient nonverbal decoders while science majors are relatively poor nonverbal decoders; women major in fine arts and business more often than they major in science. If women are drawn to college majors that require and encourage greater nonverbal sensitivity, it is likely that they will pursue occupations that require and encourage greater nonverbal sensitivity, such as helping professions like nursing and teaching, which are professions traditionally occupied by women (Isenhart, 1980). As more men and women pursue professions that are no longer gender segregated, these encoding/decoding differences may be minimized.

Whether you accept these explanations for gendered nonverbal encoding and decoding abilities, the explanations do reflect a dominant gender ideology. Traditionally, women have been perceived to hold the submissive role in our culture, to function as facilitators and accommodators in the development of relationships, to be more attuned to the social rules that govern communication, and to seek work in the helping professions. Because of this gender ideology, women may be *expected* to become more nonverbally sensitive.

Nonverbal Cues

As discussed earlier, a great deal of meaning is communicated through nonverbal cues. These cues can be divided into five major categories: (1) *physical characteristics,* (2) *gestures, body movement, and orientation,* (3) *facial expression and eye behavior,* (4) *proxemics and touching behavior,* and (5) *use of objects or artifacts.*

Physical Characteristics.   The physical differences between males and females are obvious. Perhaps more important than physical differences themselves, however, is how males and females perceive these physical characteristics in themselves and others. After all, for both males and females, physical appearance is an important determiner of how we feel about ourselves and about those around us. Nonverbal-communication research on physical attractiveness indicates female attractiveness is a function of both face and body while male attractiveness is more a function of the face alone (Raines, Hechtman, & Rosenthal, 1990). The "Consider This!" that follows reminds us that cultural definitions of attractiveness differ.

Perceived physical attractiveness affects our behavior from a young age. Boys and girls who are considered attractive also are thought to be more independent in their behavior; they are not as afraid of others and usually require less assistance with tasks (Bennetts, 1979). In conjunction with this positive attribution of independence, attractive children of both genders also are perceived to be more sociable; that is, attractive children are more likely to relate well to others. The result of this perceived social competence is that attractive children are characterized as playing in feminine ways

CONSIDER THIS!

Beyond the Veil

I will never again see myself, see other Black women, see Black men, and Black children secondarily, through the eyes of the oppressor . . . the slave master. I will never again see my kinky hair, my big nose, or my big lips as something horrible. I don't want the bluest eyes. I don't want the long, straight blonde hair. I maintain that I will never in my life walk secondarily again—or even appear to have any secondary views. If you approach me, you must approach me on an equal level. If I see your stuff is incorrect, is racist, then I will tell you. And when I hit the stage, I know that I am just as tough as anyone there. People aren't accustomed to that kind of behavior. That is a legacy that we've gotten from Malcolm, Fannie Lou, DuBois, and Ida B. I am aggressive; I will not deny myself. I will not be one of those people talking about the need to get some training on how to be aggressive. To them, I say, all you have to do is come into a sense of yourself, announce that you are an African and intend to "be." That is some automatic aggression. And you will see that in order to defend yourself, you will have to move in an aggressive fashion. Because the moment you say that you're not sure of who you are, people will slap you down, will attempt to slap you to the right and the left, tear you up!

Sonia Sanchez, quoted in Chandler, 1990

that call for more social ability. Unattractive children of both genders are characterized as playing in masculine ways (often alone) and with masculine toys that stress independent activity rather than human interaction and sharing (Langlois & Downs, 1979).

Physical characteristics can include hair color and length, facial and body hair, skin color and complexion tones, and physical handicaps. In this discussion, we will focus primarily on the perception of body size; specifically, we will examine body shape, height, and weight. For boys, gender stereotypes concerning body build and social acceptance are clearly established by six years of age. For example, males six to ten years of age view *mesomorphs* (muscular body types) as more socially acceptable than *ectomorphs* (thin, weak, tall, and underdeveloped body types) (Staffieri, 1967). Males between the ages of nine and twenty believe that physical attractiveness leads to social acceptance, and they assign more positive behavioral descriptors to the mesomorph body type and more socially negative behavioral descriptors to the endomorph (short, chubby) and ectomorph body types (Kelck, Richardson, & Ronald, 1974).

Negative body image and concern with weight begins at an early age. In one study, 64 percent of fifth graders (both boys and girls) reported that "most people have a better body than I do" and 68 percent agreed with the statements "I wish I were thinner" and "I wish I looked better" (Flannery-Schroeder & Chrisler, 1996). Sixteen percent of these children reported dieting and nearly half of them thought they should be on a diet even though few of them were actually overweight.

In general, males are more satisfied with somewhat larger body size than females (Silberstein, Striegel-Moore, Timko, & Rodin, 1988). Women tend to feel most attractive when they are considered small and thin, characteristics they typically associate with being attractive (Silverstein, Perdue, Peterson, & Kelly, 1986). In part, the desire to be thin accounts for the rising prevalence of such eating disorders as anorexia nervosa and bulimia during the past decade; in particular, these eating disorders are typically found in adolescent females who are high achievers. Unfortunately, eating disorders have led many adolescent females to poor health and even death in their attempt to strive for social acceptance through perceived beauty.

In a national survey of women, almost one half of the respondents reported they had a negative body image due to concerns about their weight (Cash & Henry, 1995). While these women, ranging in age from eighteen to seventy, felt generally satisfied with their face, height and hair, over 45 percent were displeased with their lower torso (hips, buttocks, thighs, and legs) and mid-torso (waist and stomach). Only 16 percent of the women were satisfied with all aspects of their bodies. African American women, however, were more likely to be satisfied with their bodies than either Anglo or Hispanic women.

Research to explore perceived body satisfaction among women of color is increasing. For example, Thomas and James (1988) conducted a study among predominantly single African American females. They found that these women are just as dissatisfied with their bodies, especially body weight, as Caucasian women. The primary difference between the two groups, however, is that African American women do not perceive that they need to be thin to be attractive while an overwhelming majority of Caucasian women believe that being thin is essential to attractiveness. Furthermore, the relationship between body-image satisfaction and self-esteem is not nearly as strong for African American women as for Caucasian women. As Thomas (1989) explains, "Black women may not have internalized American society's recent standard of beauty and fashion and thus did not relate their overall self-worth with various aspects of their physical appearance" (p. 111).

A survey of college students found that white men indicated less desire than African American men to date a woman with a heavier than "ideal" body (Powell & Kahn, 1995). In addition, white college men felt they would be more likely to be ridiculed by others than African American men did if they dated someone who was "larger than ideal" (p. 191). This finding may help explain why white college women in this study also reported more weight and dieting concerns as well as feeling more pressure to be thin than did African American college women.

On the other hand, another study involving Native American women and girls noted that almost three-fourths of the female Chippewas in their sample were dissatisfied with their body image and were trying to lose weight and were using unhealthy dieting practices to do so (Rosen et al., 1988). Findings like these indicate that values of a given culture "may not be strong enough to overcome the general cultural value of thinness for females" (Jackson, 1992, p. 185).

Distorted body image is no longer the primary domain of women. Researchers asked college students to describe their weight, body shape, dieting, and exercise history (Drewnowski & Yee, 1987). About the same percentage of males and females were dissatisfied with their body weight. As expected, considerably more women (48 percent) than men (28 percent) described themselves as overweight. Yet, when asked if they wanted to lose weight, 85 percent of the women and 45 percent of the men responded affirmatively. Women, however, chose to diet while men chose to exercise in order to lose weight. Perhaps the most surprising finding was that 40 percent of the men reported they wanted to gain weight (presumably to add muscle). This phenomenon has led to an increase in the use of steroids among adolescent males. As with women's eating disorders, these men also face health risks and even death in their attempt to strive for social definitions of the perfect masculine body.

As the ideal female body image changes to include a more muscular body, the use of steroids by teenage girls has also increased (Noble, 1999). Some researchers label this phenomenon a "reverse anorexia" in which girls are using drugs to increase their athletic abilities or change their body build.

Female preferences concerning the male physique also reinforce male perceptions. For example, women say they prefer men with V-shaped physiques (medium-wide trunks or medium-thin lower trunks, and thin legs); women least prefer men with pear-shaped physiques (wider lower trunks). Women also prefer men of average height; however, if given a choice, women prefer tall men to short men. According to one survey, tall men are considered more attractive, dateable, and likable than short men (Graziano, Brothen, & Berscheid, 1978). Women who perceive themselves as stereotypically feminine prefer muscular men, and women who perceive themselves as "liberated" prefer thinner, more linear men.

Mediated messages have reinforced these body images for both males and females. Cartoon figures like Tarzan have "bulked up" (Colleary, 1999), contributing to the image that an exaggerated muscular body should be the norm for active males.

One study of high school girls found that watching television shows that emphasized thinness contributed to a drive for thinness, lack of body satisfaction, and bulimic behaviors (Botta, 1999).

In general, being perceived as attractive is important to both males and females, but can one ever be too attractive? Research suggests that attractive males and females are more effective than unattractive males and females in influencing others, but that males are allowed to be more attractive than females and still retain credibility. On an interpersonal level, men sometimes report feeling intimidated by a woman who is extremely attractive. Beyond a certain level of attractiveness, very attractive women are perceived as less effective persuaders than are unattractive women (Hoffman, 1977). In a professional situation, if a woman is perceived as too attractive, she loses credibility in presenting her ideas to others. In fields such as sales or broadcast journalism, moderately attractive women may be more successful than extremely attractive women; for men, however, extreme attractiveness does not appear to be as closely tied to credibility.

Gestures, Body Movement, and Orientation

In television advertisements for pantyhose, we see women dressed in professional business suits, moving at a brisk pace with long strides and heads held high. They communicate self-confidence and control as well as sex appeal. Obviously, the producers of these commercials and the makers of these products hope to appeal to independent, self-confident women who are comfortable with their own professional image as well as their own sexuality. Now think about a few of the beer commercials you have seen. The men in one commercial, for example, "have it all" and communicate this fact through their confident body postures and attitudes. The manner in which men and women move and carry themselves communicates a great deal about how they perceive themselves and others. These nonverbal aspects of individual behavior reflect not only personality traits and attitudes, but also gender ideology.

Differences in body movement and posture begin to emerge in toddler and preschool children. For example, by three and four years of age, girls use three specific gestures significantly more often than boys—the limp wrist gesture, arm flutters, and flexed elbows (Rekers, Amoro-Plotkin, & Low, 1977). By four and five years of age, girls use these same gestures as well as hand claps and palming gestures (indicating questioning), significantly more often than boys (Rekers & Rudy, 1978). Gestural differences remain consistent throughout early adolescence, but some of these gestures (limp wrists and arm flutters) are stereotypically associated with femininity in adulthood.

Other gestural behaviors that reflect gender ideology in toddlers and preschool children include the use of **emblems,** *gestures that represent direct verbal equivalents.* Common emblems such as gestures that communicate "I don't know," "yes," "no," "I'm tired," and "come here" are frequently used by children as early as three years of age (Kumin & Lazar, 1974). As a child's repertoire of emblems increases, such common emblems as "I won't listen," "blowing a kiss," and "I won't do it" are added by four years of age. In general, girls use more emblems than boys at both three and four years of age, a phenomenon consistent with the development of early language competency in girls. Although boys generally are better at decoding the meaning of such emblems at age three, girls surpass boys in decoding capability by age four and, as we noted earlier, maintain this superiority into adolescence.

The development of gendered behavior in body movement for children often occurs during free play. After observing videotapes of children (whose average age was eight and one-half years) in free-play sessions with parents, Tauber (1979) noted that parents of girls were more likely to engage them in social play that focuses on the development of interpersonal relationships and enhances socialization. Parents of boys were more likely to engage in physical play that focuses on the development of physical activity. In addition, daughters of supportive mothers were more likely to engage in physical contact-seeking behavior than were daughters of supportive fathers. This study showed that, in general, the relationship between mother and daughter during play is similar to the relationship between mother and son during play; fathers, however, do not relate to daughters in the same way they relate to sons. Fathers tend to be very supportive of boys who engage in active play, but they tend to withhold support from girls who engage in the same type of play. Thus, fathers' behavior toward their children during free play encourages male independence and activity as well as female affiliation and passivity.

Adult men and women may also differ in their body movement and posture. Women tend to present their bodies as a moving entity; they walk with their legs close together (taking small steps) and their arms close to their sides, presenting the image of a moving whole. Men tend to be more independent in their movement from the trunk up; their legs are spread at a 10- to 15-degree angle, and their arms are angled 5 to 10 degrees away from the trunk of their bodies (Eakins & Eakins, 1978).

In comparing gestures used by males and females, Peterson (1976) notes several differences. While gestures are used by both men and women to illustrate and supplement the verbal message, men generally use more gestures than women. Further, men use or display more dominant gestures such as pointing, sweeping gestures, and the closed fist. Women are more likely to engage in gestures such as holding their hands in their laps or playing with their hair and clothing. Women tend to use more gestures when communicating with men than when communicating with other women. In posturing, men may sit with their legs open or stretch their legs out and cross them at the ankles while sitting, but women often tuck in their legs or cross them at the knees. In this way, men use more space than women.

Posture differences in males and females may reflect a perceived status difference. Women sit with their arms closer to their sides and their legs crossed at small angles. Men sprawl out more, stretching their arms and legs out in front of them and crossing their arms and legs at larger angles. Despite women's superior anatomical flexibility, they are generally less relaxed in their posture than men. Relaxed posture is most likely a reflection of a perceived higher status among men because high-ranking men are comparatively more relaxed than low-ranking men when communicating (Mehrabian, 1972).

Thus, both movement and posture reflect our conceptions of gender. Many males use body movements and postures that take up more space; females are more compact in both their body movement and posture. These behaviors, begun in childhood and maintained throughout adulthood, tend to reinforce gender stereotypes of male independence and activity and female dependence and passivity.

Facial Expression and Eye Behavior

Recall the scenario involving the department head described at the beginning of this chapter. Chris never spoke, yet we made judgments about this individual based on nonverbal cues, including facial expressions and eye behavior. Remember, Chris looked intently at the staff members, frowned, and glanced quickly at the clock before beginning to speak. Facial expression and eye behavior are typically thought to be the keys to an individual's personality and emotional state. When we try to determine if someone is happy, sad, frustrated, lying, or telling the truth, we most often focus our attention on the person's facial expression and eye behavior. It seems appropriate, then, to explore gender in this key set of nonverbal cues used to communicate vital aspects of our personality—our feelings, attitudes, and relationships with others.

Affect displays are *facial expressions that convey our emotions.* Affect-display differences begin to appear in young children. Boys inhibit and even mask their overt responses to emotion as they get older, while girls continue to respond more openly. Buck (1976) finds that mothers who view televised images of children watching emotionally arousing slides report that six-year-old boys use fewer facial expressions in general than four-year-old boys.

According to researchers who studied the eye-gaze behavior (length and direction of eye contact) of toddlers ranging from three to five years of age, gender differences are readily apparent (Kleinke, Desautels, & Knapp, 1977). Girls in this age range use eye gazes directed toward others longer and more often than boys. In addition, boys tend to react more negatively than girls to others (both males and females) who gaze at them for longer periods of time. Girls, on the other hand, tend to like and respond more positively to others who gaze at them for longer periods.

Finally, through facial expression, toddlers and preschool children demonstrate a marked preference for same-sex peers rather than for other-sex peers. Preschool children smile more often when they are interacting with their peers than at other times (Cheyne, 1976). However, both boys and girls smile considerably more with same-sex peers than they do with other-sex peers. Consistent with child development literature, children at this stage of development are most comfortable with and even prefer same-sex peers.

As children continue to develop, girls both receive and use more affect displays than boys. Feldman and White (1980) report an interesting discovery concerning children's use of facial expression to deceive others. According to their research findings, the degree to which deception is revealed through facial expression *decreases* for girls as they get older; however, the degree to which deception is revealed through facial expression *increases* for boys as they get older. It appears, then, that boys are less able to control "leakage" of deception cues as they get older.

Most of the research that compares facial expressions of adult males and females focuses on smiling and eye contact. The findings of these studies tend to reinforce the previously reported research findings about children. In general, women use more facial expression than men (Mehrabian, 1972). More specifically, women smile more often than men (Parlee, 1979a), are more likely to return smiles from others (Henley, 1977), and tend to be attracted to people who smile (Lau, 1982). Further, males who are androgynous (a blend of stereotypically feminine and masculine psychological traits described in Chapter 2) smile more than males who are more stereotypically masculine, while androgynous females smile less than females who are more stereotypically feminine (LaFrance & Carmen, 1980). These findings suggest that gender helps explain affect-display differences; androgynous males and females reflect a blend of traditionally masculine and feminine behavior.

In addition, women engage in more overall eye contact than men. This finding has led researchers to conclude that visual information plays a far more significant role in the social field of women than in the social field of men, and that the visual activity of women is more sensitive to situational conditions than that of men. For example, women in same-sex dyads spend a higher percentage of their time in mutual gaze that is affiliative and supportive of the relationship, while men in same-sex dyads spend a higher percentage of their time in aversive gaze (one person talking and less attention given to one's partner) that focuses on the instrumental and task-oriented aspects of the conversation. Perhaps most interesting is that women engaged in female-male dyads adopt the instrumental, task-oriented gaze/talk behavior of men almost immediately. This finding leads researchers to believe that women in these dyads accommodate to the gender stereotypes associated with men from the outset of female-male interaction (Mulac, Studley, Wiemann, & Bradac, 1987).

Proxemics and Touching Behavior

Sommer (1959) defines **personal space** as *an invisible bubble that surrounds us, moves with us, and separates us from others.* Each of us has a personal space. Think for a moment about the last time you used an elevator. Imagine the door opening and imagine walking into that empty elevator. Where did you stand? You probably stood at the back of the elevator or near the buttons. What happened when the elevator stopped at a floor and another person stepped in? Did you move or stand firm to defend your territory? The two of you probably moved to opposite corners of the elevator. How would you feel if you were on an elevator with only one other person and that person stood directly next to you? Would you feel uncomfortable or crowded? This example illustrates the concept of personal space. In some situations we prefer to maintain our distance from others, but in other situations we prefer closeness and even touch. **Proxemics** is *the study of how we use personal space.* The influence of gender on our use of personal space and perception of touch begins in infancy and continues into adulthood.

Much of the research on proxemic behavior in children was conducted in the 1970s and 1980s. Given the dramatic changes in parental roles since that time, this research needs to be updated to reflect the reality that many mothers today are not the sole or even primary caregivers for young children. Nevertheless, the research presented in the following section is still relevant to many of today's college students who were raised during the times in which these studies were conducted.

Touching behavior and the use of space between parents and infants may reflect the effects of gender ideology. Previous studies have found that girls seek and receive more touch and less space than boys. By about six months of age, boys may experience less touching contact with their mothers, who often believe that boys should be independent and should explore the world around them. Perhaps as a result of this parental behavior, by as early as 13 months of age boys demonstrate more exploratory and autonomous behavior than girls. Boys tend to venture farther away from their mothers than girls, remain away from their mothers longer than girls, and look at (as well as talk to) their mothers less than girls. With this newly discovered independence, boys may play more actively with toys and other objects such as doorknobs and light switches (Lewis, 1972). Since mothers may no longer be sole primary caregivers, this behavior may be changing.

In general, infants ranging from 10 to 16 months of age demonstrate strong attachment behaviors toward their mothers. However, girls look at, touch, and remain significantly closer to their mothers than boys of the same age (Brooks & Lewis, 1974; Cohen & Campos, 1974). Two-year-old girls ask to be held by both parents almost three times as often as boys (Fagot, 1978).

When interacting with adults, both male and female toddlers appear to be more comfortable approaching females. They move closer to adult females than to adult males, though the distance for both males and females decreases with increased social interaction (Eberts & Lepper, 1975). Toddlers and preschool children interacting with adults during free play are more likely to approach female adults than to approach male adults (Beach & Sokoloff, 1974). One explanation for the ease with which children may approach female adults may be that children still typically spend more time with female adults—with mothers or other female relatives, or with day-care workers or babysitters, who are usually female.

Children maintain a gender ideology in assigning personal space to others. When asked to position cutout characters engaged in interactions with differing emotional contexts, girls place significantly greater distances between cutouts of two angry men or cutouts of an angry man and an angry woman than between cutouts of two angry women (Melson, 1976). This difference suggests that both toddler and preschool girls perceive male anger as an emotion that commands more space than female anger, regardless of the other person's gender. More significantly, however, this difference may suggest that toddler and preschool girls perceive males as higher in status; therefore, males are given more space regardless of the emotional context.

Differences in the use and perception of personal space continue as children grow. Boys use more space than girls during childhood and adolescence. Boys learn to need and use more territory at earlier ages than girls (Harper & Sanders, 1975). For example, boys tend to spend more time outdoors, cover more geographical areas, and use between 1.2 and 1.6 times the amount of space as girls. When confronted with situations involving crowding (a psychological perception of closeness that may or may not be related to physical proximity), fourth-grade to eleventh-grade boys report feeling considerably more uncomfortable, tense, and annoyed than girls.

To gain a better understanding of the socialization process during childhood and adolescence, let us examine the use of personal space and touch among peers.

Specifically, boys and girls position themselves closer together when using space in same-sex dyads than when they are in mixed-sex dyads. This preference shifts during adolescence, however, when attraction to the other sex may become an important consideration. Male-female dyads require more space than same-sex dyads (Severy, Forsyth, & Wagner, 1980). In general, however, sixth-, seventh-, and eighth-graders move closer to other-sex peers (Whalen, Flowers, Fuller, & Jernigan, 1975). Although the proxemic preference for other-sex peers comes earlier for girls, the preference is clearly established in most boys by the time they reach the ninth grade. When children and adolescents do interact with same-sex peers, both boys and girls move closer to same-sex peers they describe as interpersonally attractive (Guardo, 1976).

Same-sex peers engage in touch more frequently during childhood; in fact, both boys and girls engage in same-sex touch twice as often as other-sex touch (Major, Schmidlin, & Williams, 1990). Children in kindergarten through sixth grade touch frequently (for example, boys may be seen holding hands in kindergarten), and their touch includes a greater variety of body areas when it occurs between same-sex peers rather than other-sex peers (Whalen et al., 1975; Willis & Hofmann, 1975).

These patterns in touching behavior may reflect differences in the ways parents touch their children. For example, one study found that fathers touch their daughters more frequently than their sons, but they touch both sons and daughters in the same general regions (primarily the head and arms). In contrast, mothers touch both sons and daughters the same amount (Rosenfeld, Kartus, & Ray, 1976). This research confirms the continued existence of a stereotype that male–female touch and female–female touch are more appropriate than male–male touch.

In adulthood, the personal-space bubbles that surround women are generally smaller than those that surround men (Evans & Howard, 1973); in other words, women use less space than men. Women react more negatively to an indirect, side-by-side invasion of their space; men react more negatively to a direct, face-to-face invasion of their space (Fisher & Byrne, 1975). These patterns, as well as the observation that women tend to be more cooperative and less aggressive than men in high-density situations (Freedman, O'Hanlon, Oltman, & Witkin, 1972), reflect gender ideology. Women are perceived to be more social, more affiliative, and of lower status; as a result, the space surrounding women is considered more public and accessible than the space surrounding men.

Willis and Dodds (1998) observed couples seated together in public places such as restaurants, bars, shopping-mall food courts, and parties. They found that women initiated touch more often than men and that all participants used their hands to initiate touch. Although men were more likely to initiate touch in intimate body areas (such as the face, lips, knee, or thigh), most of the touching occurred on less intimate body areas (such as the hand and lower arm).

Jones (1986) reports that male and female college students recording their own touching behavior reveal two interesting findings: (1) females initiate more other-sex touches than males and (2) females specifically initiate more other-sex control touches than males. Though these findings may appear to contradict those of earlier studies, Jones acknowledges that these college students reported only touch between equal-status peers. Other male-female differences in touch may still exist in other settings where status differences are more prevalent and gender stereotypes are reinforced. In less public, more intimate settings, however, gender differences may be negligible. During greetings and good-byes, where touch is almost an expected ritual, and in recreational settings, where touch is usually more relaxed and likely to be among family and friends, there are no significant gender-linked patterns of touch (Major, Carnevale, & Deaux, 1990). However, in one study in which males and females were asked to comfort a same-sex friend they knew well, females used considerably more hugs to comfort the person than did males (Dolin & Booth-Butterfield, 1993). These apparently contradictory findings may reflect, more than anything, the complexity of communication contexts; gender is only one of several variables that may influence touching behavior in specific situations.

Research has also examined the relationship between homophobic attitudes and levels of same-sex touch. While there appears to be a correlation between these two variables for both men and women (the greater the homophobic attitude, the less the level of same-sex touch), men in general score considerably higher on homophobic attitude scales and report considerably higher levels of discomfort with same-sex touch than do women (Roese et al., 1992). Floyd and Morman (1999) found more discomfort with same-sex touch when participants were told that the embrace was sexual in nature. Regardless of who initiates or receives more touch, research continues to support the finding that women make greater distinctions concerning the meaning of specific touching behaviors. Women perceive intimate touch as a greater sign of commitment than men and the more sexually intimate the touch, the greater the commitment perceived by women (Johnson & Edwards, 1991).

Clearly, male and female perceptions of personal space and touch begin with parental influence in infancy. As children reach adolescence, personal space and touching behaviors continue to reflect traditional gender ideologies; males use more personal space than females and more other-sex rather than same-sex touching occurs. Although there may no longer be a clear-cut distinction of who initiates touch more often (it may be more a function of the type of relationship or the level of commitment), men and women continue to attach different meaning to touch.

Artifacts

When friends brought their baby girl home from the hospital, she was wrapped in a soft pink blanket. Her new room had been painted pink; it was filled with pink toys and pink stuffed animals. One of her first gifts from a loving grandmother was a frilly pink dress designed to make her look as feminine as any female infant only one week old can look. If the baby had been a boy, these parents would have painted his room blue, and he probably would have received a baseball glove from his loving grandfather. Even though many parents are attempting to avoid the "pink and blue treatment," these stereotypes persist. A student who works at a restaurant told us that as she was handing out balloons to a group of children, one mother said to her young son, "Oh, you don't want the pink one; take the green one instead."

The *artifacts* or objects with which we surround infants and children are often reflections of the attributes we believe the child possesses. This important link between objects and perceived attributes is underscored when we note that by about three years of age, infants' toy and activity preferences during play are gendered (Bell, Weller, & Waldrop, 1971). For example, observations of infants ranging in age from twelve to twenty-four months indicate that boys engage in active play with transportation toys and potentially dangerous objects, such as electrical outlets, more often than girls. Girls more often play with soft toys and dolls (Smith & Daglish, 1977). As early as eighteen months of age, both boys and girls display greater involvement when playing with gender-typical toys than when playing with gender-atypical toys, and parents show subtle signs of excitement and positive reinforcement when a child plays with a gender-typical toy (Caldera, Huston, & O'Brien, 1989). In general, boys are given more play objects that encourage activities directed away from the home, while girls may be given play objects that encourage activities directed toward the home ("Poll: Parents see pink for girls," 1995).

Research confirms earlier studies that both preschool and elementary school-children typically request gender stereotyped toys. Girls' liking and requests for feminine toys decrease throughout the elementary school years more than boys' requests for masculine toys; however, children are likely to receive the gender-typical toys they request more often than the gender-atypical toys they request. Children who ask for and receive gender-typical toys are also more likely to have same-sex friends and engage in gender-typical play activities (Etaugh & Liss, 1992).

However, there is some evidence to indicate a shift in gender ideology regarding toy preferences. Zucker and Corter (1980) observed the interaction of adults with four-month-old infants during play and noted that both male and female adults spent considerably more time using neutral toys than they spent using toys traditionally identified as masculine or feminine. Since these findings include male and female adults as well as male and female infants, the implications are wider in scope than previous research. Parents who use neutral toys may encourage a less stereotyped orientation toward play, one that becomes acceptable and even preferred by both male and female infants. Once toys become more gender neutral, the attributes that accompany them when given to infants will become less stereotyped. As a result, infants may be better able to explore and develop a wider range of behaviors at an early stage of development.

Our discussion of artifacts has focused primarily on children and their toys, but these artifacts often serve as the foundation for reinforcing gender ideology in our culture. The powerful masculine and feminine images created by the media and discussed in Chapter 8 carry tremendous impact in reinforcing artifacts associated with masculine and feminine gender ideologies for adults. The use of dress, makeup, jewelry, and hairstyle often becomes an extension of gender expectations in social settings. In addition, the toys we give children are often associated with jobs and occupations traditionally·considered masculine or feminine—a nurse's kit rather than a doctor's bag, G. I. Joe versus a Barbie doll, or a sewing kit versus a chemistry set.

Giving Mom a vacuum cleaner for her birthday and Dad a power drill for his reflects gender ideology for mothers and fathers. Even a man's choice of a particular model of car to purchase may differ from a woman's choice because very different images may be associated with different models, and a portion of that image may be gender related. It appears, then, that from the toys of childhood to the toys of adulthood, the objects with which we surround ourselves communicate, in part, our gender identity.

The use of bookbags or backpacks among college students is an interesting example of changing use of artifacts. Both men and women have adopted this means of carrying books and personal items. As an example of a nonverbal cue, this trend can either be interpreted as freeing women from the necessity of carrying a purse or as giving men "purses" to carry too.

Implications and Consequences of Nonverbal Cues

In his book *Silent Messages*, Albert Mehrabian (1981) examines the impact of nonverbal communication by asking one question: How is it possible to have agreement in using and understanding nonverbal cues when, unlike language, definitions for nonverbal cues are rarely if ever explicitly discussed or taught? His answer to this question is based on the premise that three basic dimensions of human feelings and attitudes are conveyed nonverbally: immediacy (liking-disliking), status and power (degree of influence), and responsiveness (activity-passivity). In this next section, we will explore how nonverbal cues influence and reflect these three dimensions in communication between women and men.

Nonverbal Cues of Immediacy

Nonverbal cues of *immediacy* indicate the degree of liking felt in the communication. In general, we are drawn toward people or objects we like, evaluate positively, and prefer. At the same time, we tend to avoid people or objects we dislike, evaluate negatively, or do not prefer. Regardless of the verbal message, the degree of liking or disliking felt by a communicator may often be detected through nonverbal cues. Mehrabian explains that nonverbal cues usually considered to indicate a high degree of immediacy or liking include the following: standing close to rather than far from an individual; leaning forward rather than leaning backward in a chair while listening; facing another person directly rather than turning to one side; touching; establishing direct eye contact, and using gestures that indicate a desire to reach out to the other person. (Remember that these cues are culture-bound and may not carry the same meaning in other cultures.)

Although use of nonverbal cues probably varies more from situation to situation than from males to females, females traditionally are more likely to demonstrate immediacy cues of liking than are males. Girls are more likely to move close to other people, to touch other people, and to make eye contact with other people than are boys. As a result, females may be more comfortable demonstrating nonverbal cues typically associated with liking, and males may be more comfortable with the nonverbal cues of independence and distance often associated with disliking. Unfortunately, some men may be perceived as being cold and unfeeling because they do not feel comfortable demonstrating the immediacy cues of liking; women may be perceived as passive or as constantly seeking approval because they demonstrate the immediacy cues of liking.

Nonverbal Cues of Status and Power

Nonverbal cues of *status and power* indicate a degree of *influence or control* rather than a submissive and dependent attitude. The person who is perceived to have a high degree of status and power is able to regulate the degree of immediacy that will be demonstrated in interactions with others. At the same time, the individual who is perceived to be of lower status and power may be viewed as weak or subordinate; this person does not have the "right" to increase immediacy cues with someone of higher status and power.

Mehrabian (1981) discusses several nonverbal privileges that are often accorded the individual perceived to be of higher status and power. For example, in U.S. culture, high-status individuals are provided a greater expanse of space in which to move and use gestures. As a result, high-status individuals usually feel comfortable assuming a confident, relaxed posture and using expansive gestures that encroach on the space of lower-status individuals. Furthermore, high-status people are often allowed to refuse eye contact or to initiate touching behavior with lower-status people.

The implications and consequences of men being perceived as having higher status than women are obvious. One of the most significant consequences can be found in the workplace, where higher status usually translates into higher salaries. If women are perceived as subordinate to men in the workforce, their ability to demonstrate power and control will be limited. Women, however, may not be the only losers in this status disparity. If men are consistently perceived to have higher status, the burdens associated with power and control can create tremendous stress for men in our society.

Nonverbal Cues of Responsiveness

Nonverbal cues of *responsiveness* indicate the *extent of awareness of and reaction to people*, the sheer intensity of our communication with others. According to Mehrabian (1981), the highly responsive individual is able to easily communicate a wide range of emotional responses such as anger, frustration, happiness, and pain. The less responsive individual, however, appears withdrawn and oblivious to those around him or her.

Several nonverbal cues are associated with responsiveness. The highly responsive individual typically uses body movements and gestures that are lively and larger-than-life, uses more space, and initiates more touching behavior.

In general, men are more responsive on some nonverbal cues, and women are more responsive on others. For example, men may use more space, use broad gestures, have a greater body expanse, and initiate more touch. Women, on the other hand, demonstrate a wider range of facial expressions and more direct eye contact. Men tend to demonstrate more responsive cues indicating status and power, and women tend to demonstrate more responsive cues indicating emotional affiliation. Responsiveness may be found in both men and women, but the nature of that responsiveness and the attributes associated with it may differ. A gender ideology that views men as having higher status and women as having lower status and women as affiliative and men as nonaffiliative may constrict the opportunities for both genders to explore these attributes in their personalities.

Strategies for Change

Just as verbal communication cannot be interpreted out of context, nonverbal communication cannot be interpreted independently from the verbal message and the situation; furthermore, one set of nonverbal cues cannot be viewed separately from other nonverbal cues. Both verbal and nonverbal messages come together to complete the communication process. Using Mehrabian's (1981) framework of dimensions that may be communicated nonverbally, we can identify nonverbal cues that people may wish to explore in order to develop an awareness of and sensitivity to gender.

Immediacy Cues

Traditionally, females more easily display the immediacy cues of liking than do males. Almost from birth, girls are encouraged to express their feelings and emotions, including the immediacy cues of liking. Boys may be encouraged to mask their true feelings, especially the immediacy cues of liking. Since these behaviors are learned, they can be adapted for more effective communication. Consider the following suggestions to encourage more effective communication of immediacy cues.

Both males and females could be encouraged to use nonverbal cues that accurately reflect feelings and emotions, including the immediacy cues of liking. Although females appear to be more comfortable in doing this, both boys and girls can learn that masking true feelings (liking or disliking) may be unproductive in the communication process. For communication to be effective, we need to use both verbal and nonverbal cues that are consistent and accurately reflect our intended message. Masking one set of cues (usually nonverbal cues) will only confuse our intended message. A key to success in interpersonal relationships is openness on both sides.

Because the immediacy cues of liking are learned, parents play a vital role in encouraging the development of those cues, especially in boys. For example, parents may encourage boys at an early age to feel comfortable seeking affiliation with people they like. Boys may be reinforced for engaging in social play as well as independent play. They can be encouraged to move closer to people around them (both male and female), to use a wider range of facial expressions to express feelings of liking, to use more eye contact directed toward both males and females to draw people into relationships, and to touch both males and females as an indication of liking rather than as an indication of power and control. Parents who encourage and reinforce these behaviors for boys in childhood lay the foundation for modifying rigid gender ideologies.

Women, too, can play a significant role in assisting men in adopting nonverbal immediacy cues. Women can encourage and positively reinforce men's use of appropriate nonverbal immediacy cues to indicate liking. Whether in the interpersonal relationships of friend, spouse, parent, or coworker, some men may need to be encouraged to open up and express their feelings. If men are able to do so, however, women may face a challenge they have never encountered before; since some women have become adept at ignoring men's feelings, women may find they are uncomfortable with such feelings. The challenge comes with expressing feelings and seeking to understand feelings as part of the total communication process; only then will gender expectations be broadened.

Status and Power Cues

Status and power cues are the nonverbal cues stereotypically associated with men rather than with women. Men may possess some physical attributes in adulthood that enhance the perception of power and control (larger body physique, greater height, and deeper, louder voices), but research suggests that most power and status cues are learned. Because they are learned, they can be adapted for more effective communication. Consider the following suggestions to encourage more effective communication of status and power cues.

Both males and females can be encouraged to use nonverbal cues that reflect status and power when such cues are appropriate to the communication situation. Instead of using these cues as a reflection of gender ideology (men are always dominant and women are always submissive), both sexes can use these cues when the situation calls for them. For example, it may be appropriate for a woman to use status and power cues as the manager of her office just as it may be inappropriate for her male secretary to demonstrate such cues in the office. We should remember that the nature of the situation, not gender stereotypes, dictates the use of status and power cues in interpersonal communication.

Because status and power cues are learned, parents can encourage the development of those cues. To accompany the verbal strategies discussed in Chapter 3, girls should be encouraged to use voice and body cues that convey competence and self-confidence in a variety of communication situations. For example, girls might be encouraged to use more space and to use more expansive gestures when assuming leadership roles. These nonverbal cues, coupled with verbal assertiveness, can enhance a female's ability to command the authority and respect often necessary to influence others.

Men, too, can play a significant role in supporting women who use status and power cues. Sometimes when a woman uses assertive nonverbal cues to communicate status and power, she is labeled as *aggressive* or *abrasive*. For example, if a woman raises her voice or pounds her fist on a desk to emphasize a point, she may be criticized for behaving aggressively and inappropriately for her gender. If a man demonstrates these same behaviors, he may be considered *assertive* or a *strong leader*. Both men and women are guilty of negative gender stereotyping and bear the responsibility for change. While women can learn to demonstrate these cues, men can view them as assertive and appropriate rather than as aggressive and inappropriate. Assertive communication behaviors should be an option afforded everyone and viewed positively whether used by females or males. (See Chapter 9 for a more extensive discussion of assertive behavior.) After all, an equal distribution of power and control between women and men provides the foundation for a truly democratic society, one that grants everyone the opportunity to succeed.

Responsiveness Cues

Finally, we have noted that both men and women have the capability to be responsive and should be encouraged to expand the range of responsiveness in their repertoire of nonverbal cues. From an early age, boys may be encouraged to use more affiliative behaviors (moving closer to others, using more touch to demonstrate caring, using more facial expression to reflect emotions). Learning to use nonverbal responsiveness cues is crucial if men are to become more expressive in the communication process. Women need to explore and develop responsiveness that reflects power and control in their communication (using more space, using more expansive gestures to create an image of confidence). In addition, both men and women need to understand each other's behavior. Society's institutions need to change to accommodate various kinds of effective communication behaviors.

A willingness to explore the range of responsiveness available in the use of nonverbal cues and a willingness to encourage and reinforce new behaviors in both men and women will provide the foundation for changing gender ideology. These behavioral adaptations should reduce gender stereotypes and enhance the quality of communication between men and women.

Summary

Gender is reflected in nonverbal cues. In general, women are more adept at encoding (forming) and decoding (translating) nonverbal cues than men, a difference that emerges in childhood and continues into adulthood. In body movement and posture, female and male toddlers and preschool children tend to use different gestures. Girls tend to use more emblems (nonverbal gestures with verbal equivalents) than boys. Throughout childhood development and into adulthood, men use more space than women use in both posture and general body movements. Boys tend to inhibit and mask their overt responses to emotion as they grow older, and girls continue to respond freely. As children develop, girls both receive and use more affect displays than boys. As a result, females tend to be better than males at encoding and decoding affect displays throughout their lives.

Boys tend to venture farther away from their mothers than girls, stay away from their mothers longer, and look at and talk to their mothers less than girls. Gender differences in the use and perception of personal space continue as children grow: boys are given and use more space than girls during childhood, adolescence, and into adulthood. Men also initiate more touch than women, usually for the purpose of communicating power and control rather than nurturing and affiliation.

Although a common gender ideology holds that women are more concerned than men with personal appearance, the majority of what we know from research about perceptions of physical appearance is about men. Perceptions of the "best" body build and its link to social acceptance are clearly established in boys by six years of age. Mesomorphs (people with athletic bodies) are perceived as more socially acceptable than ectomorphs (people with very thin bodies) or endomorphs (people with chubby bodies). Unfortunately, some men have taken dangerous drugs such as steroids to make their bodies more muscular and to improve their athletic performance. Many women believe that being small and slim is an important determinant of their physical attractiveness, and therefore disorders such as anorexia nervosa and bulimia have increased as a result of young women's striving to meet gender expectations.

Gender ideologies are also reflected in artifacts such as toys. As infants, boys play with transportation toys and potentially dangerous objects, such as electrical outlets, more than girls; girls more often play with soft toys and dolls. Boys are more likely to be given play objects that encourage activities directed away from the home; girls may be given play objects that encourage activities directed toward the home. Recent research, however, suggests that parents are beginning to offer neutral toys to their children. This finding indicates a shift away from some traditional gender ideologies.

Overall, nonverbal behaviors reflect the same gender ideologies we observed in verbal behavior in Chapter 3. Many boys and men demonstrate nonverbal cues that conform to gender expectations of independence and dominance. Many girls and women demonstrate nonverbal cues that conform to gender expectations of dependence and submission. Unfortunately, conforming to these gender expectations leads to behaviors that can have negative repercussions for both men and women.

CONSIDER THIS!

Too Pumped Up?

Researchers have identified a new psychiatric disorder for the gymnasium set: pumped-up people in top physical shape who worry constantly that they "look puny."

Many of the muscle-bound men and women found to have the disorder were so preoccupied with their bodies that they had given up good jobs and intimate relationships to spend hours in the gym. And yet they typically wore baggy sweat-shirts and pants even in midsummer to conceal their bodies, refusing to go to the beach or swimming pool. Many reported taking anabolic steroids to build up muscle, constantly weighed themselves and checked in mirrors, suffering great distress if they missed a day of weight-lifting.

"Bound to be muscular," 1997

Because these nonverbal behaviors are learned, everyone can expand their repertoire of nonverbal cues to break away from a rigid gender ideology. We hope that exploring new behaviors used in appropriate contexts and understanding more about others will expand everyone's communication options and will enhance all of our communicative capabilities.

FINDING YOUR VOICE

1. Spend an hour in a location where people gather, such as a shopping mall, a fast-food restaurant, or park. Observe the proxemic behavior (use of space) of as many people as you can. Be sure to note their sex and approximate age. What can you conclude about how people use space? Do men and women use space differently? How much touching behavior did you observe? When did it occur? Were there any differences in touching behavior between men and women as well as in people of different ages? What did the touching behavior you observed indicate to you about the relationships between the people you observed? What are the implications of the nonverbal behavior you observed for communication between men and women?

2. Look through magazines and newspapers to find pictures of male and female mesomorphs, male and female ectomorphs, and male and female endomorphs. Try to find people who are approximately the same age and who are approximately equal in attractiveness except for their body type. Ask 10 males and 10 females to rate each of the pictures on the following scales:

I think this person is attractive.	Yes	No	Maybe
I would like to be friends with this person.	Yes	No	Maybe
This person is intelligent.	Yes	No	Maybe
I would like to date this person.	Yes	No	Maybe
This person must be lonely.	Yes	No	Maybe
This person is happy.	Yes	No	Maybe

   Tabulate the results you obtained for male and female respondents and for males and females of different body types. How are people with each body type perceived? Are males and females perceived differently? Do males and females perceive people with the same body type differently? How do gender stereotypes affect our perception of body type?

3. Wear (or bring) your favorite T-shirt to class. Does your T-shirt directly convey a message about gender stereotypes (e.g., "A woman's place is in the house—and in the Senate," "Men control the world—but women control men")? Could your T-shirt be interpreted differently when worn by a man or a woman (e.g., "It's not easy to be a sex symbol," "Born to be hugged")? Is your T-shirt more likely to be worn by a woman than a man (e.g., "I like the simple things in life—men") or vice versa (e.g., "Ten things I like about beer")? In general, what does the choice of T-shirts say about the role of gendered behavior and gender stereotypes in the communication process?

FURTHER READING

Barthel, D. (1988). *Putting on appearances: Gender and advertising.* Philadelphia, PA: Temple University Press.
    An interesting discussion of the ways in which advertising affects our perceptions of physical attractiveness. Good discussion of how advertisers develop male markets for products previously associated with women.

Jackson, L. A. (1992). *Physical appearance and gender: Sociobiological and sociocultural perspectives.* Albany: State University of New York Press.
    This book brings together a variety of empirical research to support the assertion that women's physical appearance is more important in determining life outcomes than it is for men. Perhaps most beneficial is Jackson's discussion of why and when the differences between women and men are most important. Specifically, she explores the interpersonal, professional, social, and personal implications of both facial and body appearance for men and women.

Knapp, M. L., & Hall, J. A. (1996). *Nonverbal communication in human interaction,* 4th ed. Fort Worth, TX: Harcourt Brace Jovanovich.
    This text provides an overview of nonverbal communication by exploring specific sets of nonverbal cues. These cues range from the effects of personal space and territory on human communication to the effects of facial expression and eye behavior. Relevant research findings concerning male–female similarities and differences are explored throughout the chapters.

Peiss, K. (1998). *Hope in a jar: The making of America's beauty culture.* New York: Henry Holt.
    This book is a fascinating history of cosmetics and the women who played a significant role in the development of the cosmetics industry. Peiss reveals both the positive and negative aspects of this topic.

CHAPTER

5   Friendships

As we discussed in Chapter 1, shared meaning created through communication allows us to convey our own identity to others and to convey to others our expectations for their identities. One of the primary settings in which we communicate and develop our identities is in interpersonal relationships that involve direct, face-to-face encounters between people. In particular, these relationships include friendships, marriage, and family. In this chapter, we will explore the nature of these interpersonal relationships and then specifically examine gender ideologies in friendship. We will deal with gender in families, courtship, and marriage in the next chapter.

Interpersonal Relationships

According to Wilmot (1987), interpersonal relationships function as open communication systems that possess four important qualities. First, these relationships possess *wholeness*, the elements of the system are related such that a change in one element affects all other elements in the system. For example, two college friends may form a relationship based on the fact that they are both single and free to do things together. When one of them enters a romantic partnership, their relationship may change.

Second, these relationships create *synergy*, that is, people in a relationship create an energy that is greater than the energy brought to the relationship by the two people individually. While this energy may be positive or negative, synergy explains what occurs between and among individuals as they come together to form a relationship. If you have ever studied for an exam with a friend and discovered that the knowledge you acquired studying together was more than the knowledge either of you could have acquired individually, you have experienced a positive effect of synergy. Parenting together is another example of the positive effects of synergy.

Third, interpersonal relationships possess the quality of *circularity*, mutual influence made possible through the process of feedback. Consider how circularity is reflected by two people who begin a dating relationship: she asks him to study, so he asks her to a concert; she asks him to go out for coffee, and then he asks her to a movie; she introduces him to her parents, and the relationship continues to grow and develop. Simply put, each of us behaves, monitors the other's response to our behavior, and responds to the other's response. Circularity creates and fosters mutual influence in relationships.

Finally, interpersonal relationships exhibit *equifinality*, the ability to reach the same end state in many different ways and from very diverse beginnings. For instance, two marriages may be characterized as intimate and mutually satisfying, even though the marriage partners may be quite different and those two marriages develop in very different ways over the years. Because interpersonal relationships are composed of individuals who bring their unique qualities and capabilities to their relationship, every relationship has the potential for equifinality.

Friendships, marriages, and families are the primary interpersonal relationships in our lives. They differ in significant ways. Perhaps most important is that in most cultures people choose who they want to marry, but we generally do not get to choose our parents, siblings, or children. Of course, current societal changes such as blended families and the adoption of older children are changing some of these issues, but in general we have to learn to deal with the personalities of the people in the families into which we are born.

While friendships, marriages, and families may appear to be very different in nature, however, they share several common features. First, although marriage and family relationships may be more institutionalized than friendships, all three types of relationships are uniquely defined and privately negotiated among people. We strive to create relationships that meet our needs. Friendship, marriage, and family give us the opportunity to fulfill such basic relationship (and communication) functions as expressing our feelings, confirming another's identity, serving as a catalyst for change in others, and accomplishing goals outside the relationship. Participating in any or all of these relationships can lead to a fuller, more complete life.

Second, friendship, marriage, and family require a considerable investment of emotional energy; all demand commitment from the people developing the relationship. Friendships may range in level of intimacy from mere acquaintances to casual friends to "best" friends. The amount and depth of information we disclose to another person generally increases as we develop a more intimate interpersonal relationship. Intimate friendships, marriage and families all require continual sharing of one's self, ideas, and feelings, as well as a respect for the other person in the relationship. Since disclosing intimate information makes us vulnerable, trust is an essential ingredient for intimacy in each of these interpersonal relationships.

Finally, all of these relationships are highly rhetorical in nature; that is, they involve people who are self-conscious, intentional, and purposeful in their communication with one another (Rawlins, 1992). Communication is the underlying process used to define, negotiate, and develop these relationships. In this chapter we will explore gender in friendship, the implications and consequences of gender ideology in this relationship, and strategies for change to enhance the quality of our friendships.

Defining Friendship

Blieszner and Adams (1992) define friendship by asking:
What does friendship mean to you? If you were to ask that question of a group of people, you would receive almost as many answers as there were people in the

group. Oh, of course you would be able to categorize the responses. Sharing, caring, helping, and the permanence of the relationship would be mentioned. You would also be able to discern patterns in your "data." The men would tend to mention the importance of doing things with their friends, and the women would remark on the value of intimacy. Young children would mention sharing toys, and older adults would refer to shared life experiences. Rather than the loose clustering of these responses and these patterns, however, the tremendous variation in emphasis across individuals would be most obvious. (p. 1)

Blieszner and Adams indicate that friendship occurs in structural, cultural, and historical contexts, and present a theoretical model of friendship that we have included in Figure 5.1.

According to their model, social and individual characteristics such as age influence the kind of friendships a person is likely to have. In this model, *stage of life course* refers to the stages of life that people go through (for example, childhood, adolescence,

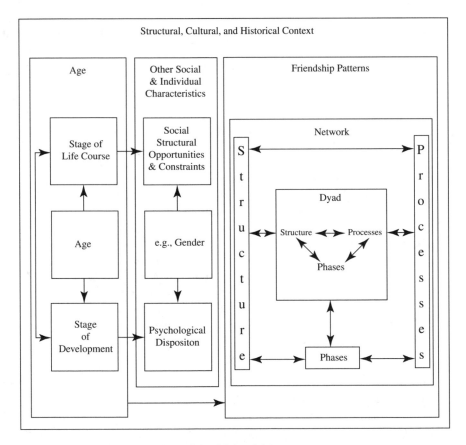

FIGURE 5.1 Theoretical model of friendship.
Blieszner and Adams, 1992

parenthood). In most cases, these stages are strongly related to age. These stages influence other social and individual characteristics, which are also influenced by gender. For example, a female adolescent may have a different "psychological disposition" (attitude) toward friendship than a male adolescent. A person's stage of life course may provide opportunities for or barriers to friendships. For example, a father who takes his children to the park may meet other fathers and develop friendships with them. A busy female business executive who puts in long hours at work may not have the time to develop friendships with people outside work. In addition, friendships vary depending on the cultural or historical setting. People from different cultures often have different ways of expressing friendships. For example, gift giving between friends may be expected or prohibited. Friendships between men and women are common today, but this was not the case in the past.

Blieszner and Adams also suggest that friendship patterns exist. These patterns consist of structure (with variables such as similarity of social positions, number of friends, how many of one's friends know one another, and the hierarchy and intimacy among them), processes (thoughts, feelings, and behaviors involved in being friends), and phases (the formation, maintenance, and dissolution of friendships). Whether discussing dyadic friendships or a person's network of friends, these three aspects of friendship (structure, processes, and phases) exist.

Having said all this and having alluded to the fact that friendship is difficult to define, we must add that research suggests friendship is perceived similarly across genders. For example, both men and women value trust (Bell, 1981), intimacy (Rose, 1985), acceptance (Sherrod, 1989), and support (Fox, Gibbs, & Auerbach, 1985) in their friendships.

Given this general introduction to friendship, let's examine specific types of friendships.

Same-Sex Friendships

Children's Friendships

Think about the friendships you have experienced over the years. When you first began elementary school, your friends were probably both boys and girls. You walked to school together, you ate lunch together, and you played games at recess together. As you grew from childhood to early adolescence, your circle of friends probably narrowed to include primarily friends of your own sex. Again, you probably rode the bus or walked to school together, ate lunch with these friends, and attended after-school activities with them. Although an interest in the other sex may emerge with the onset of middle adolescence, our early experiences with same-sex friends and our continued development of these friendships play an important role in our lives.

Consistent findings concerning childhood same-sex friendships have emerged from the literature. Rawlins (1992) reviews literature that indicates that by around age seven, boys tend to prefer to play in groups, and girls tend to prefer to play with one other girl. By fifth and sixth grade, the number of boys' friendships becomes more expansive while girls' friendships become more exclusive.

Several researchers have concluded that girls' friendships are more intimate than those of boys. For example, fourth-grade girls share more secrets than boys do (Rotenberg, 1986). In their study of fifth- and sixth-graders, Furman and Buhrmester (1985) report that girls indicate significantly more intimacy and affection in their friendships than boys. Buhrmester and Furman (1987), studying second-, fifth-, and eighth-graders find that girls exhibit a steady increase in intimate disclosure and a "striking increase during preadolescence in the significance of same-sex friends as intimacy providers" (p. 1111). In contrast, boys' levels remained constant. It is important to note that all of these studies define intimacy based on self-disclosure. As we will note throughout this chapter, this definition is biased against men. Males, and in this case boys, are often more likely to share an intimacy based less on disclosure and more on shared activity.

Adolescent Friendships

Adolescent same-sex friendships have some of the same characteristics as children's same-sex friendships. Once again, adolescent female friendships have been described as more intimate because they are more inclined toward disclosure and discussion of personal topics (Youniss & Smollar, 1985), and are generally more exclusive (Rawlins, 1992). In contrast, adolescent male same-sex friendships are more inclusive or group related (Rawlins, 1992). Males disclose less and talk mostly about activity-oriented issues rather than about personal issues (Youniss & Smollar, 1985).

Adult Friendships

As you might guess, adult same-sex friendships are similar to those of earlier ages. Aries and Johnson (1983) asked women to discuss the most important benefits of their female friendships. Respondents indicated that they value their friends for listening noncritically, for providing support for enhanced self-esteem, for offering comfort, and for validating personal growth. In terms of the content of their communication, women tend to focus on relational and personal material (Blieszner & Adams, 1992). Women talk more often with their friends than do men. Aries and Johnson (1983) found that women were more likely than men to talk to their friends on the telephone for 10 minutes or more, talk in depth about personal problems, reveal doubts and fears, and discuss intimate relationships.

Oliker (1989) studied women's best friends. The women in this study reported frequent visiting (at least a few times a week for the majority) and telephoning (from a few times a week to nearly every day) between best friends. Other researchers cite similar findings. Fifty percent of the women but only 19 percent of the men in a study conducted by Aries and Johnson (1983) had daily or weekly telephone conversations with their best friends.

Thus, female same-sex friendships have been characterized as expressive: talk is the central feature of women's friendships (Aries & Johnson, 1983). Male same-sex friendships have been consistently characterized as instrumental. Males do things together and share activities. Male same-sex friendships display common interests, shared activities, and sociability as their primary characteristics (Rawlins, 1992). Male friendships are "often geared toward accomplishing things and having something to show for their time spent together—practical problems solved; the house painted or deck completed; wildlife netted; cars washed or tuned; tennis, basketball, poker, or music played, and so on. Shared talk may arise during these pursuits but it usually is not the principal focus" (Rawlins, 1992, p. 181).

Bruess and Pearson (1997) believe that rituals play an important part in the maintenance of friendships for both men and women. Although contact with adult friends declines as individuals get older and take on more family-oriented responsibilities, adult friendships are important parts of many people's lives. After gathering data from adults ranging in age from twenty-three to seventy-nine, Bruess and Pearson concluded that there are six major categories of rituals in friendships (see Table 5.1 for a description of these rituals). Women's friendships are more likely to include Idiosyncratic/Symbolic Rituals (and specifically Celebration Rituals) than men's friendships. In addition, there are a significantly higher frequency of Communication and Share/Support/Vent Rituals reported in women's friendships with other women.

Seidler (1992), in the book *Men's Friendships*, suggests that men make few demands on their friends, and thus their friends find it difficult to make demands on them. "One of the ways that we sustain power and control in relationships," he writes, "is by overtly demanding very little. Others then are likely to feel bad because of the

TABLE 5.1   Friendship Ritual Types

	Social/Fellowship Rituals	
Type of Ritual	**Description**	**Example**
Enjoyable Activities	Social or recreational activities that are pleasurable, desirable and/or leisurely	Participating in a hobby together such as going to flea markets once a month; seeing a movie together every Thursday night
Getting-Together Rituals	Physically getting together to keep in touch	Visiting in each other's apartment; eating lunch together during the week
Established Events	Special, highly planned events	Going to the mall the day after Thanksgiving; going to the opening game of the baseball season
Escape Episodes	Being away from others, the routines of life or external pressures	Going on a trip together during spring break; having lunch together once a week "without the kids"

TABLE 5.1 Continued

Idiosyncratic/Symbolic Rituals

Type of Ritual	Description	Example
Celebration Rituals	Routines for holidays, birthdays, anniversaries, or other special events guided by shared expectations based on the history of celebrations of the friendship	Annual exchange of holiday gifts; treating each other to lunch on birthdays
Play Rituals	Joking, kidding, teasing, playing pranks on one another, or being "silly"	Calling a friend by a special nickname that reminds him or her of a past experience; harmless practical jokes
Favorites	Most preferred places to go, things to eat, items to purchase or give, and activities	Watching a favorite TV show together each week; going to a particular sporting event
Communication Rituals	Rituals for keeping in touch via cards, telephone calls, e-mail	Calling a long distance friend each month just to chat
Share/Support/Vent	Social, emotional or spiritual sharing and support	Complaining to a friend about problems with one's partner or job; weekly meetings of organized groups that offer emotional support for dealing with difficult issues
Tasks/Favors	Doing something with and/or for a friend	Doing grocery shopping for a friend who is ill; coloring a friend's hair
Patterns/Habits/Mannerisms	Interactional, territorial and/or situational patterns and habits friends develop	Greeting each other on the phone in the same way each time; sitting in a particular chair in a friend's apartment

Adapted from Bruess & Pearson, 1997.

demands they are ready to make on us. This holding back is an aspect of the way our denial of our needs serves to structure the power that, as men, we maintain in our relationships" (pp. 21–22). Seidler also suggests that it is difficult for males to learn to listen to friends because men too often assume that what the friend really wants is a solution to a problem.

Communication in Same-Sex Friendships

Many communication variables have been examined in same-sex friendships. For example, Burleson and colleagues (1996) asked college students to evaluate their communication in same-sex friendships and found that women rated the affectively oriented communication skills of their friends somewhat more important than men did. In other words, women valued their friends' skills in ego support (for example, "Makes me feel like I'm a good person"), conflict management (for example, "Makes me realize that it's better to deal with conflicts we have than to keep things bottled up inside"), comforting (for example, "Almost always makes me feel better when I'm hurt or depressed about something"), and regulation (for example, "Takes time to work through my mistakes with me") as more important than men did. Men, however, rated instrumental skills as more important for same-sex friendships. Men want their friends to possess narrative skill (for example, "Often comes up with a witty remark in conversation") and persuasive skill (for example, "Can talk me into doing things that he wants me to do"). While women's intimate bonds may be enacted through talking, disclosing, and sharing, men's relationships are often located in shared activities and common interests (Bruess & Pearson, 1997). To test this assumption, Goldsmith and Dun (1997) asked college students to indicate how they would respond to someone who had a common problem such as failing an exam, having a registration problem, or being dumped by a boyfriend or girlfriend. They found that although women's responses to another person's problem were longer and contained more talk about emotions, they also talked more about instrumental actions (actions to solve the problem) than men. Men responded by talking more about the problem or by spending more time denying the problem existed.

We will discuss three of the most important variables in same-sex friendships (conflict, intimacy, and self-disclosure) here.

Conflict.   Davidson and Duberman (1982) find that conflict is low in best friendships for both women and men, but men report more conflict in their relationships in general than do women. Within same-sex friendships, Argyle and Furnham (1983) report that conflict is low on issues dealing with criticism, but higher on emotional issues related to competition and differing values and beliefs. Interestingly, in Oliker's (1989) study, adult women often expressed their anger about someone in another relationship to their best friend, thereby diffusing their anger so that conflict could be avoided in the other relationship.

Healey and Bell (1990) studied disputes between friends. No differences were found between males and females in terms of which conflict-management strategy they employed: exit—ending or threatening to end the friendship; voice—discussing problems or changing behavior to resolve them; loyalty—passively waiting for the relationship to improve; or neglect—passively allowing the friendship to wither. However, females are more likely than males to discuss their conflicts with other friends, receive advice about dealing with conflict from a larger number of friends, and rate their conflicts as more serious and having a more harmful effect on the friendship (also see Duck, Rutt, Hurst, & Strejc, 1991).

Tannen (1990a) analyzed videotapes of six pairs of same-sex best friends from second, sixth, and tenth grades. She reports that the girls try more often to avoid anger and disagreement than the boys, and are more uncomfortable when it occurs.

Intimacy and Self-Disclosure.   One of the most often studied communication variables in friendship is intimacy (closeness) and the related concept of self-disclosure. **Self-disclosure** occurs when *people voluntarily communicate information about themselves that other people are unlikely to know or discover from other sources* (Pearce & Sharp, 1973). Disclosure should not be confused with intimacy (we can know a great deal about someone and still not feel close to that person). Many authors contend that both disclosure and self-disclosure are essential for the development of any intimate interpersonal relationship. Remember, however, that this research has a definite cultural and perhaps gender bias. Women in U.S. culture may place a high value on self-disclosure. This is not always true of men or of women from other cultures. Some people form intimate interpersonal relationships without a great deal of self-disclosure. For example, in Chinese culture, friendship is not based on self-disclosure. When one of the authors of this book asked students at the Chinese University of Hong Kong, "If you don't get to know one another through self-disclosure, how do you get to know one another?" they responded, "We do things together."

In general, based on traditional measures, women have been described as having a greater degree of intimacy in their friendships than men (Barth & Kinder, 1988; Blieszner & Adams, 1992; Sherrod, 1989) because women disclose more to their friends than men do (Blieszner & Adams, 1992). In addition, females emphasize expressive aspects (such as sharing feelings and emotions) as important to their friendships, while males emphasize instrumental aspects (such as working together) (Hays, 1989; Rawlins, 1992; Tannen, 1990b). (We will discuss the gender bias of this research later in this chapter.)

Women tend to rate themselves as more appropriate users of disclosure than men (Duran & Kelly, 1985). Women disclose more in-depth, evaluative, and emotional messages than men (Morton, 1978), and women are likely to increase the amount of their disclosure as the interaction becomes more intimate (Lombardo & Berzonsky, 1979). In fact, men who are high self-disclosers are often perceived as less competent communicators, but women who are high self-disclosers are perceived by others as affiliative and supportive. As a result, women usually are expected to disclose more than men (Jones & Brunner, 1984).

Several communication behaviors used by men and women in same-sex friendships demonstrate that women tend to be facilitators of disclosure and that men may be controllers of disclosure. Talk among female friends is generally characterized by noncritical listening and mutual support. Women are more likely to sense when their women friends are in trouble and, as a result, provide a sympathetic listening ear that conveys understanding and concern. If a man senses that a close male friend is depressed, his first impulse may be to ignore that depression and change the subject of their conversation. While this behavior is insensitive by female standards, it is considered appropriate among men. Men sometimes respond to another person's self-disclosure as if it were a request for advice. Instead of responding with their own self-disclosure, they may take the role of expert and offer advice (Coates, 1986). In addition to this advice giving, men may tend to comfort each other by switching to inconsequential topics during the course of a personal conversation. This strategy is seen by other men as a common courtesy and not as insensitivity (Howell, 1981).

Topic Choice. Disclosure among female friends typically focuses on topics that involve personal and family matters. Such topics are closely related to self and tend to be characterized as more emotion-based in nature than men's talk (Haas & Sherman, 1982). Women often are more willing to share intimate details of their personal lives with other women than men share with other men; women are more likely to confide worries to a friend than men are; and women often discuss the self-enhancement that results from self-disclosure while men do not (Mark & Alper, 1985). Disclosure among young men generally focuses on topics such as current events, sports, money, and music—topics that may reflect images of competition, power, and status (Rawlins, 1992; Sherman & Haas, 1984).

In other words, women's talk tends to be expressive; men's talk is more likely to be instrumental. Women traditionally talk to each other about personal and affiliative issues that reflect *who they are;* men traditionally talk about task and power issues that reflect *what they do* (Aukett, Richie & Mill, 1988).

Women and men also tend to follow different norms for interacting in same-sex groups (Coates, 1986; Harriman, 1985). Women may get together "just to talk" and discuss one topic for half an hour or more. As they share information with each other, they reveal a great deal about their feelings and relationships. Men, on the other hand, are more likely to prefer participating in activities together (such as playing video games, eating, listening to music, or participating in sports). Their talk accompanies the activity. When they do talk, they may jump from topic to topic, competing with each other to prove themselves better informed about current events, sports, or what-ever topic comes up. Women are more likely to respect each other's speaking turns and attempt to equalize participation in same-sex groups. Women feel uncomfortable when these norms are not followed. Conversely, individual men may dominate an all-male group while the others just listen. This behavior is seen as appropriate for this type of group.

Differences in Intimacy and Self-Disclosure. There are some basic differences between disclosure in female friendships and disclosure in male friendships. Although males tend to report more same-sex friends than females, females describe a deeper level of intimacy (as measured by amount of and type of self-disclosure) with their same-sex friends. The amount of disclosure and the nature of that disclosure differ between male and female friends.

Caldwell and Peplau (1982) suggest that males and females may employ separate standards for evaluating the intimacy of their friendships. Too often the female model of what constitutes intimacy has been applied to male friendships (Wood & Inman, 1993). For women, verbal disclosures tend to constitute intimacy. Duck (1988) reviews "clear evidence that . . . men appear to regard intimacy as being embodied in joint activities, while for women, the specific activity that signals intimacy is sharing of information, feelings, secrets and insights into oneself" (p. 80). Wood and Inman

(1993) suggest the importance of not applying a model based on one gender to judge the behavior of the other.

Cross-Sex Friendships

While romantic relationships and same-sex friendships have received considerable research attention, male/female platonic friendships have not (Kaplan & Keys, 1997). This lack of research may result, in part, from the fact that societal norms discourage friendships between females and males. Think of all the movies and televisonshows in which the main characters begin as friends and inevitably end up in a romantic relationship. Nevertheless, platonic friendships do exist and are worthy of further examination.

As one reads the literature on cross-sex friendships (friendships between women and men), a recurrent theme seems to be the difficulty of these friendships (Rawlins, 1993). As Swain (1992) says:

> Since cross-sex friendship is not a clearly defined or expected social relationship it is often interpreted in terms of heterosexual love relationships. For example, many heterosexual love relationships begin as platonic friendships, thus promoting a view of cross-sex friendships as a stage of development in the coupling process, rather than as a legitimate relationship in and of itself. When an adolescent develops a friendship with a cross-sex friend, family members often tease, hint at, or praise the person for establishing a possible heterosexual dating, sexual, or love relationship. Claims that "we're just good friends" are often viewed as withholding information, or as an indication of embarrassment or bashfulness about the sexual content of the relationship. (p. 154)

In general, cross-sex friendships occur less frequently than same-sex friendships and have shorter longevity (Swain, 1992). Males report more cross-sex friendships than females (Rawlins, 1992). Sapadin (1988) reports that men rate their cross-sex friendships as more enjoyable and nurturing than their same-sex ones, although they rate both similar in perceived intimacy. In contrast, women rate their same-sex friendships as more intimate, enjoyable, nurturing, and higher in overall quality than their cross-sex ones. Further, they feel much more nurtured by their female friends, in both personal and career areas than by male friends (Sapadin, 1988, p. 401).

Why are cross-sex friendships so difficult to achieve and to maintain? Several possibilities come to mind. The first one is the one we've already alluded to: society's lack of acceptance of this type of friendship. Rawlins (1993) suggests that cross-sex friendships are socially "deviant." Often others simply won't believe the "just good friends" explanation of a cross-sex friendship.

In addition, sexual attraction is often present in platonic friendships, especially for men (Kaplan & Keys, 1997). Because our societal norm for friendship is same-sex friendship, we may have difficulty understanding how a male and female can be just good friends, particularly in light of what we know about the differences between male same-sex friendships and female same-sex friendships.

This brings us to a second possibility, differing attitudes toward friendship. Remember our earlier discussion about same-sex friendships. In terms of intimacy, females tend to show intimacy through self-disclosure, while males are more likely to base their intimate friendships on shared activities. Another difference in attitudes relates to romantic involvement and sexual activity. Women often believe that men's motive for friendship is sexual and are, therefore, reluctant to form friendships with men if they have no desire for a more romantic involvement (Rose, 1985). A final factor influencing cross-sex friendships concerns emotional needs. If, as research suggests, men look to women rather than to other men to meet their emotional needs (Rand & Levinger, 1979), and women think men cannot meet their emotional needs and so form female friendships (Gilligan, 1982), then a cross-sex friendship may be difficult to maintain.

Closely related to the different perceptions of how best to meet emotional needs, Rubin (1983) finds that males have a more difficult time recognizing the feelings of another person. This is particularly true when the other person is female. Women, on the other hand, are better able to recognize others' emotions. This ability is evidenced by the fact that women use more affectionate touch, expressions of empathy, and feedback after disclosure than men (Buhrke & Fuqua, 1987). As Ivy and Backlund (1994) suggest, differences in the recognition of feelings can create problems for cross-sex friends if an imbalance is perceived in the amount of emotional support one derives from the relationship.

Communication in Cross-Sex Friendships

Conflict, intimacy and self-disclosure, and communicator style have been studied in cross-sex friendships. We will examine briefly each of these issues.

Conflict. Every relationship has conflict. However, in some ways, men and women handle conflict differently. If conflict or tension occurs in cross-sex friendships, women are more likely to blame themselves for relational failures and credit others for relational successes (Martin & Nivens, 1987). Also, if problems arise, women are more likely than men to end the relationship. Men are more likely to ignore relational problems by focusing on positive aspects of the relationship.

A recent study on deception (Powers, 1993) sheds some light on why females might choose to end a relationship that is difficult. Women tend to be more sensitive to relational deception than men. In addition, women evaluate the character and competence of a deceiver lower than do men. If a woman discovers deception has occurred, she may decide to end the relationship because deception is so unacceptable to her (see also Levine, McCornack & Avery, 1992).

Intimacy and Self-Disclosure. Dindia and Allen (1992) examined more than 200 studies on self-disclosure and found that women self-disclose more than men. It is important to take into account whether the conversational partners are male or female since women disclose more than men in same-sex dyads but do not disclose more than men when they are talking with a man.

In terms of disclosure in cross-sex friendships, men report that they disclose more intimate information to women than they do to other men. Women, however, claim they disclose more intimate information to other women (Aukett, Richie, & Mill, 1988). In addition, there are some interesting differences in the nature of disclosure in cross-sex friendships compared with disclosure in same-sex friendships (Hacker, 1981). Specifically, unlike self-disclosure in same-sex friendships, there is no significant difference in the amount of disclosure between men and women in cross-sex friendships. Instead, differences emerge in the nature of the self-disclosure between men and women. For example, when talking to female friends, men tend to confide more about their weaknesses while they *enhance* their strengths (Stephen & Harrison, 1985). Women tend to confide about their weaknesses and *conceal* their strengths.

To illustrate this disclosure pattern, consider the following scenario. Don is very upset with his boss. Lately, every proposal he presents to her is turned down. Don discloses this information to his co-worker and friend, Karen. During Don's disclosure he tells Karen all the wonderful things he has done for the company during the last year. He dismisses the fact that he hasn't done as well this year and blames his boss for not knowing a good idea when she sees one. In reply, Karen admits that she too has had some of her proposals turned down, but fails to mention that three out of her four proposals have been accepted and used.

These two different disclosure patterns are reflective of common gender ideology. Men are expected to assume a superior or dominant position through disclosure, so they include and even enhance their strengths when they confide to women about their weaknesses. Women are expected to facilitate the disclosure process by playing a subordinate role in which they confide only their weaknesses and discuss none of their strengths. This superior–subordinate role relationship often found in cross-sex conversation indicates that women may be dominated in cross-sex conversation while men are more likely to dominate the conversation (Rubin, Perse & Barbato, 1988; Tannen, 1990b).

Goldsmith and Dun (1997) asked college students to respond to typical problems encountered by their friends, including failing an exam, registration problems, or being "dumped by a boyfriend or girlfriend." Contrary to the stereotype that women are concerned with emotions while men are concerned with problem solving, when asked to talk about a problem both men and women spent the same amount of time talking about what action to take. Men, however, did use more time to discuss the problem and more of that talk dismissed or denied the other person's problem. Neither men nor women talked much about emotions but focused more on the problem presented.

Communicator Style. **Communicator style** refers to *"the way one verbally and paraverbally interacts to signal how literal meaning should be taken, interpreted, filtered, or understood"* (Norton, 1978, p. 99). Such characteristics as dominant, animated, relaxed, attentive, open, and friendly often are used to describe a person's communicator style, and these characteristics contribute to a person's effectiveness in the communication process.

When men and women are asked to describe their own communicator styles, they report minimal differences (Staley & Cohen, 1988). For example, of all the variables that constitute communicator style, women perceive themselves as more animated than men, and men perceive themselves as more precise than women. Both men and women rate themselves similarly on all other aspects of communicator style (Montgomery & Norton, 1981). Thus, both men and women claim they have more similarities than differences in their communicator style. In addition, both men and women report similar self-perceptions concerning stylistic characteristics considered to be indicators of effective communication.

Although men and women claim that they use a similar communicator style, their actual behavior is perceived differently. Women generally use a communicator style that others consider attentive and open, but men are more likely to use a style perceived by others as dominant, relaxed, and dramatic (Montgomery & Norton, 1981; Tannen, 1990b). These perceived communicator styles coincide with gender stereotypes. For example, as we discussed earlier in this chapter, females are perceived to be facilitators of communication. Both attentiveness (letting other people know they are being heard) and openness (receptivity to communication) facilitate the interpersonal communication process. Being dominant (taking charge of the interaction), dramatic (manipulating verbal and nonverbal cues to highlight or understate content), and relaxed (anxiety-free) convey control in the communication process—a control often associated with status and power.

Most research that examines the communicator style actually used by men and women in cross-sex friendships focuses primarily on men's use of dominance as a means of controlling the communication. Specifically, this dominance includes men talking more than women, men receiving more positive evaluations for their performance in dialogue from both men and women, and perceptions of greater male influence (Berger, Rosenholtz & Zelditch, 1980; Tannen, 1990b). But dominance may be affected by the other person's level of dominance. Davis and Gilbert (1989) found that when high-dominant women were paired with low-dominant men, the women took a leadership role 71 percent of the time. However, when high-dominant women were paired with high-dominant men, the women assumed the leadership role only 31 percent of the time. Thus, high-dominant men are somewhat more likely to become leaders than high-dominant women.

Language choice in conversations between cross-sex friends also indicates differences in perceptions of male and female communicator styles. In general, there is a tendency for females to judge verbs used in their interpersonal communication with friends as more emotional than men do; in contrast, males tend to judge verbs used in their interpersonal communication with friends as more reflective of control (Thompson, Hatchett & Phillips, 1981). For example, a woman may characterize her own behavior toward a man as protecting him (intending to communicate positive emotions), but she may be surprised when he responds to her actions in terms of the control he perceives her communication conveys. For a man, protecting may imply that the protector is stronger and the person needing protection is weaker.

In conclusion, amount and type of disclosure are important in creating and maintaining gender ideologies in cross-sex friendships. As in same-sex friendships, disclosure (and specifically self-disclosure) is essential to the development of cross-sex friendships. Although men and women use an equal amount of disclosure in mixed-sex friendships, women's disclosure is more self-related and more intimate in traditional terms than men's disclosure. In relationships where men and women are of equal status, both men and women perceive that more disclosure occurs. Perhaps more important in this discussion, however, is the introduction of differences in the communicator styles used by men and women in cross-sex friendships. A variety of language strategies—including duration of speech, language choice, and interpretation—reflect and reinforce gender stereotypes in these relationships.

Implications and Consequences of Gender in Friendships

In examining friendship, one observation is apparent: traditional gender ideologies associated with male and female communication remain relatively consistent in friendships. In general, females disclose more and are perceived as using a communicator style that is facilitative and expressive. Males disclose less and are perceived as using a communicator style that is seen as controlling and instrumental.

Within same-sex friendships, women are more likely to focus on topics related to people: self, family, and friends. Female friends encourage disclosure in their interactions and provide a supportive communication climate to facilitate disclosure. Expressive and facilitative behaviors are typically associated with traditional gender stereotypes for women. It is not surprising, then, that these behaviors are prevalent in female interactions and are often the focus for the study of communication among women. Men are more likely to focus on topics related to status, power, and competition. They may avoid rather than facilitate disclosure, usually to control the focus and direction of the interaction. These functions are consistent with gender stereotypes for men.

Many men and women also continue to maintain traditional gender ideologies as communicators in cross-sex friendships. Many men tend to use communication behaviors that reinforce images of power, status, and control, while women tend to use communication behaviors that reinforce images of expressivity and facilitation. Although men both initiate and receive more verbal communication in cross-sex friendships, the participants seem to compromise on certain topics. In conversations among college undergraduates, men tend to speak less about competition and physical aggression, while women tend to speak less about home and family than they would in same-sex groups (Aries, 1987). In cross-sex friendships, women initiate more topics (facilitation), but men decide which of those topics will be discussed at length (control). In cross-sex friendships, men's topics and language choices are more task-oriented (instrumental), and women's topics and language choices are more personal and emotional (expressive). Women generally encourage disclosure (facilitation), and men are more likely to avoid disclosure (control). When men and women do disclose, men may disclose strengths and conceal weaknesses (superiority), while women disclose weaknesses and conceal their strengths (subordination). These communication behaviors reinforce traditional gender stereotypes for both men and women.

Strategies for Change

Given our changing society, corresponding change in the basic interpersonal relationship of friendship is inevitable. The mobility of our population makes it likely that you will initiate, maintain, and terminate both same-sex and cross-sex friendships many times throughout your life. While these social changes reflect the quantity of friendships you may develop in a lifetime, the quality of those relationships is the far more important issue to consider.

A growing shift away from traditional masculine and feminine gender ideologies is beginning to change the nature of our interpersonal relationships by introducing ambiguity and uncertainty into our friendships. We need to create ways to cope with the evolving roles available to women and men because of changing social conditions, and we should be willing to redefine and renegotiate changes in the roles typically associated with friendship. Effective communication in our friendships will allow us to negotiate changing behaviors that can enhance relationship satisfaction (Petronio, 1982). Consider the following suggestions to facilitate adaptation and change in your friendships.

Develop a Supportive Climate for Change

Because any change in relationships carries with it an implicit message of dissatisfaction from the one seeking change, it is important that one or both parties in a friendship avoid feeling defensive or threatened by the possibility of change. Using communication that creates a supportive climate establishes a positive context for change. Likewise, viewing change as an opportunity to create a mutually satisfying relationship rather than as an attack or a negative assessment of the current definition of the relationship is essential to the process of change. For example, someone who asks a housemate to do more of the housework may believe that their relationship is very positive but that more active participation from the housemate in doing household chores would give them more time to spend in social activities together.

If you find yourself in relationships that you want to change, try to use communication strategies that encourage your friends to describe their feelings about your relationship and their role in your friendship. Suggest a willingness on your part to cooperate in a mutual problem-solving orientation that will help establish a communication climate supportive of change. Do not judge or evaluate feelings; rather, describe or attempt to understand those feelings. Do not imply your superior ability to define change, but emphasize equal participation by both parties in this process. Do not manipulate or control the defining and negotiation process; instead, approach it as a mutually directed process involving both parties in the relationship. Creating a defensive communication climate rather than a supportive one will only serve as a barrier to negotiating relational change.

One of the best ways to faciliate supportive change in a friendship is to engage in new activities that help produce a closer relationship. Go to a movie together. Volunteer to serve meals to the homeless. Participate in a community clean-up day. People who share enjoyable, worthwhile activities together strengthen the bonds of their friendship.

Encourage Effective Disclosure Patterns

Earlier we noted differences in disclosure patterns for males and females. Women traditionally tend to disclose about self and personal topics for the purpose of serving expressive and affiliative needs. Men tend to disclose about task- or goal-oriented topics for the purpose of serving instrumental needs. Perhaps one of the greatest frustrations expressed by women in cross-sex friendships is that men do not disclose on the expressive or feeling level. While men may find it difficult to alter the nature of their disclosure, they may become comfortable disclosing about self in interpersonal relationships where trust has been established.

Since men appreciate this type of disclosure from women in relationships, men obviously value it. Men may strive to share their feelings more openly with their close friends when increased disclosure is appropriate, and women may facilitate and positively reinforce such disclosure in their relationships.

Women may also respect men's desire to refrain from disclosure. As long as the absence of disclosure is an indication of satisfaction with the relationship and not a control tactic, men's lack of disclosure should not be criticized. Tavris (1992) suggests that women appear to: "be better than men at intimacy because intimacy is defined as what women do; talk, express feelings, disclose personal concerns. Intimacy is rarely defined as sharing activities, being helpful, doing useful work, or enjoying companionable silence. Because of this bias, men rarely get credit for the kinds of loving actions that are more typical of them" (p. 100).

Communicator Style Awareness

As we examined friendship, we noted some differences between men and women in their communicator styles. Women generally initiate topics in an attempt to facilitate conversation. Men may subtly control interaction because they often choose the topics that will be discussed more fully during the course of the conversation. Women use verbal and nonverbal turn-yielding cues to facilitate the continuation of interaction with men, but men often use avoidance strategies to control the continuation or discontinuation of a conversation. Women tend to be more adept at encoding and decoding the nonverbal cues that are related to expressiveness. Men tend to use a style that enhances the instrumental functions within a relationship.

Although the traditional male–female relationship in most communication situations has reflected male dominance and female subordination, these traditional roles are changing. Any power structure in a relationship may be satisfying if it is negotiated by the people involved. Examine the power structures in your friendships and assess your satisfaction with them.

Relationships that reflect patterns of communication based on inequality or difference are said to be *complementary* in nature. Much like a parent–child relationship, complementary patterns of communication generally imply a superior–subordinate relationship. Relationships that reflect patterns of communication based on equality and similarity are said to be *symmetrical* in nature, such as among peers who form friendships based on equality. For example, one person in a relationship may be responsible for organizing social engagements outside the home while the other is responsible for organizing the daily activities within the home. While the complementary pattern of communication may be closer to traditional gender stereotypes, where men dominate and women are subordinate, the symmetrical pattern of communication is more closely aligned with independent or nontraditional relationships. In these relationships, all participants are committed to growth and change in the relationship based on the recognition that there will be equal input from everyone into that growth process.

These two patterns of communication establish clearly dichotomous categories of power in relationships. The reality, however, is that most relationships probably reflect both of these power structures at various times and on various issues. Rather than using only complementary or only symmetrical patterns of communication, consider the benefits of using both at given times in your relationship. Consider a variety of communication options so that no person is superior or subordinate all the time. For example, in an apartment, one of the roommates may buy the food and do most of the cooking while another pays the bills and is responsible for cleaning the kitchen. In this instance, both of them serve the instrumental function of decision maker at different times and concerning different decisions. At the same time, symmetrical patterns of communication based on equality in a relationship should become apparent. Relationships that employ a combination of both complementary and symmetrical communication patterns within the relationship are said to be using a *parallel* communication pattern. Again, the key to redefining and changing a friendship is being open to a variety of communication choices, adopting a parallel pattern of communication that is both complementary and symmetrical at appropriate times and in appropriate situations.

Summary

Interpersonal relationships found in friendships are developed, maintained, and terminated through the process of communication. Because of the intimacy that can develop in these relationships, they may provide us with the ultimate opportunity for personal satisfaction in our communication with others. Men and women, however, may communicate differently in these relationships. An examination of the communication occurring in these interpersonal relationships generally confirms the traditional gender ideologies associated with communication between men and women in other situations. Women may be more likely to use expressive and facilitative behaviors, while men may use instrumental and control strategies.

If we are to encourage greater satisfaction with our communication in friendships and adapt to the shifting roles of men and women in our society, we must explore the need to redefine these relationships and negotiate change. Men should explore using appropriate expressive and facilitative behaviors, and women should explore using appropriate instrumental and control behaviors to enhance the communication process. Both parties can participate in mutually satisfying activities. A communication climate supportive of change and exploration of alternative communication styles can enhance the quality of communication in our friendships. The most effective communication in these relationships will not rely on gender stereotypes; instead, effective communication will come from both women and men exploring their use of a variety of communication behaviors appropriate to the nature of the relationship and to the demands of the situation.

FINDING YOUR VOICE

1. Think of your best same-sex friend and best friend of the other sex. Answer each of the following questions concerning each relationship:
   - What general topics do you discuss when you are together?
   - What topics do you discuss in greater depth?
   - Who typically initiates these topics?
   - Who most often changes the topics discussed?
   - Who usually asks more questions during conversation?

   Compare your answers to these questions for both of the relationships. What are the similarities and differences between the communication in these two relationships? What is the level of disclosure in each relationship? Does one person tend to disclose more than the other? Why do you think these similarities and differences exist? How do your answers agree with the research concerning communication in same-sex and male-female friendships presented in this chapter?

2. Think about your male-female friendships. Are you basically satisfied with them? Why or why not? If male-female friendships are to be satisfying, in your opinion, who would need to change the most—men or women? Why? Compare your answers with others in your class. Do all of you agree?

3. Define intimacy. Ask several of your friends to define it. What do their definitions tell you about how males and females define intimacy? What impact will your definition have on the friendships in which you are involved ?

FURTHER READING

Goodman, E., & O'Brien, P. (2000). *I know just what you mean: The power of friendship in women's lives.* New York: Simon & Schuster.
   Goodman and O'Brien have been friends for over 25 years and share their story and insights with readers. Topics include competition among friends, dealing with difficult times, and taking chances.
Macdonald, A. L. (1988). *No idle hands: The social history of American knitting.* New York: Ballantine.

Macdonald traces the history of this popular pastime for women and sees it as a reflection of their changing historical roles. Women use knitting as a practical craft, art form, and way to maintain connections with others.

Nardi, P. M. (Ed.). (1992). *Men's friendships.* Newbury Park, CA: Sage.

This book is a collection of 12 readings of empirical research on men's friendships. Specifically, this research examines various perspectives on men's friendships, structural differences in men's friendships, and some of the cultural diversity found in these friendships. Of particular interest is the focus on male bonding as it relates to male–female relationships in the larger social context.

Rawlins, W. K. (1992). *Friendship matters.* Hawthorne, NY: Aldine De Gruyter.

Rawlins examines the varieties, tensions, and frustrations that characterize friendships of children, adolescents, young adults, adults, and older adults. In each developmental stage discussed, Rawlins specifically addresses the impact of gender-related issues. The author supplements these observations with excerpts from more than 100 open-ended, in-depth interviews.

CHAPTER

6

Family, Courtship, and Marriage

W e live in a relatively transient society, one that allows us to move in and out of relationships with greater frequency than ever before. It is likely that most of us moved at least once during our childhoods. In fact, because our parents often moved wherever job opportunities led them, many of us have lived in a variety of cities, states, and perhaps even countries. Since approximately one out of every two marriages ends in divorce today, the primary relationship that people previously expected to develop only once in their lifetimes is more likely to occur more than once and result in a blended family. As a result, both the number of our relationships as well as the nature of those relationships may be considerably different from those developed by past generations (Cooney, 1993).

For example, in 1955 the Ward and June Cleaver family of the *Leave It To Beaver* TV program represented the typical family: working father, housewife mother, and two or more children. At that time, 60 percent of U.S. families fit this description. Today, however, this nuclear family is far from the most common, representing only 7 percent of all families in the United States (Otto, 1988).

Richmond-Abbott (1992) suggests that the major changes in the past 20 years in terms of number of women in the workforce, and number of divorces, single-parent families, and gay/lesbian families, have had a significant impact on American family life. In this chapter we will focus on one of the aspects greatly affected—gender and communication. We will discuss communication and gender in the family first, because our experiences in our families often influence our courtship and marriage behavior. Next, we'll discuss couple communication, and finally, we will move to a discussion of marriage partners. It is important to note that the focus of this chapter will be on heterosexual relationships. This focus in no way suggests that other relationships are not important but that there is relatively little research on other types of relationships.

Family

Your parents possessed a set of gender-specific ideas about males and females that they learned from their experiences. Based on these experiences, they influenced—both verbally as well as nonverbally—your developing gender identity.

As we noted in Chapter 2, this gender identity begins at an early age. Fagot, Leinbach, and O'Boyle (1992) indicate that the year between a child's second and third birthdays is the time during which gendered perceptions of toys, clothing, household objects, games, and work are acquired. During this time period, children learn to label boys and girls accurately and to become aware that they themselves belong in one category or the other.

Martin, Wood, and Little (1990) argue that gender ideologies develop through a series of stages:

> Children in the first stage . . . learn what kinds of things are directly associated with each sex, such as "boys play with cars," and "girls play with dolls." . . . [A]round the ages of 4–6, children seem to move to the second stage, where they begin to develop the more indirect and complex associations for information relevant to their own sex but have yet to learn these associations for information relevant to the opposite sex. By the time they are 8, children move to the third stage, where they have also learned the associations relevant to the opposite sex. These children have mastered the gender concepts of masculinity and femininity that link information within and between the various content domains. (p. 1901)

Parenting Styles

Do parents differ in their rearing of boys and girls? Lytton and Romney (1991) review 172 studies that suggest that, in general, fathers tend to differentiate more than mothers between boys and girls.

Prenatal Preferences.   Before we examine more closely how parents relate to their children, it is interesting to note that some studies have examined parent–child relationships in terms of the parents' prenatal preferences for their child's sex. Feldman, Nash, and Aschenbrenner (1983) report that satisfaction with fatherhood when the child is six to eight months old corresponds to the stated preference for the child's sex prior to its birth. More satisfaction is reported by fathers of children whose sex matched their stated prenatal preference. Children whose sex does not match the stated preference of their parents experience more negative consequences from the parent in the amount of time spent playing with the child, the number of perceived problems in the child, and other parent–child relations. However, female children whose sex does not coincide with parental wishes experience stronger negative consequences in the long run than do male children who do not match expectations, particularly in father–daughter relations (Stattin & Klackenberg-Larsson, 1991).

One of the most well-researched issues concerns the beliefs that parents hold in connection with the sex of the child. Studies show that the baby, even before birth, elicits gendered responses and treatment. Aspects that are perceived as masculine (for example, big, sturdy, hungry, curious, vigorous, or irritated) are more often attributed to a baby if it is believed to be a boy, whereas feminine attributes (for example, pretty, cute, little, fine-featured, cuddly) are given to a baby if it is believed to be a girl. Stattin and Klackenberg-Larsson (1991) state that: "An extensive literature has documented the differential physical handling and socialization practices, depending on the sex of the child, with regard to physical contact, communication style, amount and type of playing with the child, choice of toys, clothing, showing affection" (p. 141).

What does this have to do with the family? As Arntson and Turner (1987) suggest, "since sex-role development begins at an early age . . . it follows that the family is the preeminent agency for socializing children" (p. 305).

Traditional Behaviors in Children.   Compelling evidence for differences in parents' behavior toward boys and girls comes from Block (1984). Her work reveals some consistent sex-of-child differences in child rearing that begin in infancy and extend throughout childhood. These distinctions are found along a variety of dimensions and are plausibly related to differences in power and assertiveness observed in boys and girls. Parents respond more often to their infant sons' vocalizations, whereas they reinforce daughters for being quiet. Parents continue to reinforce gender-congruent behavior with toddlers in the form of play and toy selection. In general, boys' toys and play encourage activity and involvement with the world outside the home, providing objective, contingent feedback. In contrast, girls' toys and play foster engagement with the social world, providing subjective, noncontingent feedback (Block, 1984).

In their study of household chores, Etaugh and Liss (1992) report that parents who assign traditionally masculine chores to boys, such as yardwork and taking out the garbage, also are more likely to give masculine toys as gifts to boys. Those who assign typically feminine chores to girls such as kitchen work and dusting are more likely to give feminine or neutral toys and less likely to give masculine toys to girls. In addition, both girls and boys who are assigned masculine chores and who receive masculine gifts are more likely to have masculine career aspirations, whereas girls who are given feminine chores and feminine toys as gifts have traditionally feminine occupational preferences.

Traditional Behaviors in Parents.   In addition to assigning toys and household chores, some parents speak to their children in ways that promote more rigid gender ideologies. For example, Bellinger and Gleason (1982) note differences in the amount, as well as the content, of communication. Mothers speak to sons in an active manner focusing on the son's activities while speaking to daughters in softer tones, with more emphasis on thoughts and feelings (Buerkel-Rothfuss, Covert, Keith, & Nelson, 1986).

Recently, more research has focused on the parenting behaviors of fathers. Fathers who have sons exhibit fewer traditionally feminine (expressive) behaviors than fathers who have daughters, while mothers of sons exhibit more traditionally feminine behaviors. Fathers of daughters tend to retain their traditionally masculine behavior but also acquire some of the traditionally feminine (expressive) behaviors in their parenting skills. Thus, sons seem to influence parents' gender roles toward the traditional—fathers exhibit more traditionally masculine behaviors, and mothers exhibit more traditionally feminine behaviors (Bozzi, 1988).

Communicator Styles

When examining communicator styles within the family unit, we must consider how parents and children influence one another as they communicate, because there is mutual influence among family members. In play, fathers control and direct their children (both boys and girls) more than mothers; however, both boys and girls direct and control their fathers more than they do their mothers. Boys praise their fathers more than girls and display more physical warmth to their mothers than girls. Mothers engage in more quiet play with boys than do fathers. In general, women are more likely to be encouraged to relate to children; consequently, the number of words spoken to children and the amount of response elicited from children indicates considerable interaction between mother and child. For example, mothers are more likely to ask questions such as "Do you want to look at any of the trucks over here?" or "What else shall we put on the truck?" On the other hand, fathers may use directives that elicit little response from children ("Why don't you make a chimney?" or "Take it off") and that reinforce the traditional masculine behaviors of control and dominance in interaction (Bright & Stockdale, 1984).

Influence of Fathers.   In longitudinal research on a small group of families in which the father served as the primary caregiver, researchers report that children raised primarily by men are often active, vital, and vigorous babies, toddlers, preschoolers, and school-age children. In addition, the majority of these children function somewhat above expected norms on standardized developmental tests (Pruett, 1987; Pruett & Litzenberger, 1992). In a related study, Pruett (1993) finds that gender stereotypes are less likely to occur if the relationship between a father and his child is more intimate.

A gender-related issue that does not change when fathers assume primary caretaking responsibilities is gender difference in the management of same-sex and other-sex children. Female children are generally more compliant with mothers, and male children are generally more compliant with fathers (Pruett, 1993). Although research indicates that mothers working outside the home tend to raise daughters who show more competitiveness and aggressiveness, there is a question as to whether fathers' changing involvement in parenting will influence gender expectations for their sons. Specifically, as men become more involved in the parenting process, will boys develop more warmth and empathy as they grow older? Research demonstrates that because fathers' beliefs and expectations clearly influence their sons' beliefs (especially during adolescence), it is unlikely there will be drastic changes in boys in adolescent gender identity unless fathers encourage such change. It seems that fathers are still the key factor in helping adolescent boys perceive their gender differently from traditional views. More important, there is evidence to suggest that such changes will not occur soon. Some men still hold very traditional gender expectations for themselves and, if anything, express a fear that their sons may become too "feminized" or forget what it is to "act like a man" (Emihovich, Gaier, & Cronin, 1984).

Influence of Mothers.   While some fathers continue to reinforce traditional gender ideologies for their sons, mothers are also instrumental in reinforcing these behaviors.

Although many mothers hope their sons will develop personal characteristics such as emotional honesty, sensitivity toward others, and acceptance of an equal partnership with women at work and at home, mothers may be no more effective than fathers in encouraging boys to develop these traits. Research has shown that mothers place their sons' needs ahead of their own more often than doing the same for their daughters; as a result, they tend to reinforce with their sons the traditional male/female relationship of male control and female accommodation. Also, mothers report that they often feel compelled to prepare their sons to be tough enough to compete in a "man's world." Mothers may, in fact, encourage aggressiveness and emotional distance as they raise their adolescent sons (Emihovich, Gaier, & Cronin, 1984).

In their study of gender labeling, stereotyping, and parenting behaviors, Fagot, Leinbach, and O'Boyle (1992) conclude that the onset of labeling is related to several maternal behaviors and attitudes. Mothers whose children succeed at labeling males and females correctly initiate gender-typical play more often, respond more positively to their children's gendered play, and initiate less other-gender toy play than do mothers whose children do not succeed. Mothers of labelers are also more traditional in their attitudes concerning appropriate behavior for women and traditional gender roles within the family, and rate themselves as having fewer other-gender traits when describing their own behavior.

High Value of Masculine Traits.   Because masculine traits have historically been valued more than feminine traits in our society and probably because some people fear the unwarranted social stigma attached to homosexuality, boys may be encouraged by both mothers and fathers to develop traditional masculine traits rather than feminine traits. In various ways, many parents have played a greater role in encouraging girls to expand their communicator style to include masculine traits. Because of the changing role of women in today's society, girls are often encouraged to develop competitive and aggressive styles that are typically considered masculine. Traditionally masculine traits continue to be reinforced for boys while both mothers and fathers are more likely to encourage girls to retain feminine traits while acquiring some masculine traits necessary to meet the demands of changing gender expectations.

Why do some parents communicate more rigid gender ideologies for boys? Martin (1990) sheds some light on the reason. In her study to assess attitudes toward tomboys and sissies, she finds that boys labeled *sissies* are more negatively evaluated than girls labeled *tomboys*. Martin suggests that one reason for the negative evaluation of sissies may be more serious concern for their future outcomes than for those of tomboys. Analyses of predictions concerning future behavior show that sissies, more so than tomboys, are expected to continue to show cross–gender behavior into adulthood. Also, sissies are rated as likely to be less well adjusted and are negatively perceived due to adults' homophobia.

In viewing parent–child communicator styles, then, it seems that parents may reinforce gender ideologies for their children, but especially for their sons. While personal views of gendered behavior may be changing and some of these changes may be seen in marriage, many parents are still concerned that their children be raised to fit into a society that in many ways still holds a gender ideology of traditional views of masculinity and femininity.

Intimacy

As is true in courtship and marital relationships, self-disclosure may be important in creating intimacy in families. Galvin and Brommel (1991), reviewing studies of parent–child self-disclosure, conclude that:

1. Most mothers receive more self-disclosure than fathers.
2. Mutual self-disclosure exists mainly between parents and children of the same sex.
3. Parents perceived as nurturing and supportive elicit more self-disclosure from children.
4. College students are more likely to disclose more information to same-sex friends than to either parent. (p. 90)

The relationship individuals form with their parents during childhood, created through disclosure, may affect their views of love and their beliefs about love relationships as they grow older (Roberts, 1987). For example, secure adults who believe it is easy to get close to other people usually have happy and trusting love relationships throughout life; they tend to view their parents as loving, responsive, and warm people. Anxious or ambivalent adults who want close relationships and do not believe most partners are willing to develop such intimacy, experience more emotional extremes and jealousy in their love relationships. These people view their parents with mixed positive and negative feelings when recalling their own parent–child bond. Avoidant adults feel uneasy getting close to people and often report a fear of intimacy, emotional highs and lows in their relationships, and jealousy. In general, avoidants view their parents somewhat harshly, "seeing their mothers as rejecting and not likable and their fathers as uncaring" (Roberts, 1987, p. 22). Thus, the disclosure patterns children observe between their parents and develop with their parents during childhood carry a strong impression as they develop into adult disclosure patterns.

Conflict

How family members communicate during conflict determines whether the outcome is constructive or destructive. Constructive conflict promotes cooperation, relational growth, and positive affect. These cooperative strategies include disclosing and soliciting disclosure, initiating problem solving, emphasizing commonalities, accepting responsibility, and showing empathy.

Destructive conflict can be either covert or overt (Galvin & Brommel, 1999). Overt (competitive) strategies include assigning blame, finding fault with the other, and making prescriptions that demand unilateral behavior. Covert (avoidance) strategies include immediately yielding to the other's demands, shifting topics or avoiding, being unresponsive, acting hurt, and focusing on the inappropriateness of words used.

In her study of parent–adolescent conflict, Comstock (1994) finds that daughters' accounts of conflict show that destructive patterns dissipate by late adolescence and more constructive patterns prevail. In contrast, sons' accounts of conflict with their fathers showed the presence of both destructive and constructive patterns.

Vuchinich (1987), studying the question of who initiates conflict in a family, concludes that parents start about 48 percent of the conflicts, and children start about 52 percent. Fathers have less conflict initiated against them, and children start conflicts twice as often against their mother. Sons initiate conflicts three times more frequently with their mothers than with their fathers. Fathers initiate disagreements with their daughters three times more often than with their sons. Mothers, sons, and daughters share the same number of conflict attacks.

In terms of closing conflicts, mothers are more frequently involved in working out compromises. Daughters, more readily than sons or fathers, participate in working out compromises or standoffs in which the family members agree to disagree and no one really wins. After standoffs occur, women initiate nonconflict activities twice as often as men.

Individuals learn how to deal with conflict in family situations and continue to use these strategies throughout their lives. Fathers have a large influence on the conflict styles used by their children. Dumlao and Botta (2000) found that college students were more likely to use a conflict style that was similar to their father's. For example, students who tended to use collaborating (e.g., finding a solution that is mutually beneficial to everyone involved) as a conflict style had fathers who promoted communication within the family. Students who are accommodators (e.g., giving in to another person to end a disagreement) had fathers who encouraged conformity and discouraged communication.

Summary

Gender in families is a complex issue. In general, we know that gendered behavior begins early and develops through a series of stages. Research also demonstrates that fathers and mothers treat their sons and daughters differently and that this treatment generally reinforces gender ideologies. Finally, gender ideology influences intimacy and conflict, two important aspects of family communication.

Courtship

In the last 30 years, courtship has changed in three important ways: opportunities increased for informal other-sex interaction, dating became less formal than in previous eras, and a set progression of stages from first meeting to marriage disappeared (Rice, 1990). Cate and Lloyd (1992) present a historical perspective of courtship and suggest that "the dating system became more pluralistic" (p. 30). For example, it is acceptable for women to initiate dating activities and to share expenses or even to be economically responsible for a date. However, it is important to note that while dating has become more egalitarian, some traditional ideas about courtship and marital partners nevertheless remain intact. For example, Ganong and Coleman (1992) report that partner asymmetry, sometimes called the "marriage gradient," is still accepted and even encouraged in American culture. The marriage gradient is the situation in which a husband is superior to a wife in certain characteristics (age, education, occupational success). In their study of gender differences in expectations of self and future partner, Ganong and Coleman find that young women expect that their husbands will be somewhat superior to them in intelligence, ability, success, income, and education. In fact, fewer than 10 percent of the women in the study expect to exceed their marriage partner on any of these variables.

Traditional ideas about courtship are also reflected in the contemporary vision of the perfect relationship, which emphasizes the importance of togetherness as well as individuality, other-orientation as well as self-fulfillment, and communicating openly while protecting a partner's feeling (Prusank, Duran, & DeLillo, 1991).

Several researchers have written on the tensions in courtship relationships. For example, Goldsmith (1990) describes five: whether to move the relationship to a romantic level, whether to date others, balancing other priorities such as being with one's other friends, whether one person's will should be imposed on the other ("I wish you wouldn't go to bars with your friends"), and the degree of commitment. Bell and Buerkel-Rothfuss (1990) see these tensions in dichotomies such as: honesty versus the protection of feelings (for example, being totally honest even if it hurts the other person's feelings versus glossing over a problem to avoid hurting the other person); self-disclosure versus privacy (for example, telling each other everything versus keeping some things to oneself); and personal autonomy versus interdependence (for example, doing things separately versus only doing those things you can do together).

In terms of communication variables in courtship, five have been studied to some extent: self-disclosure, language, touch, conflict, and aggression. We will look at each of these briefly.

Self-Disclosure

Self-disclosure seems to facilitate relationship development. For example, Berg & McQuinn (1986) note that for men, increased levels of self-disclosure to a partner are related to greater relationship stability. Interestingly, Sprecher (1987) finds that the most important type of disclosure is the amount that men perceive their partners have disclosed to them, not what was actually disclosed.

Among dating couples, both males and females indicate that they disclose fully to their partners in almost all topic areas. Analysis of the actual disclosure in these relationships, however, indicates that women disclose more than men in several areas, including disclosure of their greatest fears. In general, women are more likely to be the partner who discloses more in dating relationships (Rubin, Hill, Peplau, & Dunkel-Schettes, 1980). Further, couples who describe their relationships as egalitarian (based on equality), disclose more to each other than couples who describe their relationships as traditional (based on inequality). Thus, a masculine role based on equality encourages more self-disclosure and emotional intimacy in a close male–female relationship. As a result, couples who hold more egalitarian attitudes perceive each other as a source of emotional support as well as an emotional confidant.

In an interesting study of romantic and nonromantic partners, Nezlek (1995) asked college students to keep diaries of their interactions with others and found that women perceived interactions with romantic male partners to be more emotionally rewarding than interactions with nonromantic male partners. But for men the emotional rewards did not differ for interactions with nonromantic or romantic female partners. Overall, these individuals spent more time with romantic partners than with nonromantic friends.

Language

In addition to the language issues we discussed in Chapter 3, several interesting uses of language apply specifically to romantic relationships.

Perhaps one of the most frequently used statements in a romantic relationship is "I love you." Many people assume that it is most often initiated by women, but research indicates that men are more often the initiators of this declaration (Owen, 1987). Owen posits several reasons for this, among them that women are more able to discriminate among love and related emotions and that women wait for men to say "I love you" because they traditionally play a more reactive than proactive role in romantic relationships.

Several researchers have examined what have been termed "secret tests," covert tests of commitment and trust. Baxter and Wilmot (1984) present test categories that individuals might use to determine the feelings of their romantic partners:

1. Endurance—if one partner puts up with "costly" behavior such as criticism, one can assume that partner is committed to the relationship
2. Indirect suggestion—hints of increased intimacy such as flirting, to see if the partner responds
3. Public presentation—one partner introduces the other as "my girlfriend/ boyfriend" to see how the other reacts
4. Separation—a couple separates for a while to see if the relationship "can take it"
5. Third-party questioning—one partner asks a friend to find out the other partner's feelings
6. Triangle tests—using someone else to make the partner jealous or setting up a situation to see if the partner gives in to temptation

These researchers report that men are less likely to use secret tests than women. As a possible explanation for this difference, Baxter and Wilmot suggest that "the use of tests by females more than by males may reflect their greater relationship monitoring. . . . It is through secret tests that females monitor a relationship's pulse" (p. 197). Other researchers (Honeycutt, Cantrill, & Greene, 1989; Peplau, 1983) report similar results, indicating that women are more attentive to the relational process than men. Duck, Rutt, Hurst, and Strejc (1991) argue "even at the level of individual conversations, women monitor their relationships more seriously than do men" (p. 247).

Touch

As noted in Chapter 4, gendered touch in U.S. culture has been well documented. A gender asymmetry exists, with men touching women more than women touch men. Men and women also may interpret touch differently (Willis & Briggs, 1992).

In their study of the effects of gender and type of romantic touch on the perceptions of relational commitment, Johnson and Edwards (1991) surveyed 152 people concerning their perceptions of commitment for seven intimate touches. The progression of touches from least intimate to most intimate was: holding hands, kissing on the lips, walking with arms around each other, light petting of upper bodies, light petting of lower bodies, heavy petting while unclothed, and intercourse. Their findings indicate that a distinct level of relational commitment is inferred for each type of intimate touch except holding hands and kissing. Men infer significantly less commitment from intimate touch than do women, however. When compared with men, women believe there is an increasingly greater level of commitment as touch becomes more sexually intimate.

Willis and Briggs (1992) report that men are more likely to initiate touch during courtship and that women are more likely to initiate touch after marriage. The researchers explain that men are more likely to initiate intimate touch to obtain sex while females are more likely to welcome and later initiate touch to preserve the relationship bond.

Conflict

Women see relationship problems as more important in breakups than do men (Cate & Lloyd, 1992). For a woman, the key issue contributing to relationship dissolution appears to be difficulty in resolving conflicts, particularly those she has initiated herself. For a man, the key issue is the stability of the conflict issue (in other words, how often the issue keeps coming up). Lloyd (1987) suggests that the female partner's "pursuit of resolution" may initiate a cycle of relationship decline if the male partner perceives that the couple is rehashing the same old issue.

Baxter (1986) examines the reasons that couples break up. Women are more likely than men to mention autonomy, lack of openness, and lack of equity. Surprisingly, men are more likely than women to mention lack of romance.

Duck, Rutt, Hurst, and Strejc (1991) asked undergraduate students to record their interactions with others and found that the typical interaction with another person lasted for 30 minutes and was generally perceived as satisfying. Nevertheless, people rated female partners more positively (that is, higher on communication quality) than males. Conversations with lovers were rated as of lesser quality than conversations with relatives, best friends, and other friends. The authors speculate that this result may result from the fact that lovers spend more time talking about relationship problems; however, conversations with lovers scored higher on conflict than conversations with friends and best friends but lower on conflict than conversations with acquaintances.

Aggression/Physical Violence

More and more research suggests that aggression and physical violence are prevalent in our society. Mack (1989) reports that therapists have identified spouse abuse as near the top of the list of areas in which people desire treatment information. Depending on how one defines abuse, it affects anywhere from 25 to 60 percent of the population (Straus, 1991).

Guerrero (1994) developed a system for measuring anger expression. Her category descriptions are included in Table 6.1. Results of a study indicate that partner perceptions of integrative-assertive anger expression are positively associated with relational satisfaction. In addition, individuals perceive themselves as using more integrative-assertion when expressing anger than their partners perceive them to use. Women perceive themselves as using less aggression when dealing with anger than their partners perceive them to use. Women are perceived as using more nonassertive denial than their male partners.

Lloyd (1991) proposes a conceptual model of what he terms the "dark side" of courtship—physical violence and sexual aggression. He posits two major reasons for these problems: the different contexts of courtship for men and women, and the highly romanticized nature of courting relationships. For many men, the predominant theme for courtship is "staying in control"; for many women, the predominant theme is "dependence on the relationship." Cate and Lloyd (1992) hypothesize that these themes contribute to violence:

> The male theme of control justifies his imposition of his will on the partner; it is his prerogative to demand compliance from his partner by whatever means necessary, even through violent or exploitive means. The theme of control also means that he is concerned with regulating commitment in the relationship; the use of aggression may be one means to maintain emotional distance or closeness in a close relationship. . . .

TABLE 6.1   Modes of anger expression

Threatening	Nonthreatening
Direct	
Distributive–Aggression	*Integrative–Assertion*
■ yells and screams at partner	■ listens to partner's side of the story
■ criticizes partner	■ discusses problems with partner
■ tries to prove s/he is "right"	■ tries to be fair
■ slams doors or throws objects	■ clearly shares feelings with partner
■ tries to "get even" with partner	■ tries to "patch things up"
■ threatens partner	
Indirect	
Passive–Aggression	*Nonassertive–Denial*
■ gives partner silent treatment	■ hides feelings from partner
■ ignores partner	■ denies feeling angry
■ gives partner cold/dirty looks	
■ leaves the scene	

Guerrero, 1994

The female theme of dependence may constrain her to remain in a relationship that is violent or exploitive. Given that marriage and relationships are viewed as key components of female identity, the cultural ideology of "any man is better than no man" may cause her to accept aggression as part and parcel of courtship. (p. 108)

Courtship, for both males and females, is surrounded by the romantic ideal that "love conquers all" (Hendrick & Hendrick, 1992). This ideal encourages that violence be downplayed by attributing it to situational factors such as anger, or too much alcohol consumed, or any factor other than a fundamental problem in the relationship or with the partner. Henton, Cate, Koval, Lloyd, and Christopher, (1983) find that both victims and aggressors may strive to ignore, overlook, or reframe aggressive behavior. In their study, more than 50 percent of those experiencing a violent incident indicate that the violence either had no effect on or improved their relationship.

Summary

Gender influences communication in courtship relationships. Specifically, women disclose more than men. Men, contrary to popular belief, more often initiate saying "I love you." Men touch women more than women touch men. Men touch women more during courtship while women touch men more after marriage. In addition, men infer significantly less commitment from intimate touch than do women.

Women see relationship problems as more important in breaking up than men and are more likely than men to mention autonomy, lack of openness, and lack of equity as reasons for a break-up.

Although violence is increasing in courting relationships (Lloyd & Emery, 1990), too often both the victim and the aggressor strive to ignore or reframe the violence.

Marriage

Let's suppose for a moment that a couple has made it through all the pitfalls of courtship and gotten married; as the honeymoon period comes to a close, they will begin to find that marital bliss takes hard work.

In a study of African American and white couples, Ruvolo and Veroff (1997) looked at spouses' perceptions of how different their spouses were from their idea of an ideal spouse. There was a significant relationship between marital happiness and wives' perceptions that their husbands significantly deviated from their view of an ideal spouse. Men's ratings of the discrepancy between their wife and the ideal spouse predicted men's marital dissatisfaction but not their wives' dissatisfaction. Simply put, when a wife is dissatisfied, both marital partners are unhappy, but a husband may be unhappy without affecting his wife's happiness.

Rituals (shared activities, ways of communicating, and other symbolic situations) are important communication aspects of marriage that help bind a couple together. Bruess and Pearson (1997) have identified seven major ritual types that are important in marriage (see Table 6.2 for a summary of these rituals). Many rituals are developed

TABLE 6.2   Rituals in Marriage

Couple-Time Rituals

Type of Ritual	Description	Example
Enjoyable Activities	Pastimes that relate to pleasure, leisure, and/or recreation	Travel, sports, hobbies, and movies
Togetherness Rituals	Spending time with each other regardless of activity	Drinking coffee and reading the paper together on Sunday morning
Escape Episodes	Designed to satisfy a couple's needs to be alone and to avoid others or external pressures	Taking a drive in the country without the children along

Idiosyncratic/Symbolic Rituals

Type of Ritual	Description	Example
Favorites	Most preferred places to go, things to eat, items to purchase or give, and activities	Favorite TV show, restaurants, or places to visit
Private Codes	Repeated use of jointly developed words, symbols, means, or gestures for communicating a unique, private, and special meaning to the couple	Nicknames, nonverbal symbols
Play	Kidding, teasing, silliness and/or playful bantering, games and contests	Seeing who can be the first person each morning to wish the other person a nice day
Celebration	Acknowledging holidays, birthdays, anniversaries, or other special events	Going to the restaurant where you had your first date

Other Rituals

Type of Ritual	Description	Example
Daily Routines and Tasks	Accomplishing day-to-day, mundane activities	One person washes the dishes while the other dries them
Intimacy Expressions	Physical, symbolic and verbal expressions of love, fondness, affection or sexual attraction	Touching, kissing, or other nonverbal behavior
Communication Rituals	Specific times and means for talking, sharing or getting in touch with each other	Daily phone calls, scheduled time spent each day catching up on plans or activities

TABLE 6.2   Continued

Patterns/Habits/Mannerisms	Interactional, territorial and/or situational patterns or habits	Sitting in the same position while watching TV together
Spiritual Rituals	Prayer, attending worship together, or other forms of spiritual fulfillment	Going to a religious service each week, praying together before meals

Adapted from Bruess and Pearson, 1997.

around couples' daily lives, including everything from specific celebrations to daily phone calls. These rituals play an important role in maintaining intimacy between partners.

Gendered Roles

The roles we play in relationships reflect the rights, responsibilities, obligations, and duties typically expected of those who occupy these positions. The shifting roles of men and women in relation to one another and the impact of these shifts on the family unit represent two of the greatest social changes we will experience in our lifetimes. How women and men view themselves and one another has changed drastically in the last three decades, and this change has had a significant impact on communication within marriage and the family. Nevertheless, major differences in behavior considered appropriate for males and females still exist today.

Traditionally the husband was considered the breadwinner, whose primary task was to provide sufficient income to meet the family's needs. With the explicit role of breadwinner often came the implicit role of chief decision maker within the marriage and family structure. At the same time, upper- and middle-class wives traditionally were not employed outside the home, and their role focused primarily, if not exclusively, on housework and child care. With the explicit role of homemaker often came the implicit roles of nurturer and caretaker for both husband and children.

In the last 40 years, however, gender roles and their corresponding expectations have changed considerably. In 1950, only 28 percent of married women with children between the ages of 6 and 17 worked outside the home; by 1986, 68 percent of all women in that same group worked outside the home (Hochschild, 1989). This basic shift within our workforce, in conjunction with other factors, has prompted considerable change in the traditional roles held by husbands and wives. While 56 percent of marriages in 1950 fit the traditional husband/breadwinner and wife/homemaker model, only 34 percent of marriages in 1975 fit this same model (Klein, 1984). By 1988, only 7 percent of marriages fit this pattern (Otto, 1988). Husbands no longer exclusively hold the role of wage earner; instead, women share this role with their husbands or occupy it themselves as the sole financial support of their families. By 1995, more than 20 percent of families were one-parent households and 7 million children were living in two-parent homes in which one of the adults was a stepparent (Gartner, 1995).

Having a family and a career has created a new set of opportunities and challenges for women. Increasingly, women have become concerned with education and career development. In many cases, women have chosen to postpone marriage and childbearing until well into their 30s and even their early 40s. If they marry, many women become concerned about juggling the traditional expectations of wife and mother as well as the new role expectations associated with being an upwardly mobile member of the workforce.

In her book *The Second Shift: Working Parents and the Revolution at Home*, Arlie Hochschild (1989) explores the burden carried by women who work full-time jobs (35 hours or more weekly) outside the home while maintaining full-time jobs inside the home. As she explains:

> Adding together the time it takes to do a paid job and to do housework and child care, I averaged estimates from the major studies on time use done in the 1960s and 1970s, and discovered that women worked roughly fifteen hours longer each week than men. Over a year, they worked an extra month of twenty-four-hour days. Over a dozen years, it was an extra year of twenty-four-hour days. (pp. 3–4)

This double workload becomes what Hochschild terms "the second shift," a workload that women juggle as they maintain traditional roles while acquiring new ones.

Men are also facing a new set of opportunities and challenges due to the shifting role of women. Men who are no longer the sole breadwinners in their homes may not automatically assume the control and power they once did. Some men are full-time caretakers of their home and children; others are adjusting to working beside or for women in the workplace. Sharing the workplace with a social group that may have been barred from that same setting just 30 years earlier creates new challenges for men. In addition, as women gain greater career opportunities, men increasingly consider career development opportunites for their wives and themselves and the shifting role of child-care responsibility.

CONSIDER THIS!
Stepmoms versus Stepdads

We've all read the fairy tales about wicked stepmothers, but who would think this perception still exists. Nevertheless, when asked, half of adult children think of their stepfathers as "parents" while only one-third think of their stepmothers as "parents" (Peterson, 2001). In addition, more children say they "feel close" to their stepdads than to their stepmoms. While the reasons for this discrepancy are unknown, the researcher who conducted this study speculated that since moms are more likely to get custody of young children, when the moms remarry these children get to know their stepdads and develop a closer relationship. If Dad gets remarried, the children may not get as much chance to know his new wife as a mother, especially if she is a much younger woman.

Evidence is growing that men are beginning to share more of the household tasks and childcare in the home. Although men continue to spend less time on household chores, their domestic participation has been increasing. Whereas men spent only 30 percent as much time as women on domestic chores in 1977, by 1998 this number increased to 75 percent (Lewin, 1998). In addition, this survey found that working fathers spend more time doing things with their children than they do on themselves. Nevertheless, 56 percent of working mothers say they wish fathers would spend more time with their children, and 45 percent want men to do more household chores. In dual-income households, mothers are still much more likely to take time off from work when their children are sick (83 percent) than fathers (22 percent).

In addition to changes resulting from the increasing participation of women in the paid workforce, the rising divorce rate in the United States is changing the structure of yesterday's nuclear family. In 1990, Bumpass estimated that almost half of the more than two million couples who marry each year would divorce. While this chapter will not specifically address the unique issues that confront single-parent families and blended families, these changing family structures influence the husband–wife dyad as well as the family unit as a whole (see, for example, Galvin & Brommel, 1999).

Two issues that have been widely examined in marital communication are intimacy/self-disclosure and power/dominance. Researchers indicate that these two variables are important factors in a couple's satisfaction with their marriage.

Self-Disclosure and Intimacy

As discussed earlier in this chapter, disclosure is the primary communication behavior assisting the initial development of relationships. Dainton, Stafford and McNeilis (1992) find that an important factor of a highly satisfying marriage is a high mutual level of self-disclosure (see also, Pearson & Spitzberg, 1990). Because no relationship—even a marriage—can sustain complete openness and intimacy over a long period of time, marriages move through cycles of greater and lesser intimacy. According to Bochner (1983), conversation in ongoing relationships serves five primary functions that may account for disclosure message choices in any given marital exchange: (1) fosters favorable impressions between the couple, (2) organizes the relationship for the couple, (3) constructs and validates a "joint worldview" for the relationship, (4) serves as a means of expressing their individual thoughts and feelings in the relationship, and (5) serves as a means of protecting their individual vulnerabilities in the relationship. Because marriage is an open system that changes over time, the amount of disclosure increases and decreases over time as relationships move through stages of development and deterioration (Baxter, 1985).

Gender differences in approaches to intimacy are present in marriages. Wives are more likely to use a range of affective responses and greater emotional expressiveness than husbands (Notarius & Johnson, 1982). Wives are also more affectionate than husbands (Thompson & Walker, 1989). While there appears to be little conversation about these differences, wives are more likely than their husbands to talk about them (Rubin, 1983; Shimanoff, 1985).

Counter to the idea that satisfaction with conversations is directly correlated with level of intimacy of the relationship, undergraduate students rate conversations in the following order according to quality: stranger, acquaintance, lover, friend, relative, best friend (Duck et al., 1991). These authors conclude that "behavioral, communicative, or conversational realities of intimacy do not clearly accord with the graduated ways in which intimacy might be represented through intuitively ordered relationship labels based on emotion or commitment alone" (p. 248).

In categorizing marital relationships, Fitzpatrick (1988) identifies three basic types of marital couples: (1) *traditional* couples, who conform to traditional gender stereotypes within the context of marriage; (2) *independent* couples, who agree to change and redefine their marital relationship over time; and (3) *separate* couples, who share little contact and few common bonds in their marriage. Traditional couples value self-disclosure in marriage; however, they find it easier to communicate positive feelings rather than negative feelings. Their primary conversation topics focus on their marriage partner as well as on the relationship itself. Separate couples do not value openness and disclosure in marriage as highly as other couples do. To maintain a moderate degree of satisfaction in their marriage, they preserve autonomy and separateness in their relationship while minimizing disclosure that might link them closely. Finally, independent couples place a high value on self-disclosure. Of the three marriage types, only independents use communication behaviors to develop roles based on the personal preferences of each spouse. Unlike traditional couples, they are more open to expressing both positive and negative feelings about their partners and their relationships. Independent couples openly confront disagreements and conflicts while striving for cohesion (Fitzpatrick, 1988).

Of the 700 married couples studied by Fitzpatrick, she notes that approximately 60 percent clearly classify themselves in one of these three types. The remaining 40 percent represent a mixture of marital types; as Fitzpatrick explains, in these couples "her description" of the marriage is considerably different than "his description" of the marriage (p. 79).

Interestingly, research suggests that in terms of gender ideology, husbands and wives are more content and have higher levels of marital satisfaction when they both occupy traditional gender roles (see research reviewed in Blair, 1993), or when both partners share similar attitudes toward female participation in the workforce (Lye & Biblarz, 1993).

No matter what type of couple, most husbands perceive their communication as primarily serving an *instrumental function* (associated with task completion, problem solving, and concern for oneself as an individual); most wives perceive their communication as serving both *instrumental and expressive functions* (related to nurturing and concern for others) (Fitzpatrick, 1988; Wood, Rhodes & Whelan, 1989). These perceptions affect the quality of marital relationships. Specifically, marriages perceived to be of the lowest quality are marriages between traditional husbands whose communication serves primarily an instrumental function and nontraditional wives who prefer their husbands to reflect both an instrumental and expressive communication function (Aries, 1982).

The topics discussed by couples tend to vary depending on the type of relationship they have. Traditional couples often have conversations that focus on the theme of togetherness that is typically associated with marital satisfaction. On the other hand, separate couples develop conversational topics that emphasize themes of individuality and separateness typically associated with marital dissatisfaction (Sillars, Weisberg, Burggraf, & Wilson, 1987). When asked what factors motivate spouses to disclose their problems and tensions, both husbands and wives offer many of the same reasons for this disclosure: they believe that it provides benefits such as emotional release, a novel perspective on a problem, and enhanced interpersonal understanding between the marital partners (Burke, Weir, & Harrison, 1976). Husbands choosing to avoid disclosure, however, often cite the desire to maintain control, to avoid confronting issues about themselves that may require personal change, and to avoid negative evaluation by others. Wives, on the other hand, tend to avoid disclosure when they predict it will lead to distress for someone else or for themselves; thus, they fear hurting others or being hurt themselves (Rosenfeld, 1979).

A conversational variable that is important to intimacy in marital communication is the use of idioms. **Idioms** are *"private expressions and gestures shared by a couple that can help define the norms of their relationship and promote its cohesiveness"* (Hopper, Knapp, & Scott, 1981, p. 23). Idioms stabilize as the couple's communication patterns stabilize over time. They are generally perceived to have a positive impact on the relationship. Over half the idioms used by couples are restricted to private contexts. Idioms that express affection are generally nonverbal cues, such as holding hands or caressing; negative idioms such as teasing insults are more likely to be expressed as verbal play. Both men and women credit men with originating most of the idioms used in marital relationships, but we do not know if husbands generate more idioms than wives, if men's idioms are more likely to become adopted as a part of the couple's private code, or if male-generated idioms are better remembered by the couple (Bell, Buerkel-Rothfuss, & Gore, 1987). We do know, however, that men think the nicknames they use for their wives (such as "doll," "cutie pie," and "piglet") are terms of endearment, but wives are more likely to perceive them as insults or criticism (Hopper, Knapp & Scott, 1981).

Timmer, Veroff, and Hatchett (1996) looked at marital happiness among African American and white couples during the first three years of marriage. African American couples were less likely to argue over matters pertaining to family and visited their families more often than white couples did. While close family ties did not affect marital happiness for white couples, African American couples with close family ties were significantly happier in their marriages than those without such ties. The authors note that these result indicate it is important to study ethnicity and structural relationships in families when considering what leads to a happy marriage.

Power and Dominance

Couples who express the highest level of marital satisfaction report that they share power in their marriage (Marshall, 1985). This shared power is important in decision making. Research demonstrates a positive correlation between equality of decision making and marital satisfaction (Ting-Toomey, 1984; Yogev & Brett, 1985). Equality seems to involve three dimensions: integrity—respecting one another;

flexibility—ability to change and adapt; and reciprocity—feeling that what is good for one person is also good for the other (Bate & Memmott, 1984).

In managing conflict within relationships, communicator style may be related to gender. Conflict occurs in relationships when the participants seek incompatible goals and each person perceives the other to be interfering with attaining those goals. While conflict initially may be viewed as destructive, it actually may be necessary to clarify crucial issues and concerns in a relationship. How people manage conflict is often related to masculine, feminine, androgynous, and undifferentiated gender types. (See Chapter 2 for a discussion of these concepts.) For example, masculine types and androgynous types who have adopted traditionally masculine traits manage conflict more constructively than feminine or undifferentiated gender types. The traditionally masculine traits of independence, assertiveness, and nonemotionality facilitate positive feelings during conflict as well as focus the individual on conflict management (Yelsma & Brown, 1985). The type of couple engaged in conflict is also a good predictor of conflict-management style (Fitzpatrick, 1988).

Fitzpatrick (1988) indicates that marital interaction patterns are basically of two types, symmetrical and complementary:

> In symmetrical interaction, the husband and the wife offer similar messages designed to control the definition of the relationship . . . . There are three basic types of symmetry: *competitive*, characterized by escalation and fighting; *neutralized*, characterized by mutual respect and by not taking a stand on the issue of control; and *submissive*, characterized by mutual coalescence and surrender. In complementary interaction, one spouse seeks control over the definition and the other yields it. The participants' behaviors are compatible but fully differentiated. Examples of complementary interaction patterns are giving and taking instructions, or asserting and agreeing. (p. 116)

Table 6.3 gives examples of various spousal interactions.

White (1989) examined conflict-resolution interactions of 56 married couples. In this study, men were more likely to take a coercive stance toward their partners during conflict, while women took an affiliative stance toward their partners.

One of the major issues that wives have concerns about is unfairness in the marriage. As Blair (1993) concludes:

> It appears that for husbands' and wives' perceptions of marital quality alike, wives' assessments of unfairness in the marriage have stronger effects than do husbands' reports of unfairness. Wives may be more likely to express their distress or displeasure over issues of equity in the marriage (e.g., the division of housework, the balance of control over family income) than are husbands. This difference in the effects of assessments of (un)fairness is in keeping with previous research that suggests that wives are likely to raise issues of marital dissatisfaction with their spouse[s], whereas husbands are more likely to try to avoid any stressful confrontations (Cowan et al., 1985). Notarius [et al.] (1989) suggest that husbands are likely to detach themselves from discussions of problems, leaving wives in a situation in which they have no partner available to discuss marital concerns. In comparison to husbands, then, wives may accumulate feelings of dissatisfaction with their husband[s] and/or marriage[s] over time, until it reaches a "breaking point" (e.g., dissolution of the marriage). (p. 209)

TABLE 6.3   Examples of spousal interactions

Competitive symmetry (one-up/one-up)
Paul: You know I want you to keep the house picked up during the day.
Margie: I want you to help sometimes!

Complementarity (one-down/one-up)
Margie: With your help, Paul, I know we can get out of this.
Paul: I do know how to organize things.

Transition (one-across/one-up)
Margie: I was thinking of taking sleeping bags.
Paul: No, we don't need them.

Complementarity (one-up/one-down)
Paul: Let's get out of town this weekend, so we can work this thing out.
Margie: Okay.

Submissive symmetry (one-down/one-down)
Paul: I'm so tired. What are we ever going to do?
Margie: Please don't leave.

Transition (one-across/one-down)
Paul: I was thinking of doing household chores.
Margie: Whatever you want to do.

Transition (one-up/one-across)
Paul: I definitely think we should have more kids.
Margie: I remember my parents always wanted more grandkids.

Transition (one-down/one-across)
Margie: I'm sorry I don't want to go out very often. What can I do about it?
Paul: I don't know.

Neutralized symmetry (one-across/one-across)
Margie: I heard it was snowing in the mountains.
Paul: That's going to make driving a little slower.

Fitzpatrick, 1988

Summary

The marriage of the twenty-first century is not the marriage of the 1950s. More women work outside the home, yet continue to be responsible for the majority of home and child care responsibilities. Along with more women in the labor force, the rising divorce rate has influenced the roles of men and women in marriage.

We have examined self-disclosure and intimacy in marriage. An important factor in a satisfying marriage in many cases is a high level of mutual self-disclosure. Yet, gender may influence self-disclosure. Wives tend to be higher disclosers than husbands and disclose more negative information.

In terms of intimacy, wives may be more emotionally expressive and more affectionate. (See Chapter 5 for a discussion of the possible gender bias in this research.)

Couples may be classified as traditional, independent, separate, and mixed (Fitzpatrick, 1988). In terms of self-disclosure, independent couples appear to disclose more.

In addition to self-disclosure, idioms are a means of communicating intimacy. Idioms may be verbal or nonverbal. Both men and women credit men with originating most of the idioms used in the marital relationship.

Conflict, it seems, is inevitable as two people live together, but it can have possible positive outcomes. In her analysis of power in marital relationships, Fitzpatrick (1988) says:

> Couples in which the partners have little commitment to traditional sex roles will be more likely to engage in manifest conflict, negotiation, and bargaining with the marital partner. The roles, rules, and norms of this marriage need to be defined and renegotiated with changes in the relationship. (p. 155)

Strategies for Change

Gender issues in families, courtship, and marriage are changing. As a result, well-defined adult roles may be confusing. No wonder tension and conflict occur! Lye and Biblarz (1993) write that "the profound shifts in attitudes toward marriage, family life, and gender roles that have marked the postwar period present complex new challenges. . . . Each partner must struggle to balance the competing demands of the relationship, for intimacy, and commitment, and the self, for personal autonomy and fulfillment" (p. 183). Many of the strategies for change discussed previously in regard to friendship also apply to the relationships we have discussed in this chapter. However, a few additional strategies are also helpful.

The first strategy for change is for couples and family members to communicate about differing expectations. If we do not know what is expected of us, we cannot make any decisions about what we need or want to change. Too often in relationships, people assume too much and fail to check out assumptions with one another.

Beebe and Masterson (1986) distinguish between position-centered and person-centered communication patterns in families. In a position-centered pattern, family members focus on the relatively stable position each person holds. Each person has a job, and they are to do it. Person-centered families place a high value on the individuality of each person. Person-centered communication patterns encourage flexibility.

Flexibility and adaptability appear to be important variables in any relationship, and particularly in relationships between women and men. As noted by Fitzpatrick and Indvik (1982), couples who are open to redefinition and changes in their relationships will find perhaps the greatest satisfaction because they explore new communication behaviors rather than remain with traditional ones.

Satir (1988) maintains that healthy families demonstrate the following characteristics:

> Self-worth is high; communication is direct, clear, specific, and honest; rules are flexible, human, appropriate, and subject to change; and the linking to society is open and honest. (p. 4)

In general, then, if couples, marital partners, and families hope to define new gender roles, communication about these roles seems to be the key.

Of course, not all people will find themselves in long-term intimate relationships. People may remain unmarried for a variety of reasons, including choice and barriers such as the perception that "All good partners are taken" or "I haven't met the right person." Contrary to the belief that women desire long-term relationships more than men, a study of unmarried adults over the age of 30 found that men desire marriage more than women do (Frazier et al., 1996), but that men express more fear that their relationships will not work out. In this study, divorced women had the least desire for marriage. The authors argue that men desire marriage more than women because they have less social support in their lives and seek to find it through marriage. Women are more likely to get emotional support from their friends.

FINDING YOUR VOICE

1. In a group of three to five people of the same sex, choose descriptors from the following list (Bem, 1974) that best describe the ideal partner:

acts as a leader	flatterable	self-reliant
adaptable	forceful	self-sufficient
affectionate	friendly	sensitive to the
aggressive	gentle	needs of others
ambitious	gullible	shy
analytical	happy	sincere
assertive	has leadership	softspoken
athletic	abilities	solemn
cheerful	helpful	strong personality
childlike	independent	sympathetic
compassionate	individualistic	tactful
competitive	inefficient	tender
conceited	jealous	theatrical
conscientious	likable	truthful
conventional	loves children	understanding
defends own beliefs	loyal	unpredictable
does not use harsh	makes decisions	unsystematic
language	easily	warm
dominant	masculine	willing to take a
eager to soothe hurt	moody	stand
feelings	reliable	willing to take risks
feminine	secretive	yielding

After you have completed that task, choose the descriptors that you think someone of the other sex would choose to describe the ideal mate. Compare your lists with the lists made by other groups. What are the major differences between the male view of an ideal partner and female view of an ideal partner? What are the major differences between what males think females want in an ideal partner and what females say they want? Or between what females think males want and what males say they want? Did all groups assume that the ideal partner was the other sex? Which of these perceptions are based on gender stereotypes? What are the implications of these differing perceptions for communication between women and men?

2. In analyzing the conversations of couples, researchers have found a direct link between happiness and the frequency with which two people refer to themselves as "we." Couples are most likely to resolve conflicts when their conversations shift from "You (or I) have a problem" to "We've got a problem."

    Research psychologist Linda Acitelli, Ph.D., of the University of Michigan, has coined the phrase *relationship awareness*, referring to how often couples discuss their relationship and refer to themselves as a unit ("we").

    She found that couples who scored high in relationship awareness early in their marriages were happiest in the years to come and that relationship talk seemed to be especially important to women.

    According to Acitelli, "relationship talk" can be as simple as saying "I really value what we share." She also suggests that women might tell their partners that a relationship is like a fine car. "You don't just take it into the shop when there's a problem. You do maintenance. You take care of a marriage or long-term relationship the same way."

    How much "relationship talk" do you have in your romantic relationship? Does one partner enjoy this talk more than the other? Why? Are there other things (such as shared activities) that you do instead of "relationship talk" that contribute to the strength of your commitment to each other?

    [Adapted from *New Woman*, February 1994, p. 36]

3. Watch a rerun of a television program from the 1950s or 1960s that portrays family life (e.g., *I Love Lucy*, *The Dick Van Dyke Show*, *Leave It to Beaver*, or *My Three Sons*). List the behaviors of mothers and fathers that reflect traditional gender ideologies in families (for example, father goes to work and mother stays home).

    Watch a current television program that portrays the same type of situation. How have the family structure, behaviors identified with specific roles, gender expectations, and role conflicts changed? Did you observe the same types of behaviors that reflect gender stereotypes? Why or why not?

4. Select a dating or marital relationship you can observe. This relationship can be one in which you are involved, one that you observe directly, or one that is portrayed in literature, on television, or in a film. Answer each of the following questions:

    ■ What general topics do they discuss when they are together?
    ■ What topics do they discuss in greater depth?
    ■ Who typically initiates these topics?
    ■ Who usually asks more questions during a conversation?
    ■ Who most often changes the topics discussed?

    From the answers to these questions, what can you learn about communication in intimate relationships? What is the level of disclosure in this relationship? Does one person tend to disclose more than the other? What communication behavior does the male in the relationship exhibit that the female does not and vice versa? Why do you think the similarities and differences in communication behavior that you observed exist? How do your answers agree or disagree with the research presented on courtship and marriage in this chapter?

FURTHER READING

Bender, D. L., & Leone, B. (Eds.). (1992). *The family in America: Opposing viewpoints.* San Diego, CA: Greenhaven Press.
This book presents opposing viewpoints on family issues such as family leave, day care, working mothers, and two-career families.

Biller, H. B. (1993). *Fathers and families: Paternal factors in child development.* Westport, CT: Auburn House.
Biller cites compelling evidence that fathers are very important to sound child development. Biller also establishes that variations in paternal involvement influence not only children, but general family well-being including spousal relationships.

Galvin, K. M., & Brommel, B. J. (1999). *Family communication: Cohesion and change*, 5th ed. Reading, MA: Addison-Wesley.
Using a systems approach, the authors consider the communication processes within the family as well as the extent to which these processes affect and are affected by larger social systems.

Walters, M., Carter, E., Papp, P., & Silverstein, O. (1988). *The invisible web: Gender patterns in family relationships.* New York: Guilford Publications.
This book, divided into four sections, represents one of an emerging group of clinically focused feminist writings. The first section examines the barriers to establishing egalitarian relationships between men and women. The second section explores the impact of gender-based socialization processes on such family relationships as mothers–daughters, fathers–daughters, mothers–sons, and couples. The third section focuses on three major life cycle events: divorce, aftermath of divorce and single-parent families, and remarriage. The final section of the book discusses the impact of major issues faced by single women throughout these life stages.

CHAPTER

7

Education

Despite great strides in the field of education, the social movement for gender equity in schools still has far to go. Unfortunately, the educational system faced by students today continues to reinforce gender stereotypes in important ways (Sadker & Sadker, 1994; Wolfe & Rosser, 1997). Inequities still exist despite federal laws and regulations that prohibit gender-based discrimination in educational institutions (Sadker & Sadker, 1994).

> The combination of research efforts and the social movement for sex equity has . . . brought about some difference in the past 15 years of educational practice. These changes include increased expenditures for women's athletics, a greater number of female students enrolled in science and mathematics courses, some increase in women elementary school principals, and including of "missing" women in curriculum materials. Yet, despite years of work on sex equity issues in education, large-scale change of gender inequities in the schools or in the wider society has not come about. (Leach & Davies, 1990, p. 321)

For example, one father who attended an awards ceremony for his daughter's kindergarten class found that the boys were given awards for "Very Best Thinker" and "Most Eager Learner" while girls were awarded "Sweetest Personality" and "Best Helper" (Deveny, 1994).

Think about your junior-high and high-school years. Were there some subjects in which females seemed to do better than males? Or vice versa? Who participated in the sports with the biggest audiences? Who organized the homecoming dance, and who was the class clown? Regardless of whether we examine the educational system from a historical perspective, or on the basis of differences in male-female occupational choices, or according to the content of curriculum subjects, we find that the educational system helps to construct more dominant roles for males and to channel females into less dominant roles. This gender stereotyping results from what has been termed girls' "below stairs" relationship to education (Mahony, 1983; Rubin, 1988).

This relationship is not solely the product of the content of the school curriculum. Male and female teachers may communicate differently with male and female students. For example, a common practice for teachers, both male and female, is to give male students specific instructions on how to complete a project, but to *show* female students how to do it. For example, you will probably learn how to use a computer more quickly if someone tells you what to do while you type on the keyboard. It is more difficult to learn if the other person sits at the keyboard while you just watch. Yet this is an example of the type of situation females often face in school. Although teachers may believe they are helping young women by demonstrating specific tasks and taking time with them, this behavior may actually have negative consequences. Such behavior on the part of teachers may communicate that males are more capable and more important than females, since it takes more time to explain something than to demonstrate it.

It is important to note that gender-based discrimination in education affects males as well as females. Sadker and Sadker (1994) report:

- From grade school to high school, boys receive lower marks on their report cards.
- More boys than girls drop out and repeat grades.
- Seven out of ten suspended students are boys.
- Boys represent 71 percent of those designated as learning disabled and 80 percent of those labeled emotionally disturbed (p. 221).
- Boys are four times as likely to commit suicide as girls (Chethik, 1994, p. 5).

Inequities in Education

In the past traditional gender ideologies existed in both the content of educational materials and in classroom interaction patterns and to a lesser degree this is still true. Often gender bias is subtle. In terms of educational content, gender bias occurs in textbooks as well as in other educational materials, such as college catalogs and counseling materials. Gender bias exists in classroom communication patterns and also as a result of teacher expectancy. In this section, we will examine the types and extent of gender ideologies in education. Later in this chapter, we examine the consequences of gender bias and suggest strategies for change.

Textbooks and Literature

Textbooks constitute an important part of the educational material provided to students. As Smith (1985) notes:

> Students are less free to disregard or be critical of educational materials than they are of the media. In fact, they are frequently required to absorb and assimilate this material in minute detail. Second, people attach a great deal of credibility and authority to educational and reference material and are, therefore, probably much more attentive to the messages they convey and susceptible to the sway of their influence. (p. 37)

In addition, children are read stories in other types of books, and young adults choose their own fiction to read. Gender ideologies may be reinforced in each of these types of books through numerical differences and gendered behavior patterns and characteristics.

It is important to note that major changes have been made in both textbooks and trade books over the past two decades. In the 1970s, it was common to find differential treatment of males and females or even the complete absence of females in popular textbooks and similar types of discrepancies in non-textbooks. Today, authors and publishers are more sensitive to such issues and follow established guidelines to ensure fairness—although this goal is not always achieved. The following sections summarize many of the changes that have taken place in publishing over the past 30 years. Remember that although current and future generations will benefit from improved publishing practices, many of us were raised reading texts and trade books much like the ones described below.

Textbooks.   In the 1970s researchers examining the most heavily used elementary textbooks in first through sixth grades reported disturbing results (Weitzman & Rizzo, 1975). For example, in social studies textbooks, only 33 percent of the illustrations included females. In one series designed to teach reading, 102 stories were about boys and 35 were about girls. In 1972, researchers reported that of the 2,760 stories examined, there were approximately three males for every one female (Women on Words and Images, 1972). In biographies, the number of males increased to six males for every one female. Curious about the relevance of these findings for the 1990s, Purcell and Stewart (1990) replicated the study. Although the numbers of male and female characters represented were more equal, inequalities still existed. For example, men were featured in two-thirds of the photographs and pictures, and both males and females were portrayed in gender-stereotyped ways: males were shown in a wider range of careers, were engaged in more adventurous activities, and often rescued females. In a study of elementary readers (Tetenbaum & Pearson, 1989), male characters were more visible, more active, and more involved in areas of life considered important in our society.

Mliner (1977) examined elementary and junior-high school math and science texts. In these textbooks, females were pictured as Indian dolls or witches, or participating in activities such as skipping rope and buying balloons. Males were pictured as sailors, kings, bakers, circus performers, band members, and balloon sellers. Males were pictured 15 times for every one female pictured. Although many changes have been made since that time, comparing three decades of science materials, Nilsen (1987) found that artists were still drawing three times as many pictures of males as females. In addition, in the majority of books examined in this study, the word *man* was used to describe people in general, and few books depicted women in scientific careers. Bazler and Simonis (1991) found a 3:1 ratio of male to female images in high school chemistry textbooks. Such discrepancies present negative images of females and reinforce gender stereotypes. Thus, although more females may be taking math and science classes, some curriculum materials still tend to reinforce traditional gender stereotypes.

Discrepancies also exist in the number of male and female authors included in textbooks. In an early survey of English literature anthologies, the 17 books examined included selections by 147 male authors and only 25 female authors (Arlow & Froschel, 1976). Another survey of 400 selections revealed 75 female authors and 306 male authors (Arlow & Froschel, 1976). Carlson (1989) reports that a survey of high-school–level anthologies still revealed a preponderance of male authors. One anthology, for example, includes more than 90 selections by male authors and only eight by female authors. Most anthologies dealing with speech communication feature more speeches by men (Campbell, 1991) and some history textbooks devote only about 2 percent of their pages to women (Sadker & Sadker, 1994) while some art textbooks discuss male artists rather than female artists (Roth, 1987; Sadker & Sadker, 1994).

In the 39 top-selling college psychology textbooks, males significantly outnumber female examples in the texts as well as outnumbering female authors and reviewers (Peterson & Kroner, 1992). In sociology textbooks (Ferree & Hall, 1990), as well as in historical accounts of the United States (Kramarae, Schultz & O'Barr, 1984), women are glaringly absent. In virtually every academic discipline, the contributions of women have been minimized or neglected (Spender, 1989).

Generally, gender bias may be found in all types of textbooks. In speech communication textbooks, for example, hypothetical applications of communication skills sometimes perpetuate gender ideologies, such as a man arguing in court and a woman making an announcement at a PTA meeting (see Randall, 1985). Rarely are women's experiences represented in theories of small group communication, public speaking, or other areas (Bowen & Wyatt, 1993). Similarly, prominent theories of human moral and cognitive development have historically been based on studies using males as subjects (as discussed in Chapter 2). Female development was assumed to be the same as male development (Gilligan, 1982; Wood & Lenze, 1991), and, as a result, women were often seen as inferior because their development was judged in comparison to a standard not representative of them.

In some math textbooks, men are depicted as active, alert, and scientific. They are more often pictured doing math. Women are sometimes depicted as dull and insignificant and are rarely involved in career situations. In science textbooks, males may control the action while females watch the action; boys perform experiments, girls clean up. In addition, adult women are almost never presented in scientific roles (Nilsen, 1987). Bazler (1989) examines the seven best-selling high school science texts and reports that only one of the texts provides a balance of pictures of men and women. Calling for a change, Bazler argues:

> If women do not see women in science, if their teachers are 95 percent men, and if textbooks are predominantly male, they won't go into science unless they're specifically out to break down those barriers. (p. 33)

Feiner and Morgan (1987) analyzed 21 major introductory economic texts and found that the number of pages that even make a passing reference to economic topics of special interest to women and minorities is externally small. The number of pages referring to women and/or minorities ranges from 2 to 22. The average number of pages per book is 800. As Feiner and Roberts (1990) write:

> The almost total silence of the texts on the economic status of minorities speaks louder than words: The student cannot help but absorb the message that these are matters of relative unimportance. (p. 179)

With the adoption of nonsexist guidelines during the past decade, many textbook publishers have made substantial progress. Harwood (1992) notes that "a cursory look through any high school Spanish or French book will, for the most part, reveal an equal number of illustrations of men and women and a fair depiction of their roles" (p. 16). Nevertheless, some authors have made relatively few changes to increase the visibility of females and to decrease the stereotyping of males and females. For example, the "nonbiased" material is often added to the center or end of a textbook without any attempt to integrate it into the overall format of the book. Peterson (1994) quotes one student as saying, "You'll see women's pictures all put in one chapter—'great women in history'—rather than throughout the book" (p. 2D). And Harwood (1992) describes a popular high-school Latin textbook that rarely uses the word *she* in practice sentences and depicts over two-thirds of the characters in the reading lessons as male.

While gaps in math and science achievement between girls and boys narrowed by the end of the 1990s, a major new gender gap in technology has developed, according to a report released by the American Association of University Women (AAUW) Educational Foundation (1998). *Gender Gaps: Where Schools Still Fail Our Children* documents the progress and failure of schools in providing a fair and equitable education since 1992. In that year, the AAUW published *Shortchanging Girls, Shortchanging America*, which propelled gender equity to the forefront of the debate concerning reforming education to provide equality for all students (this report is discussed in more detail later in this chapter). The new report focuses on emerging gaps in areas such as technology that threaten to disadvantage girls as they confront twenty-first-century demands. For example, technology is now the new "boys' club" in public schools. While more boys program and problem-solve with computers, many girls use computers for word processing—the latest version of typing.

Synthesizing 1,000 research studies, *Gender Gaps* reviews issues of historic concern for girls—math and science enrollment, high-stakes standardized testing, extracurricular activities, and health and development risks—and new areas such as technology and School-to-Work programs. The report indicates that from 1990 to 1994, girls' enrollments in AP (advanced placement) and honors calculus and chemistry improved relative to boys. And the 1997 addition of a writing skills section on the PSAT raised girls' scores and narrowed the gender gap between boys' and girls' scores (from 4.5 to 2.7 points).

Despite the progress in these areas, however, gender gaps persist:

- High school girls and boys take similar numbers of science courses, but boys are more likely than girls to take all three core science courses—biology, chemistry, and physics—before they graduate.
- Girls take fewer computer science and computer design courses.
- Boys take fewer English courses.
- Girls are enrolling in AP classes in larger numbers, but fewer girls than boys receive the high scores on TP tests needed to receive college credit.
- Girls cluster in traditionally female occupations in School-to-Work and vocational education programs.

- Girls continue to experience risks to their health and development such as sexual harassment and abuse, pregnancy, substance abuse, and delinquency.
- Boys repeat grades and drop out of school at a higher rate, but girls who are held back are more likely to drop out.
- Girls still consider a narrower set of careers than boys.

Children's Literature.   In addition to textbooks, educators are being encouraged to use other books to supplement the basic curriculum (Aiex, 1988; Holmes & Ammon, 1985). The image of males and females in literature—from a child's first picture book to adult best-sellers—can influence the way in which males and females see themselves and, thus, can influence their communication. In this section, we will examine the gender stereotypes of males and females that are communicated in children's literature.

In many ways, children's literature reflects and reinforces gender ideology. Numerical disparities and gendered behavior patterns and characteristics reflected in children's literature may help teach girls to undervalue themselves and teach boys to believe that they must always strive to be stereotypically masculine.

Although the situation continues to improve, females are not included in children's books in numbers that reflect their presence in the general population. Four studies have examined how gender is treated in books that have won the Caldecott Medal or the Newbery Award (Cooper, 1989; Cooper, 1993b; Kolbe & LaVoie, 1981; Weitzman et al., 1972). The Caldecott Medal is given by the Children's Service Committee of the American Library Association for the most distinguished picture book of the year. The Newbery Award is given by the American Library Association for the best book for school-age children. From 1967 to 1972, the ratio of male characters to female characters in Caldecott Medal books is 11:1. From 1972 to 1979, the ratio of male characters to female characters in Newbery Award books is 1.8:1. Interestingly, from 1980 to 1987, the ratio of human male characters to human female characters in Caldecott Medal books is 2:1, and the ratio in Newbery Award winners is 6:1. From 1967 to 1987, only 14 books (out of a total of 97) depict women working outside the home.

Although numerical disparities seem to be decreasing in children's books, the role models presented for children have not become less stereotyped. The three studies cited above also examine the gendered behavior patterns and characteristics depicted in children's books. The 1967 to 1972 study shows that when females are illustrated, gender-stereotyped characterizations are reinforced: girls are passive, boys are active; girls follow and serve others, boys lead and rescue others. Adult men and women in these books also are stereotyped: women are depicted as wives and mothers, while men hold a variety of occupations. In the years from 1972 to 1987, gender stereotypes are still prevalent. From 1967 to 1972, all 18 Caldecott Medal books portray traditional gender stereotypes; from 1972 to 1979, 17 out of 19 do; and from 1980 to 1987, 26 out of 31 do. Of the 29 Newbery Award books for 1980 to 1987, 22 contain traditional gender ideologies.

Two more recent studies of Caldecott Medal winners suggest similar patterns. Heinz (1987) examines the occupations of characters in Caldecott Medal-winning books from 1971 to 1984. Males are shown in three times as many occupations as females. Almost half of the females pursuing any type of work are depicted in a homemaker role. Dougherty and Engel (1987) analyze Caldecott winners and honor books from 1981 to 1985 and find that although numerical disparities decrease considerably, gender-stereotyped images do not.

Biased portrayals do not occur only in Newbery Award and Caldecott Medal books (Peterson & Lach, 1990). In an analysis of nursery rhymes and fairy tales (the first literature to which most children are exposed), Donlan (1972) finds three recurring types of female characters: the sweet little old lady, the beautiful young heroine, and the aggressive female. The first two types, sweet little old lady and beautiful heroine, are both depicted as lovable and incompetent. The aggressive female takes many forms: witch, domineering housewife (who functions as wife, mother, or stepmother), and shrew (cruel, vain, greedy, and demanding). Donlan concludes that in children's literature, women may be portrayed as ineffectual creatures who need to be dominated by men or as aggressive monsters who must be destroyed by men.

Examining 2,216 children's books published from 1900 to 1984, Grauerholz and Pescosolido (1989) find that males are the dominant characters and females conform to a passive stereotype. In a random sampling of 1,380 school library books in grades

K–6, female athletes frequently fall victim to gender stereotyping. Boys are shown participating in a variety of individual sports, and girls predominate only in traditionally feminine activities, such as dance. In team sports, 34 out of 38 baseball players are male, as are 7 out of 8 basketball players (Weiller & Higgs, 1989).

Think about the fairy tales you remember. Were the female characters generally passive, incompetent, and beautiful, like Rapunzel, who is locked in a tower, or the miller's daughter in Rumpelstiltskin who cries when faced with the task of spinning straw into gold and promises her firstborn child in exchange for Rumplestiltskin's help? Active female characters are either evil older women or supernatural characters such as fairy godmothers. Men are more often portrayed as handsome princes who have to rescue someone or as greedy characters who meet a violent end.

Cooper (1987) explores gender ideology in children's books concerning stepfamilies. She examines 42 books (1975–1983) available in libraries in the Chicago metropolitan area and finds numerous gender stereotypes. Women work, but in stereotyped jobs such as receptionists, secretaries, or nurses. When women are employed outside the home, they neglect their children or become aggressive. They are relatively passive and focus primarily on their appearance. Men are more likely to be depicted as lawyers and doctors who are usually inept at simple household duties. They are caring and sensitive, but only to a point; when problems are not resolved quickly, they become impatient. In an update to this study, Cooper (1994) finds that stepmothers continue to be portrayed in a negative way.

Barton (1984) suggests that the gender ideology of male characters in children's literature has been greatly ignored. As a result, this author analyzes more than 50 children's books and finds that books depicting a sensitive male role model do exist, but not in great numbers. Vaughan-Roberson, Tompkins, Hitchcock, and Oldham (1989) examine sexism in basal readers. The study was conducted to determine if positive female traits (such as nurturing) are attributed to male main characters. Their analysis indicates that although classically positive female traits appear in some male characters, the overall composite and, to a lesser degree, depiction of individual characters are dominated by masculine stereotypes such as independence and a willingness to take risks.

To combat some of these stereotypes, several lists of nonstereotyped children's books have been published. One researcher rates the books on a nonsexist book list entitled *Little Miss Muffet Fights Back* in terms of five categories: (1) sex of central characters, (2) sex of figures portrayed on front cover, (3) sex of characters named in titles, (4) number of illustrations with males and females, and (5) expressive and instrumental activities (St. Peter, 1979). In addition to analyzing the nonsexist books, St. Peter also analyzes titles published prior to the advent of the modern women's movement in the 1970s and titles published after that time. This analysis of 206 picture books indicates that children often are presented with gender-stereotyped models. In general, females are underrepresented in titles, central roles, and illustrations; males are overrepresented in instrumental activities and underrepresented in expressive activities. St. Peter (1979) concludes:

> As time passes, . . . children's books on conventional lists may begin to reflect changes in female representation. Even now, books on the specialized list, *Little Miss*

Muffet Fights Back, contain material that overcomes some stereotypes with females well represented in titles, central roles, and illustrations. These books overcompensate, however, by presenting highly instrumental female models and a minimum of expressive activities. In conclusion, despite the attempted improvement of sex-role models in the Miss Muffet books, the majority of children's picture books today continue to underrepresent women and to stereotype female and male characters. The fact is that, when Jack goes up the hill, Jill stays home. (pp. 259–260)

Our concern with gender ideology in children's literature stems from the fact that these books may influence children's behavior (Campbell & Wirtenberg, 1980). Several studies reveal the effects on children of traditional gender stereotypes in children's books. Koblinsky, Cruse, and Sugawara (1978) tested children's recall after listening to stories with males and females in traditional roles and report that boys recall the masculine characteristics of males and girls remember the feminine characteristics of females. When preschool children read stories with traditional and nontraditional behaviors of boys and girls, they prefer stories in which the characters display traditional behavior for their sex (Kropp & Halverson, 1983). Bleakley, Westerberg, and Hopkins (1988) studied the effect of the sex of the main character on fifth-grade boys' and girls' reading interests. Boys rate stories much less interesting when the main character is female; girls rate stories with male protagonists less interesting, although their preferences are much less pronounced than boys.

Research also demonstrates the effect that nonbiased stories can have on children. Children who are asked their career preferences after hearing stories with characters in nontraditional roles make more nontraditional choices than children who only heard about traditional characters (Lutes-Dunckley, 1978). Girls who hear nontraditional stories rate male jobs and characteristics as more appropriate for females than girls who heard traditional stories (Ashby & Wittmaier, 1978). In another study, nursery-school girls exhibit more achievement behavior after listening to a story about an achieving girl than after listening to a story about an achieving boy (McArthur & Eisen, 1976). Thus, feminine gender stereotypes can be modified through the use of books that depict egalitarian gender roles (Flerx, Fidler, & Rogers, 1976). When females are portrayed in roles traditionally assumed by males, both boys and girls increase their perceptions of the number of girls who can engage in these traditionally male activities (Scott, 1986).

Young Adult Literature.   Much of what has been reviewed in this chapter relates to younger children's literature. However, young adult (adolescent) literature also has been analyzed for gender stereotypes. Wigutoff (1982) reviewed 300 young adult, contemporary realism books published between 1977 and 1980. Again, gender stereotypes are depicted: fathers go to work, and mothers stay home. Mothers provide food and clean clothes without expecting thanks from their husbands and children.

Teen romances are an extremely popular form of fiction for female adolescents. They are one of the three types of books most widely read by young girls; a single title may sell as many as 90,000 copies through book clubs. One study indicated that teen romances constitute 35 percent of B. Dalton's and Waldenbooks' combined nonadult sales (Christian-Smith, 1988). Reading romances is the primary leisure activity for many adolescent girls (Daly, 1980). Teenagers read romance novels for three reasons:

escape, enjoyment, and education (Christian-Smith, 1988). Although some of these books are beginning to deal with more serious social issues, the messages teenage girls encounter in many of these stories, however, may promote gender stereotypes for both males and females. Campion (1983) says:

> A new generation is now being subjected to the same nonsense: good looks and the right clothes are a girl's most important attributes; there is no need to take responsibility for your life because a man will do it for you; life ends (at 16 years old, if you're really lucky) when you walk off into the sunset with the perfect boyfriend. (pp. 98–99)

Counseling and Guidance Materials

Students use textbooks in the classroom, but they also use written materials in guidance-counseling offices. Often these materials contain the same gender stereotypes that are found in textbooks.

In an analysis of 100 college catalogs (which often constitute a portion of the materials high-school counselors use to advise students), Harway (1977) finds that a higher percentage of catalog content is devoted to males than to females. This research calculated the percentage of half pages in catalogs devoted to males and to females. In catalogs from four-year colleges and universities, an average of 23 percent of the half pages are devoted to men while less than one half page is devoted to women.

Gallo (1987) has conducted a follow-up to this study to determine if these data are still accurate. He examines four-year college admission catalogs from the years 1982 to 1986 and finds that women are depicted in a wide range of curricula and activities; however, the degree of status within these roles is still biased. For example, although female administrators account for 35 percent of the people pictured in that occupation, the pictures are more likely to depict female administrators in the areas of housing or student relations, while male administrators are more likely to be deans or department heads.

As Gallo (1987) concludes, males and females in college catalogs are still presented stereotypically. Men are department heads; women are working in housing offices. Men participate in contact sports; women exercise alone or in dance classes. One researcher concludes that the limited vistas for women shown in college catalogs may convince many high-school students that the options available to women in colleges themselves are also limited (Harway, 1977).

Gender ideology in educational materials is a major concern. Males and females are often offered limited role models for nontraditional gender roles in textbooks and in counseling and guidance materials. Later in this chapter we will examine the consequences of these limitations for men and women.

Classroom Interaction

Gender bias occurs not only in educational materials, but also in student interactions with teachers, with other students, and with educational personnel such as guidance counselors.

Teacher Expectancy

In a classic study, two researchers examined the expectations teachers have for various students and the effect of these expectations on student achievement. The researchers randomly labeled some elementary-school children as high achievers and others as low achievers. Then this information was given to teachers. Students who were labeled as high achievers showed a significant increase in their IQ scores from the beginning of the school year to the end (Rosenthal & Jacobson, 1968). This phenomenon is called *teacher expectancy* and works as follows:

1. A teacher expects certain behaviors from certain students.
2. These expectations influence the teacher's behavior toward these students.
3. The teacher's behavior indicates to the students what the teacher expects of them. These expectations affect the students' self-concepts, motivation to achieve, and achievement.
4. If the teacher's behavior is consistent over time, and the students do not resist it, high-expectation students will achieve well and low-expectation students will not.

Relating teacher expectancy to gender expectations, teachers do not perceive stereotypically feminine traits in high-achieving students (Benz, Pfeiffer, & Newman, 1981). Both male and female high achievers are perceived as exhibiting androgynous or stereotypically masculine behaviors. (See Chapter 2 for an explanation of these concepts.) In other words, the feminine gender role is negatively correlated with achievement. This finding does not vary significantly over grade levels or between male and female teachers. Benz, Pfeiffer, and Newman summarize the implications of these findings:

> The conclusion of this study, to fit the feminine role is not to achieve, sheds important light on evidence . . . that achievement declines the longer females are in school. Not surprisingly, the evidence implies that females may be fulfilling society's expectations for them. If teachers expect girls to be feminine and boys to be masculine, the results clearly show what playing the roles can mean in terms of academic behavior. (pp. 297–298)

A review of research at all educational levels suggests six major ways in which teachers communicate gender expectations to students (Hall & Sandler, 1982; Jones, 1989; LaFrance, 1991; Riddell, 1989). First, teachers may call on male students more often than on female students. Some female students indicate they feel invisible in the classroom. Female students raise their hands often, yet males are more likely to be asked to respond. When female students are asked why they believe teachers call on male students more often, they claim that teachers either do not expect them to know the answer or do not feel their answer would be correct or worthwhile.

Second, teachers often coach male students to help them work toward a fuller answer. Female students are not coached as often. For example, a teacher is more likely to say, "What do you mean by that?" or "Why do you believe that to be the appropriate theory?" to male students than to female students. Coaching may communicate to males the expectation that, with a little help, they can succeed. Lack of coaching may communicate to females that their ideas are not important enough to probe further or that they are not intellectually capable of succeeding.

The third way in which teachers communicate gender ideologies, waiting longer for males than they wait for females to answer a question before going on to another student, may subtly communicate to females that they are not expected to know the answer. This behavior on the part of teachers may also communicate to males in the classroom that they are more intellectually competent than their female counterparts. In addition, a male's silence following a question may be perceived as due to formulating an answer, while a female's silence may be perceived as due to her lack of knowledge.

Fourth, female students are more likely to be asked questions that require factual answers ("When was television invented?") and male students are more often asked questions that require critical thinking or personal evaluation ("How do you feel the concept of symbolic interaction affects communication?"). Once again, teachers communicate expectations regarding the intellectual capability of each student: that females are capable only of low-level cognitive processes, but males are capable of high-level cognitive processes.

Fifth, teachers respond more extensively to male students' comments than to female students' comments. Males, therefore, receive more reinforcement for their intellectual participation than females.

In 1992, the American Association of University Women (AAUW) Educational Foundation commissioned a comprehensive review of 1,331 studies of gender and educational practices in which evidence was amassed to show that female students continue to receive less attention, less encouragement, and less serious regard than their male peers. While girls enter first grade with the same or better skills and ambitions as boys, "all too often, by the time they finish high school, 'their doubts have crowded out their dreams' " (AAUW, 1991). The evidence from this study led to the conclusion that the hidden curriculum creates a downward intellectual mobility cycle in which "girls are less likely to reach their potential than boys" (p. 62).

Finally, teachers may inadvertently communicate gender bias by their use of sexist language (Jones, 1987). For example, when a teacher asks, "Why were the fathers of our country so concerned about religious freedom?" or "If a lawyer knows his client is guilty what should he do?" the teacher may communicate that males have been more important throughout history or that lawyers are usually male. Richmond and Gorham (1988), in their study of generic-referent usage among 1,529 public school children in grades 3 through 12, find that the masculine generic usage (he) is still prevalent. In addition, a heavy dependence on masculine referents is associated with self-image. Males use significantly more masculine referents than do females.

Teacher expectations are a powerful force in the classroom because they can affect a student's feelings of intellectual and personal worth. Students may sense a teacher's expectation and begin to communicate in the same way with each other.

For example, male students may be more likely to pay attention and respond more extensively to each other's comments than to comments made by female students.

Many teachers have worked very hard to overcome these behaviors. Nevertheless, they are still common (Sadker & Sadker, 1994). Elementary-school teachers are still dividing their classes into girls and boys competing against each other in spelling contests, and sending notes home to parents that say: "We will be having a holiday gift exchange. Boys should bring a gift suitable for a boy and label it, 'For a boy.' Girls should bring a gift suitable for a girl and label it, 'For a girl.' "

Expectations are also communicated by other educational personnel. As we have seen earlier in this chapter, another major influence on students, in addition to that of teachers, comes from guidance counselors. Counselors may foster gender stereotyping by displaying negative reactions toward women entering nontraditional careers (Worell, 1980). For example, counselors may ask probing questions of females who wish to enter nontraditional fields (Thomas & Stewart, 1971). In one study, the researchers report that females often do not choose science as a career if they are discouraged from doing so by their high-school counselors (Ware & Lee, 1988). Anne Bryant, executive director of the American Association of University Women, explains this type of subtle bias: "When a school counselor tells a girl failing math to switch to French to get better grades and improve her chances of getting into college, that is a very subtle message that she probably won't pick up" (Peterson, 1994, p. 2D). Similarly, if a counselor tells a young man he should take math and science instead of creative writing or early childhood education in order to get into college, gender bias also occurs. In the 1970s researchers found that some high-school counselors recommended occupations to female high-school seniors that were lower-paying, more highly supervised, and required less education than those recommended for male high-school seniors (Donahue, 1976). Some research suggests that although this behavior has changed significantly, counseling often still occurs along gender lines (Gender Gaps, 1998).

Communication Patterns

A great deal of research has explored the communication patterns that exist in the classroom in relation to the gender of both the students and teachers. Although in many areas significant changes have taken place during the past few decades, recent research regarding classroom communication (American Association for University Women, 1992; Sadker & Sadker, 1994) has found results surprisingly similar to those conducted in the 1970s. Generally, we know that differences exist in terms of initiation, discipline, and dominance (Stake & Katz, 1982). In this section, we examine each of these.

Initiation.   Male students tend to initiate more interactions with teachers than female students initiate (Brophy, 1985). In addition, the interactions between male students and teachers last longer (Hall & Sandler, 1982). Some scholars contend that this longer duration of interaction is a result of what teachers and male students discuss. As suggested earlier in this chapter, some teachers explain how to do things to male students and simply do them for female students. Interaction time increases as a teacher explains how to set up lab equipment, work a math problem, or write a thesis sentence. If a teacher is "doing for" the female student, as is often the case, interaction time is decreased.

Teachers have suggested that males are more creative and more fun to teach (Sadker & Sadker, 1985). As discussed in a previous section of this chapter, teachers may communicate this attitude to male students, who, in turn, may be more willing to initiate interactions because they feel more valued in the classroom.

Discipline.   Classroom communication patterns differ in terms of how male and female students are disciplined. Criticism of female students tends to focus on their lack of knowledge or skill; criticism of male students is more likely to focus on disruptive behaviors. Male students receive more discipline than female students and are more likely to be reprimanded in a harsher and more public manner than female students (Brophy, 1985).

You might be asking whether male students feel less comfortable in the classroom than female students since males are disciplined more. To understand why male students do not feel less comfortable than female students, we need to examine the other side of the discipline coin: praise. Although male students receive a larger number of negative messages, their ideas are used by teachers more often. For example, a teacher might say, "That's an interesting idea, Steven. Let's explore that idea for a moment." When male students are praised, they tend to be praised for the intellectual quality of their work. When they are criticized, they are more likely to be criticized for lack of neatness and form (Riddell, 1989). For example, a teacher might say, "Your ideas are very good, Danny; however, try to be neater. Your writing is difficult to read." Female students, on the other hand, often are praised for their neatness and form, but not for the intellectual quality of their work ("Your model of communication looks very nice, Laurie, but you didn't analyze it very well.")

High-achieving male students receive more teacher approval and active instruction; lower-achieving male students are likely to receive more criticism. However, high-achieving female students receive less praise than both low- and high-achieving male students (Parsons, Heller, & Kaczala, 1980). Thus, while male students receive more disciplinary messages, they also receive more praise in general than female students receive and, in particular, more praise for their intellectual ability.

Dominance.   Male students often dominate classroom talk. They are given more opportunities to respond in the classroom, and teachers direct more attention (both positive and negative) toward them. In addition, teachers ask male students a higher proportion of product and choice questions (questions that require synthesis or analysis), thereby encouraging problem-solving behavior in male students to a greater extent than in female students (Riddell, 1989). Pearson and West (1991) examine 15 college classrooms and find that female students ask fewer questions than male students in courses taught by male instructors. Another study records the types of questions asked by male and female students at various grade levels in mathematics and language arts classes. The results suggest that in advanced secondary mathematics classes, female students ask fewer questions than males. In addition, teachers subtly discourage female students from participating (Good & Slavings, 1988).

Moreover, male students tend to dominate more than just the conversation in the classroom; they also dominate many of the nonverbal aspects of classroom communication (Thorne, 1979). Keegan (1989) reports research suggesting that fourth- through eighth-grade males are not only given more time to talk, they receive more attention (for example, more eye contact) than females. In addition to dominating linguistic space, male students dominate the physical space of the classroom. For example, they have more opportunities than females to use equipment, perform experiments, and carry out demonstrations (Jones, 1989).

In addition, boys may emphasize their masculine dominance by using girls as a negative reference group. One researcher asked students, "Who would you least wish to be like?" All of the boys named girls (and only girls). The characteristic of girls most vehemently rejected by these boys was their apparent marginality in classroom encounters. The term "faceless" was used repeatedly by the male students (but by none of the female students) to describe their female classmates, and seemed to sum up their feeling that silence robs female students of any claim to individual identity and respect (Stanworth, 1981).

Male students use several strategies to achieve dominance in mixed-sex classrooms. They deny female students' academic abilities, make negative remarks about females' appearances, and overtly resist females' adopting of nontraditional roles. The following example from a drama teacher demonstrates the latter strategy:

> The problem of finding roles which girls can identify with became an acute one for me . . . and when I did manage to do so and cast a girl in an important part which might normally have been given to a boy, I found myself feeling guilty because I had denied a boy a plum role. Possibly I was also afraid that my choice might cause disruptive behavior from the boys. Sometimes the boys challenged me, "airline pilot? A girl can't be an airline pilot, Miss!" Each time this happened, I saw the girl hesitate, waiting for my judgement, waiting to be sent back to her seat. "Of course she can," I would retort. . . . Each time I did this particular lesson, three in all, . . . the girl playing the pilot approached me privately, when the others were busy and whispered was I serious? Could women be pilots? Everytime I reassured the girl that it was perfectly alright and would she please go back to her controls before the plane crashed. (quoted in Mahony, 1983, p. 113)

Not only do teachers communicate differently with male and female students, but teachers perceive male and female students differently. For example, Guttman and Bar-Tal (1982) found that teachers respond to students in a stereotypical manner when they are presented with written descriptions of students' biological sex and national origin. Gold, Crombie, and Noble (1987) found that preschool girls whose behavior is in accordance with the compliant, good student model are more likely to have their abilities perceived at a higher level than girls whose behavior does not fit the model. Evaluations of boys' competence is not affected by teachers' perceptions of their compliance.

Perceptions of Teachers

Students perceive male and female teachers differently. Male instructors may be perceived as dominant; female instructors may be perceived as supportive (Nadler & Nadler, 1990). Often female teachers are better liked. Students believe that classes taught by women are more discussion-oriented, and that classes taught by men are more structured and emphasize content mastery more (Treichler & Kramarae, 1983). Nevertheless, the more student participation female teachers generate in their classrooms, the less competent they are perceived to be (Macke & Richardson, 1980). Evidently, students equate a structured teaching strategy (such as a lecture rather than a discussion) with competence, and male teachers are more likely to use a structured teaching strategy.

Investigating student perceptions of science classes taught by male and female teachers, Lawrenz and Welch (1983) report that students believe that classes taught by females are more diverse and have more instances of teacher favoritism and friction among students than classes taught by male teachers. Students also report that classes taught by male teachers are more difficult. Cooper, Stewart, and Gudykunst (1982) examine the impact of several variables on students' evaluation of instructors, including the gender of the instructor. They conclude:

> When evaluating instructors, students give greater significance to the type of *interpersonal response* they receive from female instructors while giving greater significance to the *accuracy of the grade* they receive from male instructors. Presumably, female instructors, who are supposed to be sensitive and caring, are evaluated favorably if they confirm this stereotype through their interpersonal response. Male instructors, who are supposed to be competent, are favorably evaluated if they demonstrate their competence by awarding accurate grades. (p. 314, emphasis added)

The perceptions students have of instructors affect student communication in the classroom (Nadler & Nadler, 1990). Male and female students communicate differently with male and female instructors. When the instructor is male, male student interactions are three times more frequent than female student interactions. Male students indicate they learn more from male professors while females indicate they learn more from female professors (Menzel & Carrell, 1999). When the instructor is female, male and female student interactions are nearly equal (Karp & Yoels, 1976). Perhaps female students feel more comfortable in classes taught by females and are, therefore, more willing to communicate in an environment they perceive as more supportive (Statham, Richardson & Cook, 1991).

Rosenfeld and Jarrard (1985) examine how the perceived sexism of college professors affects classroom climate. They find that students who perceive their male teachers to be highly sexist describe their classes as less supportive and less innovative than those taught by nonsexist male teachers. In a follow-up study (Rosenfeld & Jarrard, 1986), the researchers examined coping mechanisms used by students in classes taught by sexist and nonsexist teachers. Coping mechanisms used by students in sexist male teachers' classes are passive (not doing what the teacher asks, hiding feelings) when students like the class. If students do not like the class and perceive the male teacher as sexist, students use a more active coping mechanism: forming alliances against the teacher. Generally, teachers in disliked classes are perceived as more sexist than teachers in liked classes. Also, male teachers are perceived as more sexist than female teachers.

Most of the research on sexism and classroom interaction has not directly considered gender, but several communication researchers have begun to examine this area of classroom communication. For example, teacher-effectiveness research suggests that qualities of effective teaching can be grouped according to stereotypically masculine (for example, self-confident, independent, logical, objective, and aggressive) and stereotypically feminine (for example, warm, gentle, facilitative, and showing concern for others) styles (see research reviewed by Wheeless & Potorti, 1987).

Bray and Howard (1980) find that androgynous teachers score higher than stereotypically masculine teachers in both student satisfaction and progress and higher than stereotypically feminine teachers in terms of pupil progress. Wheeless and Potorti (1987) find that androgynous teachers produce the highest levels of student learning, followed by traditionally feminine, traditionally masculine, and undifferentiated teachers. (See Chapter 2 for a more extensive discussion of these concepts.) Similar results are reported by Jordan, McGreal, and Wheeless (1990).

Bachen, McLoughlin and Garcia (1999) examined how students' perceptions of gender ideology affect how they evaluated their instructors. The researchers conclude that female students' identification with female faculty is strong and probably constitutes a measure of educational success for those students. Male students do not rate female faculty differently than male faculty, but their qualitative comments indicate that males were more comfortable with female faculty when they seemed to be adapting to a more masculine style in the classroom. In general, students are most positively affected by teachers who show concern for them as individuals but who are also able to show some sense of independence and classroom leadership (Downs & Downs, 1993; Teven & Gorham, 1999; Teven & McCroskey, 1997).

Implications and Consequences of Gender Bias in Education

As the research discussed in this chapter indicates, curriculum materials and classroom interaction patterns influence student gender ideology and communication behavior. The question now becomes, "What are the effects of gender ideology in education?" Basically, gender ideology in education affects three areas: (1) the self-concept of students, (2) the curriculum choice of students, and (3) the occupational choice of students.

Self-Concept

The research concerning women's self-confidence in achievement settings concludes that women's self-confidence is not lower than men's when: (1) the task is appropriate for females, (2) the women are informed that they have the ability to complete the task, and (3) the emphasis placed on comparison to others and evaluation by others is low (Licht, Stadler, & Swenson, 1989). Generally, these three criteria are not met in achievement settings. Thus, women's self-confidence in the educational environment may be low, and this low self-confidence may affect their self-concept (Licht, Stadler, & Swenson, 1989).

In a study comparing the self-concept scores of tenth-grade girls with the scores of their male peers, Bohan (1973) finds that girls have a significantly lower self-concept rating than boys. The self-concept scores of tenth-grade girls are also significantly lower than the scores of girls in all other age groups. Bohan offers two interpretations for these findings: (1) that the adolescent years involve a reevaluation of self, and adolescent girls may find themselves wanting in relation to the ideals that they hold or believe to be important; and (2) since adolescence is the period of most intense evaluation of roles, as well as the apex of gender-identity development, the adolescent girl may come to recognize that the role she is expected to assume as a female is relatively inferior in status and prestige to the traditionally masculine gender role. Accordingly, she may decrease her evaluation of herself. Orenstein (1994) and Brown and Gilligan (1992) also report similar results.

Equally as disconcerting as the decline in the self-concept of adolescent girls are the results of tests that seem to indicate that girls' IQ scores decrease over time while boys' scores increase (Foxley, 1982). In some cases, high-school girls with better grade averages than boys do not believe that they have the ability to do college work (Byrne & Shavelson, 1987). Seventy-five to 90 percent of the brightest high-school graduates who do not go on to college are women (Jacko, Karmos, & Karmos, 1980).

Gilligan, Lyons, and Hanmer (1990) note a remarkable change in girls' self-confidence as they mature. Up to the age of 11, girls are outspoken about their feelings and accept conflict as a part of healthy relationships. But at age 11, they begin to fear that disagreements will harm relationships. Gilligan and her colleagues report that by age 15 or 16, girls begin to say, "I don't know" as a way to try to find out what their friends or teachers know and what it is safe to say. The reason for this change, according to Gilligan, is that during adolescence girls come up against the "wall of Western culture" and begin to perceive that their straightforwardness may be dangerous, so they learn to hide and protect what they know.

In a major study, Earle, Roach, and Fraser (1987) examine female high-school dropouts. Based on their findings, they conclude that the majority of female students who drop out of high school are not pregnant, as was previously assumed. In their report, *Female Dropouts: A New Perspective*, they speculate that current school practices encourage girls to leave school by depressing their overall achievement. For example, as discussed earlier, studies have shown that teachers talk less to female than to male students, counsel them less, and provide them with fewer directions and rewards. Also, schools provide limited opportunities for students to work cooperatively, although girls may perform better than boys in such situations.

These researchers suggest that the female dropout rate can be lowered by using (1) teaching strategies that incorporate group activities and collaboration, (2) remedial instruction in abstract spatial reasoning to prepare girls for math and science courses,

(3) mentor programs that enable girls to identify with females who hold nontraditional jobs, (4) counseling and related activities to enhance girls' self-esteem, and (5) teacher training that promotes student–teacher interactions free of gender bias.

Curriculum Choice

Gender ideology in education may also affect the course of study students pursue. Traditionally, female students have perceived math and science courses, spatial ability, and problem solving as male domains (Ethington & Wolfe, 1988; Maple & Stage, 1991). Collis and Ollila (1990) note that regardless of daily participation in classroom language arts and computer activities over a period of seven to eight months, young children still perceive computer use as masculine. Males traditionally have viewed home economics, secretarial skills, and reading as feminine activities (Cooper, 1993a). Research examining differences in male/female math and science performance suggests that males are more likely to take higher-level math and science courses and that this is particularly true of physics, trigonometry, and calculus (Becker, 1990; Goleman, 1987; Gender Gaps, 1998).

Gender-biased labeling such as that discussed above is related to student attitudes and achievement in those subjects (see research reviewed in Collis & Ollila, 1990). For example, Wilder, Mackie, and Cooper (1985) find that K–12 students perceived writing as more appropriate for females than for males. Trepanier-Street, Romatowski, and McNair (1990b) examined the creative writing responses of 140 third- and sixth-grade boys and girls to story characters cast in either stereotypic (male mechanic and female nurse) or nonstereotypic (female mechanic and male nurse) occupational roles. The authors conclude:

> Strong evidence of gender-stereotypic thinking was manifested in several ways in the stories of both boys and girls. Consistent with gender-stereotypic thinking, writers had the least difficulty maintaining a character in role when the role was occupationally gender-stereotypic. All boy writers and young girl writers had the most difficulty maintaining a character in role when the character's gender did not match the occupational gender stereotype. Occupation aside, the lead character most often was developed as consistent with the gender stereotype. The one exception was seen in girl writers who developed the male nurse character as stereotypically female. (p. 67)

Of course, male and female students may be equally capable of high achievement in courses traditionally considered the domain of one or the other (Brandon, Newton & Hammond, 1987; Friedman, 1989). For example, among 13-year-olds, females' mathematical abilities are comparable, and in some areas, superior to those of males. However, by 12th grade, males catch up with and then surpass females in certain areas of math achievement. Yet, when women have the same mathematical training as men, they perform equally as well (Pallas & Alexander, 1983; Paulsen & Johnson, 1983). The same is true in science. An analysis of 13-year-olds reports no differences in science achievement. Yet females continue to move away from the sciences (Baker & Leary, 1995). Thus, although achievement in science and math may not be different when male and female students are exposed to the same material, female students tend not to take advanced math and science courses (Gender Gaps, 1998).

Occupational Choice

The choice of which curriculum to pursue is directly related to occupational choice. For example, math and science skills are critical in determining educational and occupational choices (Peng & Jaffe, 1979). A 1989 study in *Education Week* reported that students who take more mathematics courses earn considerably more in the workforce. Thus, when female students avoid science and math training, they preclude themselves from considering a wide range of occupations, not only in engineering and the natural sciences, but also in the social sciences and in business administration (Carnegie Commission on Higher Education, 1973; Eaky, 1991).

Many jobs are still segregated by gender. For example, in 1987 75 to 98 percent of the workers in clerical and health-care occupations were women (U.S. Department of Labor, 1987). The situation is similar today. Large numbers of women are not entering traditionally male-dominated fields.

Girls still consider and pursue a narrower set of career opportunities than do boys (Gender Gaps, 1998). This inequity reverberates beyond school and into the labor force, where only 6 percent of women are in nontraditional careers. In fact, women cluster in only 20 of the more than 400 official jobs categories, and two out of three minimum-wage earners are women. Statistics make it clear that students still face gender barriers when they prepare to enter the workforce (as will be discussed in more detail in Chapter 9). These barriers include:

- School-to-Work and other career preparation programs often fall short of their promise of helping girls and minorities enter fields that are nontraditional for

---

CONSIDER THIS!

The Gender Gap and Technology

We all know how important it is to use a computer today. Rarely does a day go by when we don't use a computer in some form—whether it's to check our e-mail, find out information on the Internet, or work on a paper for class. Research tells us, though, that boys and girls use computers somewhat differently. For example, according to one study, girls are more likely to use computers for word processing and skill building at school while boys are more likely to use computers for games and entertainment at home. In advanced classes, girls report less confidence in their use of computers. While technology can be a way of connecting with people for girls, it may be perceived as a way for boys to extend their power through games that focus on competition.

Dorman, 1998

their gender or race. A recent study of fourteen School-to-Work sites, for example, found that more than 90 percent of the young women were clustered in five traditionally female occupations.

- A 1997 review of School-to-Work initiatives across the country similarly found that "boys tended to dominate—almost to the point of exclusion—in many industrial and engineering programs."

Children continue to exhibit a preference for choosing occupations that are linked to traditional gender ideologies. Thompson and Zerbinos (1997) interviewed children from ages four through nine and discovered that over three-quarters of the boys chose stereotypically male jobs and only 20 percent chose gender-neutral jobs. Only 2.5 percent of the boys selected traditionally female jobs. Boys most often indicated that they wanted jobs such as firefighter, police officer, and athlete. Over half of the girls chose stereotypically female jobs such as nurse or teacher, but 25 percent of them chose stereotypically male jobs. It appears, then, that girls are more likely to exhibit a desire for male-oriented jobs than boys are to exhibit a desire for female-oriented jobs.

A study by the National Science Foundation reports that women make up 46 percent of the workforce but only 28 percent of jobs in high technology industries (McClain, 2001). This situation is unlikely to change in the near future since computer jobs tied in eleventh place in a list of occupations that girls age fifteen to eighteen desire. Medicine/health care, teaching, and art/music ranked on top, followed by law and business (McClain, 2001).

Latinas may be particularly disadvantaged in today's educational system. A report by the American Association of University Women Educational Foundation notes that Hispanic females have lower high-school graduation rates, are underrepresented in gifted and talented programs, and are least likely of any group of women to receive bachelor's degrees (Henry, 2001). Researchers have speculated that it is important to provide role models for these women and involve the entire family in preparing these students for higher education.

Strategies for Change

Teachers are the primary agents for implementing change in the gender stereotypes that exist in U. S. schools and universities (Wood & Lenze, 1991). The government publication *Taking the Sexism Out of Education* (1978) emphasizes the role of the teacher: "Teachers' behavior is probably the most critical factor in determining whether what happens in the classroom will encourage the development of flexibility or the retention of old stereotyping practices. One of the ways in which teachers can help to eliminate sexism is through their own modeling of nonsexist behaviors" (Cited in Koblinsky & Sugawara, 1984, p. 365; see also Cooper & Simonds, 1999).

Several authors have suggested the importance of developing teacher education programs that emphasize gender issues in the educational environment. Sadker and Sadker (1981), surveying 24 leading teacher education textbooks, report that:

- None of the texts provide future teachers with curricular resources or instructional strategies to counteract sexism in the classroom.
- Twenty-three of the 24 texts give less than 1 percent of space to sexism in education.
- One-third of the texts fail to mention sexism at all. Most guilty of this are math and science education texts.
- An average of five times as much content space is allocated to males as to females in the education texts analyzed.
- In the science methods texts, an average of seven times more space is allocated to males than to females.
- Continued stereotyping is evident in language-arts texts. For example, the Sadkers note one text that indicates girls will read boys' books, but boys will not read girls' books; the text concludes, therefore, libraries should buy two boys' books for every girls' book purchased.

Jones (1989) suggests these findings have not changed significantly and that teacher education programs need to emphasize gender issues because teachers still channel students into gender-stereotyped activities as early as the preschool level. She cites a 1986 research study by Kelly, who estimated in an analysis of gender differences in teacher–pupil interactions that teachers spend, on the average, 56 percent of their time with males and 44 percent with females. Over the length of a student's school career (about 15,000 hours), males would average 1,800 more hours with the teacher than females. When that attention is divided among 30 students, the average girl would end up with 60 fewer hours of individual attention than the average boy. Jones suggests that such a discrepancy should be taken very seriously by the teaching profession.

Maher and Rathbone (1986) and Roop (1989) suggest that recent research on women challenges long-held generalizations in the history, sociology, and psychology that are taught to future teachers and that these new research findings must be incorporated into teacher-training programs. Thus, teachers need to be trained in choosing nonsexist curriculum materials, classroom-management techniques designed to equalize classroom interaction, and collaborative-learning techniques (see also Higginbotham, 1990; Gender Gaps, 1998).

A feminist educational perspective begins with the assumption that males and females have equal abilities that need to be nurtured and challenged. Differential treatment of students is acceptable only if it is designed to maximize learning and opportunities for everyone. Wood (1989) says that a feminist perspective on teaching and learning is effective because feminism:

1. is inclusive so that topics representative of both sexes' experience and concerns are addressed
2. values diversity so that multiple ways of knowing are accepted and valued
3. values human relationships so that teaching becomes interactive rather than authoritative
4. values personal experience so that thoughtful consideration of how ideas/knowledge relate to personal experience is encouraged

5. emphasizes empowerment, not power, so that students have control over their own learning

6. seeks to create change so that learners perceive themselves agents of change. (pp. 4–5)

Such a feminist approach to education means that the teacher places an emphasis on individual learning styles, variety in teaching strategies, student–student interactions, collaborative learning, and requesting and reacting to student feedback on course content and pedagogy.

Several authors have written about curriculum changes from a feminist perspective. Gillikin (1989) and Dehler (1989) suggest using personal diaries as writing assignments; Hewitt (1988), Leach (1990), and Johnson (1988) present unique curriculum approaches to history; Hanice (1987) and Roth (1987) suggest new ways to teach art; Campbell (1991), Higginbotham (1990), Jensen and Carlin (1991), Beauchamp and Wheeler (1988), Carter and Spitzack (1989), and Peterson (1991) suggest curriculum materials and methods for speech-communication classes. Apple and Jungck (1990) suggest that areas such as math and science need to incorporate the concepts of feminist pedagogy into their curricula. Certainly, the above list is not exhaustive. It does, however, suggest that teachers who desire to find nonsexist curriculum materials can do so.

In terms of classroom interaction, teachers can promote more open interaction among students by integrating teams, lines, seating arrangements, and instructional groups. They can assign classroom tasks on a nonstereotypical basis. For example, girls can help carry chairs and boys can be class secretaries. One of the most extensive lists of behaviors for nonsexist teaching is presented by Hall and Sandler (1982). They suggest that communication behaviors such as asking female and male students questions that call for factual knowledge as well as critical thinking skills, coaching female students as well as male students, using language that does not reinforce limited views of masculine and feminine gender roles and career choices, and giving female and male students an equal amount of time to respond after asking questions, can begin to communicate the expectations that both males and females are equally competent intellectually.

In terms of math and science, teachers can favorably affect girls' preparation for math- and science-related occupations if they provide active encouragement, exposure to role models, sincere praise for high ability and good performance, explicit advice regarding the value of math and science, and explicit encouragement to both boys and girls and to their parents regarding the importance of developing their talents to the fullest and aspiring to the best jobs they can obtain (Eccles & Hoffman, 1984).

One report, *Sex Bias in College Admission Tests: Why Women Lose Out* (reported by Carmody, 1987) on girls' lower SAT scores, suggests the long-term impact that a lack of math and science background is having: a real-dollar loss for females in later life. Women get less prestigious jobs, earn less money, and have fewer leadership opportunities (Karen, 1991; Wolfe & Rosser, 1997). Male-dominated occupations are higher paying, on average, than those dominated by females (U.S. Department of Labor, 1987). For example, in 1990, only 19 of the 4,012 highest paid officers and directors of the 1,000 largest U.S. industrial and service companies were women. Of 225 selected corporations in the United States listing 9,293 names for positions as low in the corporate structure as division head, assistant vice president, and corporate secretary, only 5 percent were women (Fierman, 1990). And only 300 of the 3,000 institutions of higher education in the United States were headed by women. Most of these positions were at women's colleges or church-related institutions. Of the 450 publicly supported institutions who are members of the American Association of State Colleges and Universities, 26 were led by women (Kaplan & Tinsley, 1989).

The National Committee on Pay Equity has found that a woman has to work a full year plus a little more than three months (to April 8) to earn what a man earns in just twelve months (Stewart, 1999). In 1997, women earned a median pay of $24,973—74.1 percent of men's pay (Stewart, 1999).

The U.S. Department of Education suggests the following strategies for encouraging women and minorities to achieve in nontraditional careers involving math and science:

- The classroom walls would have posters of women and minorities in leadership roles and nontraditional careers.
- The teacher would plan ways to let students know about the contributions of women and minorities in the areas being studied.
- During the year there might be a parents' night on nontraditional careers where parents, too, could become aware of what women and minorities have done. (Hill, 1991, p. C2)

It is important to inform students about nontraditional careers for a variety of reasons. First, students need to discover which jobs they might truly enjoy and would be successful at doing, not just which jobs society determines are appropriate for them. Second, neither women nor men should be prevented from pursuing jobs that are economically rewarding if they aspire to these jobs. Third, both men and women should be permitted to balance work and personal/family goals. A person may decide that spending more time with family is more important than career achievement. Educational programs should be designed to help students seek a variety of alternatives that will produce a satisfying life for them. (We will discuss issues of equity at work more fully in Chapter 9.)

Guidance-counseling personnel can also strive to eliminate materials containing gender biases. When this is not possible, they can discuss the materials with parents and students. They can also model nonstereotyped behavior and encourage both male and female students to pursue nontraditional careers.

Sexist language can also be a problem in educational materials and educational interaction. As several researchers suggest, the generic grammatical structure (using *he* instead of *he* and *she*; see Chapter 3 for an explanation of this concept) "cannot fail to suggest to young readers that females are a substandard . . . form of being" (Burr, Dunn, & Farquhar, 1972, p. 843). Richmond and Gorham (1988), in their study of current generic-referent usage among 1,529 public school children in grades three through twelve, report that, in general, masculine generic usage is still prevalent. Webb (1986) provides pedagogical strategies for persuading students to use nonsexist language in class-related communication. Teachers should not only act as models by using nonsexist language but also use teaching strategies that encourage their students to do likewise.

Included in these sexist messages may be the implicit assumption that girls are inferior to boys. A report by the American Association for University Women describes one researcher's observation:

> It is just before dismissal time and a group of very active fourth-graders are having trouble standing calmly in line as they wait to go to their bus. Suddenly one of the boys grabs another's hat, runs to the end of the line, and involves a number of his buddies in a game of keep-away. The boy whose hat was taken leaps from his place in line, trying to intercept it from the others, who, as they toss it back and forth out of his reach, taunt him by yelling, "You woman! You're a woman!" When the teacher on bus duty notices, she tells the boys that they all have warnings for not waiting in line properly. The boys resume an orderly stance but continue to mutter names—"Woman!" "Am not." "Yes, you are."—under their breath. (Stubbs, cited in *How Schools Shortchange Girls*, AAUW, 1992, pp. 73–74)

This report goes on to note:

> Examples of name calling that imply homophobia, such as "sissy," "queer," "gay," "lesbo," are common among students at all levels of schooling. The fourth-grade boys who teased a peer by calling him a "woman" were not only giving voice to the sex-role stereotype that women are weaker than and therefore inferior to men; they were also challenging their peer's "masculinity" by ascribing feminine characteristics to him in a derogatory manner. Such attacks often prevent girls, and sometimes boys, from participating in activities and courses that are traditionally viewed as appropriate for the opposite sex.
>
> When schools ignore sexist, racist, homophobic, and violent interactions among students, they are giving tacit approval to such behaviors. Environments where students do not feel accepted are not environments where effective learning can take place. (AAUW, 1992, p. 74)

Hostile Hallways: The AAUW Survey on Sexual Harassment in America's Schools (1993) represents the first national scientific study of sexual harassment in public schools. Based on the experiences of 1,632 students in grades eight through eleven, this research found that 85 percent of girls and 76 percent of boys have experienced sexual harassment. The survey also found that although both girls and boys experience sexual harassment at alarming rates, sexual harassment takes a greater toll on girls; for example, girls who have been harassed are more afraid in school and feel less confident about themselves than boys who have been harassed. In addition, this research found that sexual harassment in school begins early; students are harassed by both boys *and* girls; and girls of all races experience more sexual harassment than do boys.

Summary

Women are marginalized from education by its content and by classroom interactional processes. As a result, the academic climate is a chilly one for female students (Hughes & Sandler, 1988; Moses, 1989; Nieves-Squires, 1990), and female faculty, administrators, and graduate students (Sandler, 1991; Sandler & Hall, 1986). In addition, women are not represented in significant numbers in many textbooks and works of literature, and females are portrayed in biased ways.

Some recent writing suggests that males too are shortchanged in the classroom. For example, Chethik (1994) suggests that boys find the educational system hostile to them:

> The tensions start early. When a 6-year-old boy enters school, he already knows the American way of maleness. He runs, jumps, throws, yells, and competes with anyone who comes along. Suddenly, however, he's told to sit quietly, listen, and wait to be called on—or else.
>
> For many boys this transition is jarring, and it's exacerbated by the fact that there are so few adult males to help them through it. Men account for just one in four teachers nation-wide, and they're virtually nonexistent in the lower grades. It's not unusual for the only grown man in an elementary school to be the gym teacher. (p. 55)

In the classroom, teachers communicate gender expectations to students. Teachers may call on male students more often than on female students. Teachers often coach male students to help them develop fuller answers. Waiting longer for male students than for female students to answer questions may communicate to female students that they are not expected to know the answer and place a burden on male students to always come up with the answer. Female students are more likely to be asked questions requiring factual answers, while male students are more often asked questions that require critical thinking or personal evaluation. Critical thinking (not just uninformed opinion) asks for a higher level of information processing than recitation of memorized facts. Teachers respond more extensively to male students' comments than to female students' comments.

Classroom interactions vary in terms of initiation, discipline, and dominance. Male students initiate more interactions with teachers than female students. Criticism of female students focuses on their lack of knowledge or skill, whereas criticism of male students focuses on disruptive behaviors. Overall, male students dominate classroom talk and space.

Sexism in the educational environment affects the self-concepts of students, their curriculum choices, and their occupational choices. In the educational environment, women generally lack self-confidence. Males and females may avoid courses thought to be the domain of the other sex. Because of these curriculum choices, women usually do not enter traditionally male-dominated fields, and men usually do not enter traditionally female-dominated fields.

Teachers are the primary agents for effecting change in the gender stereotypes that exist in American education. Thus, teachers need to be trained to be aware of and to avoid gender stereotypes in the materials they choose and in their classroom interactions.

FINDING YOUR VOICE

1. Bring three or four textbooks to class. With a classmate, rate the gender stereotypes in the textbooks using the following categories: (1) numerical differences in the portrayal

of males and females, (2) stereotyped behavior patterns and characteristics, and (3) sexist language. How would you rate the gender stereotypes found in your textbooks? Do some textbooks contain more gender stereotypes than others? Are gender stereotypes more prevalent in textbooks for some subjects than for others? What messages are being communicated by the authors of these textbooks? If you were the author of one of these textbooks, what changes would you make to avoid gender stereotypes?

2. Choose a popular fairy tale such as *Snow White, Cinderella, Jack and the Beanstalk,* or *Rapunzel.* Identify the gender stereotypes contained in the story. Rewrite the story to eliminate these stereotypes. (For example, a rich princess could save Cinderella from his wicked banker.) What gender stereotypes did the original fairy tale contain? How does your rewritten story avoid these stereotypes? Did you add any new gender stereotypes in your version? How difficult is it to write a children's story that eliminates gender stereotypes?

3. Think about the expectancies that are communicated to students in your classrooms. If you were a teacher, how would you communicate that you wanted your students to conform to traditional gender stereotypes? Have you observed any of these behaviors in classes that you have attended? How would you communicate that you wanted your students to have a more equal role in classroom interaction? Have you observed any of these behaviors in classes you have attended? How have you been affected by these teacher behaviors?

4. Choose one of your classes to analyze the communication patterns that occur. Answer the following questions:
   - Who initiates the communication contacts?
   - Who is criticized by the teacher or other members of the class? For what reasons?
   - Who is praised? Why?
   - Who dominates the classroom verbally?
   - Who dominates the classroom nonverbally?

   Analyze your answers in terms of gendered behavior. Are males praised more than females? Do males or females initiate the most communication? Who dominates the classroom? Do you think your observations are influenced by the subject matter? For example, do males tend to dominate engineering classes, while females tend to dominate communication classes? Compare your results with others in your class. What conclusions can you draw about communication patterns in the classroom? How do these communication patterns create and maintain gender stereotypes?

5. Try this simple test adapted from one developed by Myra and David Sadker (1994). Name 20 famous American women from history. Now, delete the athletes and entertainers. Are there any names left on your list? List real women, not advertising creations like Aunt Jemima or Betty Crocker. Does your list include any women of color? Expand your list to include women from other countries. Consult resources in your school or community library to construct a full list. What does the difficulty of this task say about the portrayal of women in our educational system?

FURTHER READING

Belenky, M., Clinchy, B., Goldberger, N., & Taruk, J. (1986). *Women's ways of knowing: The development of self, voice, and mind.* New York: Basic Books.

Based on interviews with 135 women, these researchers describe five ways of knowing. Based on these descriptions, a new approach to education is discussed.

Gilligan, C., Lyons, N. P., & Hanmer, T. J. (1990). *Making connections: The relational worlds of adolescent girls at Emma Willard School.* Cambridge, MA: Harvard University Press.
The essays in this volume discuss the views of young women on self, relationships, and morality. The overall theme of each essay concerns the crisis of connection in girls' lives during adolescence.

Grancisco, V. L., & Jensen, M. D. (1994). *Women's voices in our time: Statements by American leaders.* Prospect Heights, IL: Waveland.
A collection of speeches and public statements by American women, this book includes notable women in a variety of fields including the arts (Lillian Hellman, Elizabeth Taylor), politics (Barbara Jordan, Elizabeth Holtzman), journalism (Nina Totenberg), and political activism (Wilma P. Mankiller, Maggie Kuhn). It is an excellent complement to textbooks focusing primarily on men's rhetorical acts.

Thorne, B. (1994). *Gender play: Girls and boys in school.* New Brunswick, NJ: Rutgers University Press.
Thorne describes how children grow up, experience the world and each other, and "cross the gender divide." Thorne contends that children actively participate in the creation of their gender identities.

Weis, L., & Fine, M. (Eds.) (1993). *Beyond silenced voices: Class, race, and gender in United States schools.* Albany, NY: State University of New York Press.
Weis and Fine go beyond examining policies, discourse, and practices to call up the voices of young people who have been expelled from the centers of their schools and our culture to speak as interpreters of adolescent culture. These voices include Native American college students, lesbian and gay students, and other young people struggling for identities amid the radically transforming conditions of contemporary society.

8 Media

In our daily lives, most of us are continually exposed to the popular mass media. We read a newspaper or at least see the front page when we walk by sales boxes on the street. We hear music played in clothing stores at the mall, at the fitness center, in supermarkets. We go to movies, watch television, and hear our friends discuss the latest male or female sex symbol or what happened on yesterday's episode of their favorite soap opera or drama or talk show.

We are constantly "massaged," as Marshall McLuhan put it, by complex mediated messages, including messages about what it means to be a man or a woman in our culture. These messages both reflect our culture and influence our individual lives by affecting our cultural values and our images of each other. The mass media constitute an important type of communication in their own right—consuming an increasing percentage of people's time, often at the cost of face-to-face communication—and also affect the communication that occurs among people. On the one hand, the media reinforce traditional gender ideologies in numerous ways, as we will discuss throughout this chapter. On the other, the media occasionally offer more positive images such as Claire Huxtable, the wife and lawyer on *The Cosby Show*, or nurturing fathers in ads for popular products like cameras or breakfast cereals.

Both men and women have been stereotyped in all areas of the media. This stereotyping may be necessary for comprehension; that is, stereotypes have a descriptive or cognitive dimension (Seiter, 1986) that allows members of a cultural group to understand some textual aspects of *cultural artifacts* in the same way, whether the stereotypes themselves are positive or negative, true or false. Nevertheless, stereotypes tend to reduce real individual differences to generalizations about a group in ways that are potentially damaging to members of that group and their ability to communicate with others. In addition, all stereotypes have an ideological, evaluative dimension (Seiter, 1986). For example, the stereotype that women manipulate men in relationships, which shows up frequently in the media, is usually a negative stereotype used to belittle women, while the stereotype that men ought to remain stoic in the face of pain is seen sometimes as positive and sometimes as negative.

The issue of gender ideology in the media arises in three areas. The most obvious of these concerns gendered *images of men and women communicated directly by popular mass media*. We will discuss these images in detail throughout this chapter. The second area concerns *who produces the images* that you are exposed to by popular media.

Historically, men have been the decision makers in all media; therefore, the media images of men and women have usually been presented from a male point of view. For example, even such widely praised female-oriented television shows of the 1980s and early 1990s as *The Golden Girls, Kate and Allie,* and *Cagney and Lacey,* were largely the work of male producers, writers, and directors (Daviss, 1988). The third area concerns the *audience for a particular artifact or genre.* Men and women use different media artifacts and sometimes use them in different ways or construct different meanings from them. Many prime-time television shows are more heavily watched by women than by men. Men are more likely to watch televised football games or action shows.

It is important to remember that all popular media are businesses. We may be concerned with the gender ideologies carried by the media, but most of the people who control the media are not. They are concerned with making money. Most of these businesspeople do not see the promotion of social change to be part of their function. Businesspeople in the media tend to be conservative, following past money-making formulas and aiming for the largest possible audience. This is particularly true of popular media, such as commercial broadcast television that must reach a diverse audience; it often relies on lowest-common-denominator programming to appeal to an audience. Such programming reflects no one's cultural ideals accurately and may contain a confusing mix of traditional and nontraditional stereotypes even in the same show. For example, Tim, the central male character in *Home Improvement,* learned a humanizing, even feminizing, lesson each week—usually from his wife Jill—that points out and often criticizes some aspect of traditional masculine behavior. Still, the show frequently reaffirmed gender stereotypes; for example, Tim's sons fit traditional roles (teasing each other, roughhousing, getting dirty, being rude, and having problems expressing emotions), and everyone criticized Jill's cooking.

Research on gender and the media is not always up-to-date. Much of the existing research was done in the 1970s and 1980s and has not been updated. As we will discuss, more recent research has found change in some areas, but little change in others. In addition, despite the growth of interest in men's roles in the 1990s, we still know much more about female images in the media than about male images.

In the rest of this chapter, we will discuss five forms of popular media: film, television, music, cartoons/comic strips, and advertising. We will analyze media images of men and women, evaluate the effects of these images, suggest some strategies for changing them, and discuss some changes that have already occurred.

Film*

Watching a film may be a public, communal experience or a private pursuit. We go to a movie theater, rent videos, or watch movies interrupted by commercials on network television. The images of men and women presented to us in film has changed

---

*Material for this discussion is based, in part, on information gathered from Erens (1979) and Mellen (1974, 1977).

throughout the years. This section contains a brief summary of some of those changes and discusses some recent images of men and women in film as well as some of the meanings generated by those images.

A brief overview of male and female images in film follows. The representative films chosen for each decade were box-office hits, Academy Award winners, or films that have received considerable critical attention over the years.

The 1920s Through the 1970s

Rudolph Valentino exemplified the male image of the 1920s and provided a dominant cultural symbol of the period when he portrayed a character who drove women wild in *The Sheik*. In the films of the 1920s, women generally fit into four predominant stereotypes: working girl, chorus girl/vamp, and old-fashioned girl. Women throughout the country bobbed their hair and wore tight dresses in the flapper craze inspired by the movies.*

Sound came to film in the 1930s, and the characters suddenly became more real. Stars such as Clark Gable, Gary Cooper, and Cary Grant became popular. These new screen heroes were romantic and subtly macho. Women emerged in films as capable of making their own decisions. Mae West was one of the major screen stars who played a woman of security and independence, although usually portrayed in a humorous vein. The years from 1930 to 1934 witnessed less stereotyping of women in films than previously. Stars like Greta Garbo, Jean Harlow, and Marlene Dietrich portrayed characters who initiated sexual encounters, pursued men, and embodied masculine characteristics (such as aggressiveness) without being regarded as unfeminine or predatory.

In the 1940s, many films centered on three main themes dominated by men: sports, westerns, and war stories. Sports stories glorified the masculine, athletic male in such films as *Knute Rockne: All-American*, in which Ronald Reagan portrayed the boy next door who became a great football player. Westerns, starring actors like John Wayne and Henry Fonda, also helped to glamorize the rough and tough masculine image already prevalent throughout the 1920s and 1930s. Because of the war effort, Hollywood experienced a shortage of male actors in the 1940s. As a result, many so-called "women's films" were made (for example, *The Philadelphia Story*, *Mildred Pierce*, *Possessed*, and *Lady in the Dark*) and films that traditionally may have revolved around men found a new focus, as when the war picture *So Proudly We Hail* focused on the courage of nurses (Haskell, 1987). Nevertheless, the major focus of these movies was often on saving a man.

Many of the major films of the 1950s, such as *Blackboard Jungle*, *Rebel Without a Cause*, and *On the Waterfront*, depicted men as alienated, tormented heroes who, by the end of the film, were forced to conform to the norms of society. For the first time, men were portrayed as thoughtful, understanding of weaknesses (including their

---

*Material for this discussion is based, in part, on information gathered from Erens (1979) and Mellen (1974, 1977).

own), and perceptive. Yet other popular films still strongly reinforced the old ideas of manhood and masculinity, such as *High Noon* with Gary Cooper. The early 1950s brought us femme fatales, including the ultimate female film image, Marilyn Monroe.

One of the major male characters of films of the 1960s and 1970s was James Bond. In the original Bond films, he treated women as disposable sexual objects. Along with the Bond films came a series of Clint Eastwood films, and both instructed us in what was necessary for survival in a masculine world (for example, bloodshed, violence, and sexual potency). In this world, a man's survival depended on becoming a violent vigilante who could meet force with force.

The 1960s and 1970s were a confusing time for men in film, however, because as one group of films was glorifying the fantasies of violence and casual sex, another group was emphasizing the theme of male friendship. In films like *Deliverance, The Sting, M*A*S*H, All the President's Men*, and *One Flew Over the Cuckoo's Nest*, men built relationships with each other and did not need to use women to prove their masculinity. The male bonds in these pictures were forged by facing a common challenge or test, although the circumstances did still usually involve violence.

While men were forming friendships, the major women's roles of the 1960s and 1970s (such as Elizabeth Taylor in *Who's Afraid of Virginia Woolf*, Barbra Streisand in *Funny Girl*, Jane Fonda in *Klute*, or Ellen Burstyn in *Alice Doesn't Live Here Anymore*) were, for the most part, jilted wives or mistresses, emotional cripples, drunks or prostitutes.

The 1980s and 1990s

The most interesting trend in the images of men and women in films since 1980 is that there seems to be no central trend. Rather, a variety of treatments have been given to both men and women, with some strong negative stereotypes and some positive new images. This lack of a clear-cut trend may reflect a changing culture. One of the most prevalent roles for males in films of this period marks a return to the violent, macho image as seen in action movies starring Sylvester Stallone, Chuck Norris, Steven Seagal, Jean-Claude Van Damme, and Arnold Schwarzenegger. Sometimes the macho male has a romantic side, but more often these characters are just pumped-up, one-dimensional figures moving from one violent episode to another.

Contrasting roles for men are also seen in films of this period. The intellectual but troubled male, exemplified by Woody Allen, continues to be a mainstream staple. In *A Few Good Men* and *Unforgiven*, traditional masculine ideas about duty, honor, and moral behavior are questioned. Several films of the 1980s and 1990s further reflect changing roles for men through plots in which men take on feminine roles (for example, *Mr. Mom, Tootsie*, and *Mrs. Doubtfire*). *Philadelphia* sensitively dealt with issues of gay male sexuality and AIDS, while part of the charm of the central character in *Forrest Gump* was his inability to understand the implications of the traditional masculine roles he was expected to assume.

Women's roles are even more varied than men's. Maslin (1988a) criticizes what she calls the new sexism in films, pointing to two specific characteristics. First, she cites films in which women are portrayed as the "bad guys" who harm men (for example, in *Fatal Attraction* and *Misery*). Second, she points out the return of extended female nudity and "kittenish" roles. These two characteristics are brought together in male-oriented fantasies such as *Basic Instinct, Body of Evidence,* and *Species,* in which the female leads are both sex objects and direct threats to the male leads.

Other films present quite different images of women. *The Color Purple* shows women who are strong and united in a world of male abuse. *Outrageous Fortune* and *Thelma and Louise* twist the traditional buddy movie format by making the buddies female. Sigourney Weaver in *Aliens* presents a strong, competent female as the lead character in a science fiction movie for the first time. *Driving Miss Daisy* offers a moving view of a strong older woman. Linda Hamilton's portrayal of Sarah Connor in *The Terminator* movies provides an example of a powerful, capable action role for women.

Teen-oriented films such as *Sixteen Candles* and *Pretty in Pink* are rarities in that they attempt to focus on being a teenager from a female perspective. *Heathers* both parodies and works within this genre, again from a female-centered perspective. Movies such as *The Handmaid's Tale* and *V. I. Warshawski* attempt, if with less success, to bring strong feminist stories and roles from popular fiction to the movies. Non-stereotypic views of lesbians were provided in films such as *Personal Best, Lianna, Desert Hearts, Go Fish, Boys on the Side,* and the character played by Cher in *Silkwood*.

The late 1980s were also marked for the widespread presence of the female creator in the role of writer, producer, or director (Insdorf, 1988). One such figure is Susan Seidelman, who directed *Desperately Seeking Susan*. Barbra Streisand, who directed and/or produced movies such as *Yentl, Nuts,* and *Prince of Tides,* remains the most prominent mainstream female creator. Penelope Spheeris moved into mainstream directing with *Wayne's World* after years of making underground and documentary movies. The work of less mainstream female writers and directors in movies like *Heartland, My American Cousin, Birch Interval, Wildrose, Working Girls,* and *The Piano* is more successful at suggesting realistic roles for women or showing how real-life women live.

Although progress has been made, in 1999 only 4 percent of major motion pictures were directed by women. No woman has won an Oscar for directing, and only 3 percent of the acting awards have ever been presented to people of color ("Help the Guerrilla Girls," 2001).

Television

Most adults and children watch hours of television a day and are exposed to specific shows over and over. Children sometimes watch *Barney* daily and the *X-Men* every Saturday morning; adults may view *Friends, NYPD Blue,* or *ER* every week. Due to television's important role in our culture, the U.S. Commission on Civil Rights (1979) suggests that people who are visible on television are considered worthy of attention, and people ignored by television are invisible. Historically, females have been less visible than males in television programming. Perhaps even more important, when females are made visible, they have often been portrayed in stereotypical roles. In this section, we will discuss the past images of males and females in both children's and adult programming and examine some recent changes in these images.

Children's Programming

Many elementary-school students spend more time watching television than they do sitting in a classroom (Brooks-Gunn & Matthews, 1979). For the length of time that children watch television, the image they receive of males and females is out of the hands of parents or teachers and in the hands of scriptwriters and advertising agencies. Children's television has stereotyped males and females in three main ways. First, the ratio of males to females is greatly unequal—male roles may exceed female roles two to one (Durkin & Nugent, 1998; Sternglanz & Serbin, 1974). Second, behavior differentiates the sexes—males may be portrayed as aggressive and constructive (for example, shooting people or building and planning) and females may be portrayed as deferent, waiting to be helped or saved by men. Third, the communication patterns of males and females differ—males are generally more dominant or aggressive while females are more likely to be shown as caretakers and nurturers.

Cartoons ranging from *The Smurfs* to *Teenage Mutant Ninja Turtles* exemplify these problems (Pollitt, 1991). All of the Smurfs are male except for Smurfette and Grandmother Smurf, who only appears occasionally. The sole lead female character on *Ninja Turtles* may have an active role as a reporter but she is always getting herself stuck in situations from which the Turtles must rescue her.

In children's educational programs, even *Sesame Street* shows unbalanced representation. Although the human characters are nearly evenly divided between males and females, the Muppets (perhaps the most popular characters on the show) are predominantly male, including the best known ones such as Bert and Ernie, Big Bird, and the Cookie Monster (Hallingby, 1988). In the early 1990s the major networks refused to broadcast a series based on the successful *Babysitters Club* books (later shown on HBO), arguing that girls will watch shows that feature boys but boys will not watch shows featuring girls. And, of course, that big purple dinosaur who presents relatively positive gender images for children is male.

Finally, in an analysis of language in Saturday morning children's programs, McCorkle (1982) finds that the main character who appears most often (the white male adult) also speaks most often. Males speak more often than females, and adults speak more often than children. Main characters (primarily male) are twice as likely to be defensive as supportive and, when not giving an opinion, are usually challenging, sarcastic, belittling, blaming or personally attacking others. Female characters are more supportive as a group than are male characters.

Children appear to be aware of these discrepancies even at an early age. Children ranging in age from four to nine report that there are more boy than girl characters in children's cartoons and that boys talk more (Thompson & Zerbinos, 1997), a finding that is confirmed by a content analysis of cartoons. Boys are also more likely to describe girl characters in relationship to boys (e.g., girls "follow what boys say," are "not as adventurous," and are "left out of play"). In addition, children are less likely to describe job-related behaviors for girls, perhaps because male cartoon characters are more likely to have a job while female characters are usually cast in the role of caregiver.

Barner (1999) examined gender in children's educational programming and found that programs targeted toward young children present more traditional gender ideologies than programs for teenagers. This result, however, is mainly because male characters are less stereotyped in teen programs while female characters remain more stereotyped across all programs. Most child-oriented programs feature a single male character (such as a boy of school age), and the plot revolves around his experiences. Teen-oriented programs are more likely to have ensemble casts of high-school students and deal with relationship problems.

Adult Programming

In adult prime-time television, traditional gender ideologies have often been perpetuated in the same way as in children's programming. In the past, males outnumbered females, gender stereotypes were depicted, and stereotyped female–male relationships were presented. We will examine each of these aspects briefly and discuss some recent changes.

CONSIDER THIS!
Why Girls Don't Like Computer Games

As the androgynous Rookie One, you choose a gender, select a voice and physique to match, and head out on a pilot training run to Beggar's Canyon. "Stay tight, follow our lead, and steer clear of the walls," the captain—his sex never changes—commands as you steer your T-16 skyhopper to the triumphant strains of *Star Wars*.

Master the basics and the action builds. Soon you'll be taking out a Star Destroyer, blowing away Imperial walkers, and blasting through a Rebel base overtaken by stormtroopers. What more could a girl want? The computer game industry doesn't care to know.

In giving the players the option of being male or female, LucasArts, manufacturer of the top-selling "Rebel Assault," has defied the generally accepted limits of accommodating girls in the male-dominated field of computer games. "As far as targeting games to girls, we don't do that," Camela Boswell, spokesperson for LucasArts says. "The primary gaming audience is male". . . .

On the theory that "girls will play boys' games, but boys won't play girls' games," software game manufacturers have long pitched their wares almost exclusively to boys. Lately, however, a handful of companies have begun to challenge that thinking.

Among the renegades, computer giant Sega has launched a "girls task force," and a top executive at Viacom New Media is calling for more gender-neutral titles. Sanctuary Woods is actively experimenting in the girls' game market, and Mindplay, author of the "Ace" series, is paying attention not just to game structure but also to the balance between male and female figures.

"It's only recently that companies have discovered the human race is divided into two genders and there might be a market in the second one," says Jo Sanders [director of a gender equity program at the Center for Advanced Study in Education at the City University of New York Graduate Center]. "We're just beginning to see an effort to develop software for girls."

Morse, 1995

Domestic comedies are a particularly popular form of television series shown during primetime. These shows range from 1950s-era shows like *Father Knows Best* that portray traditional images of women as housewives and men as breadwinners and authority figures to *Grace Under Fire*, in which a single mother worked in an oil refinery, and *Will and Grace*, featuring a heterosexual woman living with a single gay man. Given the new possibilities for both men and women in contemporary society in terms of parental expectations and career opportunities, we would expect that domestic comedies on television would reflect these changes. Nevertheless, an examination of television shows from the 1950s to the 1990s reveals that the traditional husband-wife relationship continues to be portrayed (Olson & Douglas, 1997). Although spouses in more contemporary domestic comedies have more similar roles (for example, both parents work outside the home), they do not display more equality or less dominance than was portrayed in earlier shows.

Some of the stereotypical relationships between men and women that were characteristic of television programs in the past have changed in recent programming. Such popular shows of the 1980s as *The Cosby Show, Cagney and Lacey, St. Elsewhere* and *Kate and Allie* portrayed both male and female characters in roles that overcame traditional gender stereotypes. For example, in one episode of *The Cosby Show*, Dr. Cliff Huxtable screened prospective dates for his teenage daughter by asking them if they could cook and if they would support their wife's career choice. More recent shows as *Chicago Hope, My So-Called Life*, and *Buffy the Vampire Slayer*, continued this trend toward overcoming stereotypes.

Other shows also indicate some positive changes in the portrayal of women. The 1980s saw the arrival of shows that focused on groups of women or individual women with men as secondary characters. Such shows as *Golden Girls, Designing Women*, and *Murder She Wrote* helped to redress the numerical imbalance on television and provided a chance to show images of women without male partners and in relationships with other women. *L.A. Law* showed strong male and female professionals working together. While appealing to some traditional elements of the romance genre, *Beauty and the Beast* provided roles that broke traditional stereotypes. Shows such as *Northern Exposure* and *Picket Fences* examined and questioned traditional gender stereotypes and showed characters exploring the changing nature of relationships. The continuing series of *Star Trek* spinoffs feature varied male and female roles with strong women and sensitive men working together in new types of relationships. That is true especially of *Star Trek: Voyager*, which features a female starship commander in the lead role.

Roseanne and *Grace Under Fire* examined the lives of working-class women and raised questions about issues important to women such as spousal abuse. The central character of Lilly on *I'll Fly Away* provided strong, well-developed portrayal of an African American woman. And one of the most nontraditional portrayals of motherhood on television is certainly featured on *Malcolm in the Middle*.

Capsuto (2000) notes that gay male and lesbian characters were more visible on network television during the 1990s. Capsuto credits the soap opera *One Life to Live* with breaking barriers by featuring an ongoing, sensitive, and credible story about a gay male youth from 1992–1993. He notes that the first openly gay African American character with a regular role on a television show occurred in 1993 on a short-lived situation comedy called *Cutters*. It took until 1996 for a successful, strong, gay male character to have a regular role on *Spin City*. Some of the most popular network television shows during the early 1990s featured gay or bisexual women (for example, *L.A. Law, Roseanne, Friends, ER*, and *Mad About You*). Nevertheless, these shows were either mostly off the air by the end of the 1990s or the lesbian characters had disappeared from them. Of course, the character Ellen Morgan came out in April 1997 on the series *Ellen* and television finally had a show with a lead character who was openly gay.

The elderly are particularly invisible on television even though the population in the United States is graying. An examination of 1,228 adult characters on 100 primetime shows found that less than 3 percent of the characters were over the age of sixty-five and that the prominence of older male characters actually decreased since the 1970s (Robinson & Skill, 1995). During the same time period, the number of female characters between the ages of fifty and sixty-four increased slightly (from 8% to 12%). Nevertheless, only 4.4 percent of the female characters were over sixty-five. The vast majority of television characters, 79 percent of males and 84 percent of females, are between the ages of twenty and forty-nine.

There is increasing diversity in some areas of television, however. A study by the Center for Media and Public Affairs found that the percentage of women and minority correspondents on the nightly news has doubled since 1990 ("Breaking the airwaves," 2000). Eighteen percent of correspondents on one network were people of color, while women made up 32 percent of correspondents on another. Nevertheless, the study found that 86 percent of all news stories are still reported by whites and 76 percent are reported by men.

Music

Even if you are not particularly interested in popular music, you are bound to be exposed to it regularly. Students who monitor their total exposure to popular music typically find that they hear some sort of music during half or more of their waking hours. The combined elements of frequent exposure, repetition, heavy interest among adolescents, and the sociocultural power of music itself make popular music a potentially strong influence on our gender identities.

While the literature on gender ideology in film and television examines the images of both women and men, the literature on popular music focuses primarily on women. Since 1955, the predominant form of popular music has been rock and closely related genres. As a musical form, rock has been dominated by males and usually shows a strongly stereotypical masculine perspective. As several researchers have pointed out, rock songs are written in the first person and, therefore, tell us about the experience of the singer (Cooper, 1985; Endres, 1984). Since male rock performers clearly outnumber females, the gender stereotypes in rock music have largely been defined by males. Consequently the views about women expressed in rock music are the source of considerable concern.

The research literature on female images in rock music and other popular music forms reveals mainly negative stereotypes of women. According to one study, this literature reveals three recurring images of women in popular songs: the *ideal woman/madonna/saint;* the evil or fickle *witch/sinner/whore;* and the *victim* (Butruille & Taylor, 1987). In general, role portrayals are highly stereotypical: women are wives, sweethearts, mothers, or wicked witches. These stereotypical images of females can be found in all areas of popular music, including pop, country, and rock. In country music, Saucier (1986) found women portrayed as stereotypic housewives, mothers, or lovers.

There are some signs of change. Endres (1984) reports that by 1980, male figures were less likely to be stereotypically active and female figures less passive. Cooper (1985) says that eight of eleven female stereotypes improved significantly between 1946 and 1976, although 96 percent of all songs contained at least one negative stereotype. Croyle (1987) reports that although female roles are still traditional, they exhibit more power in relationships.

Many of the problems with negative stereotyping of women stem from the fact that women have been underrepresented in the recording industry and have functioned in only limited roles in rock music. Before 1975 most women working in rock music functioned in a traditional role. These female performers usually fell into the singer–songwriter genre or the so-called *girl group* genre, either playing soft rock or fronting for a male-led group or a male writer/producer team. The status of women in rock music prior to 1980 can be seen statistically in Denisoff and Bridge's (1982) demographic study of popular music artists between 1970 and 1979, in which they report that 10 of 268 acts in the rock category of their sample were women or had female group members. Traditionally, few if any women consistently worked in the hard-rock areas of popular music, wrote their own material, led their own bands, or played instruments. Thus, with a few exceptions, female artists had a basically second-class status in rock music, especially hard-rock music, in the 1950s, 1960s, and 1970s.

This situation started to change in the mid-1970s in two very different ways. The first of these is the complete withdrawal of some female artists and audience members from the mainstream to perform and listen to what is sometimes called *women's music.* Women's music at its most extreme is music by and for women, produced and distributed by female-operated companies like Redwood Records and Olivia Records. Stylistically, it tends to be acoustic, folk-based music with pleasant melodies that stress the words. Frequently this music is didactic and feminist with an emphasis on sisterhood, explicitly lesbian themes and is sometimes either directly or indirectly anti-male. Some performers include Holly Near, Cris Williamson, Meg Christian, and Alix Dobkin.

Another group of female artists is also sometimes identified with women's music but is nearer to the mainstream in some ways, recording for mainstream record companies and having a mixed-sex audience. Their music is more varied and the themes are less didactic, more particular with less generalizing, more likely to use humor and to talk about the particular texture of their own lives, especially their lives as women. The work of these women pictures a mixed as opposed to idealized world. Such artists include Suzanne Vega, Tracy Chapman, and Christine Lavin.

The second major response of female performers to the limited traditional role for women in rock music was the emergence in the mid-1970s of women performing rock and hard-rock music. This trend was marked by the emergence of performers like Heart, led by the Wilson sisters, and Fleetwood Mac, featuring Stevie Nicks and Christine McVie, artists such as Patti Smith and Chrissie Hynde of the Pretenders, and more recently by mainstream artists such as Sheryl Crow, Melissa Etheridge, and Courtney Love of Hole. Over the last decade, the number of female rock performers has gradually increased to the point where they no longer seem to be an anomaly.

Stewart (1989a), in discussing the emergence of older female rock artists like Smith, Hynde, Marianne Faithfull, and Tina Turner, says that the work of these female artists (as well as artists such as the Go-Go's, Joan Jett, and the Bangles) represents a new, significant communicative role that breaks traditional stereotypes. The biting, aggressive, emotionally intense and complex, if often unpleasant, music they are now making represents a declaration of independence from the limited, stereotyped art that women were previously expected to produce. Further, Stewart suggests a pattern to this new communicative role: the work is characterized by lyrical and musical rawness, an emotional depth and complexity, by anger, bitterness, and irony, and by a viewpoint that tends to link power, love, and sex. These artists have a control over the final product similar to that held by male artists because, like major male artists, these women often write or choose their own material, play instruments, rather than front bands, and sometimes produce their own records. For these women, rock music is a source of empowerment that frees them from past stereotypes and limitations. Stewart goes on to present a model for the way in which the works of these female hard-rock artists function as declarations of independence empowering themselves and their audiences to enter into new and deeper experiential territory. These declarations of independence fall into two distinct categories: (1) direct, even anthemic, declarations of independence and (2) indirect declarations.

Direct declarations function in one of three forms: (1) by making statements within the context of interpersonal relationships (for example, in "Sweetheart," Faithfull insists that she's not changing even for her lover), (2) by making declarations of a more general, often philosophical nature (for example, Robin Lane avows that she will not lead an "imitation life"), and (3) by making statements stressing the importance and primacy of the artist's personal experience (in "Gloria," Smith tells us that Jesus died for somebody else's sins because hers belong to her). The indirect declarations function in four different ways: (1) in terms of the music itself (just hearing a female voice in this musical context represents a new communicative role), (2) in terms of the nature of the rough performance with the emphasis on emotional impact rather than prettiness or technique, (3) in terms of transformations of previously recorded male-associated material often implicitly challenging traditional gender expectations (for example, Hynde reverses the gender stereotype in the Kinks' "Stop Your Sobbing" when the female singer tells a male that she could love him if he would just stop crying); and (4) in terms of the unexpected and untraditional, as well as frequently extreme, violent, and obsessive images, subjects, and language.

Clearly, then, despite the many recordings of female artists that still function within traditional roles, many recordings exhibit parts or all of a general pattern for a new role for female artists. This new role, as well as the existence of women's music, suggests that some aspects of popular music may be moving in a less stereotypic direction.

Male roles in rock music also are often stereotyped. One study found that males were generally depicted by female rock music performers as romantic partners who were either idealized as the perfect lover or portrayed as unfaithful or abusive (Stewart, 1989b). Males in more realistic roles such as friends, co-workers, successful breadwinners, or relatives were rare. Similar results have been found for male roles in country music (Saucier, 1989), reggae (Mulvaney, 1989), and images of African American men in songs by African American women (Garner, 1989).

Comic Strips and Political Cartoons

Comic strips and political cartoons are widely read in the United States. As a cultural form, comics reduce the complexities of contemporary life to stock figures and situations that produce humor, often enabling us to better understand their origins. In this sense almost all figures in the comics are stereotypes, although sometimes very sophisticated stereotypes: contemporary artists like Garry Trudeau, *Doonesbury;* Cathy Guisewite, *Cathy;* and *Boondocks,* by Aaron McGruder, self-consciously play on and twist those stereotypes for the purposes of social commentary.

Gender stereotypes, however, begin with the disproportionate number of male versus female characters in the comics. Different studies have found different ratios, but all studies have found more male figures than female figures. The numbers vary from a study that finds a 2:1 male-to-female ratio in minor figures and a nearly 6:1 ratio for major figures (Chavez, 1985) to a study reporting a 3.6:1 ratio of male leading or title figures to female figures (Thaler, 1987). In another study of family-oriented strips, male visibility is about 15 percent higher than female presence (Brabant & Mooney, 1986). Thus, the conclusion likely to be drawn by a regular comics reader is that the male experience is more important than the female experience. A weekly publication that reprints the daily strips for a large number of syndicated comics contains almost a four-to-one ratio of male-titled strips to female-titled strips, with many of the female-titled strips—such as *Blondie, Agatha Crumm*, and *Mary Worth*—containing some of the most traditional feminine stereotypes in the comics (*Strips*, January 10, 1993).

Content analyses of gender messages in the comics have revealed similar negative stereotyping of both sexes (Mooney & Brabant, 1987; Thaler, 1987). Women are usually presented doing housework and generally serving males. When women do work outside the home, their occupations are generally stereotypical: women are nurses but men are doctors. In some of the newer comic strips in which the female character works outside the home, however, such as *Sally Forth* and *For Better or for Worse* the double burden of the working woman is presented.

Men also suffer from negative stereotyping. They are often dominated by their bosses, friends, family, and circumstances (Thaler, 1987). In general, men are stereotyped as unwilling or unable to share housework or child care, and are defined by traditional masculine activities such as working, playing or watching sports, eating or drinking to excess, or fighting criminals (Mooney & Brabant, 1987). For example, Hi in *Hi and Lois* is often depicted as unwilling to take on or as incompetent at domestic chores since Lois has gone to work.

An important quality of comics is the visual aspect. Comics are a complex combination of visual and verbal elements. According to Turner (cited in Bailey, 1986), one way to look at how men and women are portrayed in the comics is to look at how they are drawn. Blondie is a stereotypical full-figured female while the contemporary Cathy is drawn without any shape, or with a shape that reflects not her outward appearance but her subjective self-perception. Sgt. Snorkel's fatness and Prince Valiant's traditional masculine good looks similarly serve to restrict men. In this way, the visual characteristics in comics often contribute more to stereotypical gender portrayals than the verbal elements.

Political cartoons present even more limited portrayals than most comic strips. Most figures in political cartoons are men, in part because many world and national leaders are men but also because feminine concerns rarely show up in political cartoons. When women do appear they usually represent victims or dupes or female-stereotyped occupations. Judges, lawyers, labor union members, and general figures representing the "average person" are habitually presented as male. For example, a cartoon that shows Washington lawyers celebrating a Supreme Court decision pictures all 12 of the lawyers as men (*Political Pix*, June 27, 1988). Sometimes the cartoons carry the stereotypes so far that the cartoon figures are not just unrepresentative but actually untrue. A cartoon of Governor Michael Dukakis during the 1988 presidential election showed his campaign advisors as men when, in fact, his campaign manager was a woman (*Political Pix*, May 23, 1988).

An additional perspective is the production approach. Very few comic strips are produced or drawn by women. Cathy Guisewite's *Cathy*, Lynn Johnston's *For Better or for Worse*, and Nicole Hollander's *Sylvia* are major exceptions. Men and the masculine perspective continue to dominate despite the recent emergence of female-oriented strips. Even most of the female-oriented strips—such as *Sally Forth*, *Mary Worth*, *Annie*, and *Apt. 3-G*—are written and drawn by men.

Cartoons and comic strips reflect negative ideologies not only of gender but also of racial and ethnic minorities and older people. In recent years, however, some changes have been made by cartoonists to reflect societal changes. Lois in *Hi and Lois* went from being a full-time mother and homemaker to working outside the home part-time. Miss Buxley has been given less revealing clothing in *Beetle Bailey* and strips featuring her are more likely to stress the General's sexism than her body. Blondie has developed a career outside the home, although her job as caterer more often provides a focus for jokes about Dagwood's eating than commentary on Blondie's independence. More important, there are now at least a few strips such as *Cathy* and *For Better and For Worse* that are produced by women and present life from a female perspective. In addition, comic strips such as *Doonesbury*, *Sally Forth*, and *Cathy* regularly focus on the trials and tribulations of both career women and men. Three recent strips provide frequent gender commentary: *Safe Havens* (developed by Bill Holbrook) is set in a day-care center with a racially and sexually mixed group of children, and run by women; *On the Fast Track* (also by Holbrook) centers on the female half of a couple who work for the same large company with a racially and sexually mixed workforce; and *Baby Blues* explores the challenges of parenthood for both partners. Hopefully, comic strips like these will be successful in turning the public's attention away from the traditional gender stereotyping of comic strips such as *Bringing Up Father, Snuffy Smith*, and *The Lockhorns.*

Advertisements

We are bombarded by advertisements every day in magazines, on television, on billboards, inside buses, trains, and subways, and on the radio. The gender ideology communicated in these advertisements can affect our views of appropriate behavior for each sex. The possible negative effects of advertising are multiplied by two important factors: (1) advertisements are repeated over and over, so exposure levels are higher than for any other medium, and (2) since advertisements are carefully crafted persuasive pieces designed to sell products and attitudes, so they may sell the images of men and women contained in them more powerfully than other media. In this section, we will examine advertisements in three popular media: magazines, television, and radio.

Magazine Advertising

Generally, advertisements in magazines have promoted a limited portrayal of women by communicating that: (1) a woman's place is in the home (women are frequently pictured in a domestic setting or as users of domestic products); (2) women do not make important decisions or do important things; (3) women are dependent on men and are isolated from other women; and (4) men regard women as sex objects (communicated in their use as sex objects in advertising aimed at men as well as in advertising for appearance-enhancing and other products aimed at women) (Bonelli, 1989; Kilbourne, 1990). While there may have been some recent changes in the degree of such stereotyping, a quick flip through any women's magazine suggests that much of this stereotyping still exists. And minority representation is almost nonexistent. In fact, an examination of a recent issue of a major women's fashion magazine showed 153 pages of ads with no pictures of people of color.

After examining 375 advertisements from the 1950s through the 1990s in two women's magazines, one with a "domestic" focus and one with a beauty and fashion focus, Paff and Lakner (1997) found that traditional portrayals of women persist. Almost all of the women in the ads were seen as interested in their physical appearance through actions such as applying their makeup, fixing their hair, or dressing. The women were seen in "decorative roles" with no particular function in the ad except to be attractive. Dependency was demonstrated through various poses such as reclining on the floor, leaning on men, or gazing at men. Very few women were shown in more active roles such as achievement or aggression except for women chasing children, carrying groceries, or working out. The primary difference over time that these researchers found was that the dress of women in contemporary ads has become more masculine. Women are still primarily portrayed in passive, appearance-oriented roles.

Men have been increasingly used as sex objects in ads targeted toward women. Advertisers seem to believe that women, as they achieve more equality and higher buying power, will be attracted to ads that use men as sex objects. An interesting trend shows a handsome, extremely muscular, frequently shirtless man tenderly caring for a child (Jordan, 1987).

Current ads still suggest traditional gender ideologies even when they claim to be breaking free of stereotypes. Remember the diet cola ad with the shirtless construction worker being watched by a group of female office workers? Or the magazine ad promising women who are busy juggling conflicting responsibilities as mothers, wives, and employees that their problems will be solved if they buy a cellular phone? Ads for a particular brand of exercise treadmill show a model that runs at up to six miles per hour in magazines targeted to women; in a magazine with a large male readership, the same company advertises a treadmill that runs up to 10 miles per hour.

Why is it important to consider the gender ideologies portrayed in magazine advertising? Research has demonstrated that people are influenced by these images. For example, high school students who view advertisements with stereotypical images of women were more likely to transfer these perceptions to a "neutral" photograph (Lafky et al., 1996). Researchers showed pictures of women working with household cleaning products and engaged in preparing food, child care, and teaching young children to high school students. Although there is nothing negative per se about these activities, they all focus on the home and what has traditionally been designated as "women's work." Another group of students saw advertisements portraying women as physicians, engineers, and in outdoor clothing and business suits. After viewing these images, the groups then looked at neutral photographs that portrayed a woman dressed casually who was not engaged in any obvious task. When asked to evaluate this woman, students who had previously seen the stereotyped images were more likely to identify the woman as someone who performs most of the household chores such as cooking all the meals and cleaning for her family, who would get permission from her husband before getting involved in volunteer work, and who spends part of every afternoon watching soap operas on television. Thus, even brief exposure to a limited role portrayal may influence a person's subsequent perceptions.

Television and Radio Advertising

The research on television and radio advertising finds traditional gender ideologies similar to those in magazine advertising. Studies consistently find male voice-overs approximately 90 percent of the time (Lont, 1988). Similarly, single-announcer radio ads are predominantly male (Melton & Fowler, 1987). Females are frequently presented as the users of products on both television and radio. These two trends work together to stereotype men as authorities and women as consumers who need to be told what to use by male authorities.

Interestingly, the images of women depicted in television commercials seem to have changed more since the 1950s than the images of men. Researchers (Allan & Coltrane, 1996) have found a shift in the portrayal of women in which they are more likely to be pictured in job-related activities and in more diverse occupations (such as professional jobs, sports or business owners) than previously. Working women are seen being engaged in nonstereotypical behaviors such as giving orders and leading meetings. The image of men has changed little since the 1950s, however. Although there is a slight increase in the portrayal of men as parents and spouses in commercials, there is a decrease in images of men doing housework. Thus, there seems to be some progress for women in more complex ways, but little change in male characters in television advertising.

Images of men and women may differ on television during the course of a week. Craig (1992) content analyzed 2,209 network television commercials and found that advertising during the week continues to portray men in stereotypical roles of authority and dominance while commercials shown on the weekend emphasize escape from the home and family. Daytime ads targeted toward homemakers emphasize products identified with home and family (such as cooking, cleaning, and child care) and rarely include men except in positions of authority, such as celebrity spokesman or professional. Commercials on the weekend, presumably targeted toward men, are more likely to exclude images of women (or portray them in roles subservient to men, such as secretaries or hotel receptionists) and stress physical aggressiveness, competitiveness, and independence as important values for men. Primetime commercials portrayed a much more complex world in which women were seen in positions of authority and in settings away from the home, and men were portrayed as a parent or spouse.

Lin (1998) examined the television commercials shown on major television networks during primetime (8–11 p.m.) for a week and found 505 individual commercials. In examining the characters portrayed in these commercials, Lin found that male characters were typically older than female characters, female models were more likely to be shown as fit and males were more likely to be "full figured" or muscular. Female characters were also more likely to be more physically attractive and shown in a state of undress more often than males. Both genders, however, engaged in the same amount of flirting. In addition to gender portrayal, this study also indicates the relative lack of people of color in advertising. Lin found that 89 percent of the characters were Caucasian, while 10 percent were African American and only 0.2 percent were either Hispanic, Asian, or Native American.

Children's television commercials offer no better models than commercials targeted toward adults. Browne (1998) videotaped Saturday morning cartoon programming in both the United States and Australia and analyzed 298 different commercials. She found relatively little change from previous research. The commercials contained more male than female figures, with the male-to-female ratio increasing with age. In other words, while commercials with elementary school children in them had close to the same percentage of males and females (56% boys, 43% girls), commercials with teenagers showed 70 percent males and only 28 percent females. Female voice-overs were used in less than 16 percent of the commercials, and boys were more likely to be shown demonstrating or explaining a product to girls. Girls were never shown using a product designed for boys (such as a truck), nor were any boys shown with a product targeted toward girls.

Implications and Consequences of Media Images

If there were no effects of the media images portrayed, there would be little need for concern. However, research demonstrates that images presented in the media reflect and reinforce traditional gender ideologies. We use research on the effects of television images as an example, because more research has been conducted on the effects of television than on any other media, and this research suggests that most of it can be generalized to other media.

Television promotes rigid gender ideologies. Children of both sexes identify more with same-sex television models than with other-sex models (Sprafkin & Liebert, 1978). Children who frequently watch television tend to accept more gender stereotypes than children who seldom watch television (Frueh & McGhee, 1975). Children use television characters as models for adult roles. They may also model their problem-solving behavior on the behavior of their favorite television characters (Roloff & Greenberg, 1979).

Several researchers have investigated the effects of viewing programs with non-traditional gender content. McArthur and Eisen (1976) report that after viewing televised counterstereotypical role portrayals, preschoolers recall and imitate more of the activities of an adult same-sex model than an other-sex model, even when the same-sex model displayed sex-inappropriate behavior. Eisenstock (1984) notes similar results with preadolescent boys and girls in an examination of the effects of television in promoting nonsexist role learning among children with different gender orientations. The results of this study suggest that androgynous and feminine children identify with nontraditional televised models more often than masculine children. Commercials in which females are depicted in nontraditional roles elicit fewer traditional beliefs about females (Atkin & Miller, 1975).

As we have seen, adult television programming also communicates gender ideologies (Tan, 1982). The more that people watch television, the more they tend to believe in social stereotypes. Gender ideologies are learned more easily by people who watch television a significant portion of time than by those who do not (McGhee & Frueh, 1980). Therefore, the influence of television on the formation and perpetuation of gender ideologies suggests that television can play a similarly influential role in changing gender portrayals.

The major focus of the research on gender ideologies on television has been on the negative effects of these stereotypes on females. However, the effects are no doubt as serious for males. The stereotyped macho, unemotional male portrayed in the media perpetuates gender ideologies such as that males must be in charge and in control of their emotions. As we have seen in previous chapters, gender ideologies resulting from the portrayal of traditional roles affects the communication behavior of men and women.

Strategies for Change

The major roadblock to changing media images of men and women is that much of the media is controlled by people unwilling to change the stereotypes. For example, the limited images of women in films is attributable, in part, to the makeup of the film industry itself. Filmmaker Barbara Evans summarizes the problem:

> The established film industry presents serious problems for a woman filmmaker. Even women directors find the films they make not wholly within their control, being dependent, as they are, on a large crew composed mainly of men, who are still seen as the chief bearers of technical knowledge and skills. And women's voices are far too often stifled by those who control the purse-strings. Unfortunately for the cause of women's self-expression, these are usually men. (*Media Report to Women*, 1983, p. 5)

Change is occurring. For example, advertisements more often portray women in out-of-the-home roles. Television programs are featuring male and female characters in more equal roles.

But what can you, as an individual, do to overcome some of the gender ideologies that are portrayed in the media? Perhaps the simplest answer is that you can expose yourself to a variety of media sources. Watch some of the television shows that feature men and women in a variety of nonstereotyped roles; seek out films that include strong characters, both female and male; listen to the music of some of the newer female rock stars rather than only listening to well-established male groups. You might also write letters to companies whose product advertising tries to make women feel guilty for having kitchens that are less than spotless or uses men as decorative sex objects. If men and women truly want the media images of males and females to change, perhaps the media will begin to depict people in their complex, ever-changing roles instead of in terms of outdated gender ideologies.

Summary

In this chapter, we have analyzed gender images communicated through the media of film, television, radio, music, cartoons/comic strips, and advertising. The gender images portrayed in the media are often stereotypical. Recently, some of these media images have begun to change in response to changing gender roles in society. Since the communication of gender ideology in the media serves to perpetuate stereotypes in society, we should work to support productive changes in media portrayal of both men and women.

FINDING YOUR VOICE

1. Watch an hour of children's educational programming on public television such as *Sesame Street, Mister Roger's Neighborhood* or *Barney and Friends*. In addition, watch an hour of children's entertainment programming such as *The X-Men, The Little Mermaid, The Teenage Mutant Ninja Turtles*, or *Tiny Toons*. Compare and contrast the gender stereotypes portrayed in these programs. What types of messages about the roles of males and females in society are being communicated by these shows? What are these shows doing to overcome gender stereotypes? How are these shows creating and maintaining gender ideologies images for children?

2. Obtain a copy of a magazine that is marketed primarily to women (for example, *Woman's Day, Cosmopolitan, Glamour, Good Housekeeping*) and a magazine that is

marketed primarily to men (for example, *Sports Illustrated*, *GQ*, *Popular Mechanics*, *Esquire*). Examine the types of products advertised for each sex. What gender ideologies are implied? Then examine advertisements in each magazine that are for similar products (for example, perfume and cologne ads, liquor ads, cigarette ads). How do ads designed to sell products to women differ from those designed to sell similar products to men? Describe the gender stereotypes contained in the ads, including the persuasive appeals used. Do any of the ads avoid gender stereotypes (for example, picturing a father taking care of an infant, showing a female business executive)? In your opinion, which of these ads is most effective? Why?

3. Watch a rerun of a television situation comedy from the 1950s, 1960s, or 1970s (for example, *The Honeymooners*, *The Brady Bunch*, *I Love Lucy*, *Bewitched*, *Make Room for Daddy*, *The Mary Tyler Moore Show*) and a similar show that is now on television. Compare and contrast the gender ideologies contained in these shows. Compare the portrayal of men and women. How has the portrayal of families changed on these shows? How have the gender messages contained in these shows influenced our perceptions of communication?

4. Listen to an hour each of several different radio formats in your broadcast area, for example, contemporary hits radio (top 40), AOR (album-oriented rock), classic rock, adult contemporary (light rock), dance music, college radio, country radio, National Public Radio, or talk radio. Carefully observe when and how much you hear male and female voices. Who is talking to you and when? Is the disk jockey male or female? Who typically reads the news, weather, traffic, and sports? Which sex is doing the authoritative voice-overs in the ads? Are you more likely to hear male or female performers? Do the female performers fit the traditional role for female performers or a new role? On balance, what roles for men and women are implied by the answers to these questions? Are there differences between different formats?

5. Watch several hours of MTV or similar music-video programming on television at different times and days. What are the percentages of male to female performers and video jockeys? What gender stereotypes show up frequently in the videos? How often are men and women portrayed in stereotypic roles as sex objects or conventional romantic figures? Are men stereotyped as sexual/romantic objects (for example, bare-chested or with open shirts or as stereotypically handsome lovers)? Who is most likely to be shown as active or as doing something unrelated to sex or romance? Are there differences in behavior between male and female video jockeys?

FURTHER READING

Carson, D., Dittmar, L., & Welsch, J. R. (Eds.). (1994). *Multiple voices in feminist film criticism*. Minneapolis: University of Minnesota Press.
    A comprehensive collection of essays that encourages readers to participate in the ways films are produced and received. Included are important writings in feminist film criticism and theory from the past and present.

Craig, S. (Ed.). (1992). *Men, masculinity, and the media*. Newbury Park, CA: Sage.
    A collection of essays exploring representations of men in the media and readings of mediated masculinity. Included are case studies of heavy-metal music, comic books, and beer commercials as well as more general discussions of television and advertising.

Douglas, S. J. (1994). *Where the girls are: Growing up female with the mass media.* New York: Times
      Books.
      A humorous and provocative look at the portrayal of women in American popular culture since
      the 1950s, and the unexpected effects such images have had on women's real lives. Douglas
      tells the story of young women growing up on a steady diet of images that implicitly
      acknowledge their concerns while urging them to respect traditional female roles.

Dyson, M. E. (1993). *Reflecting Black: African American cultural criticism.* Minneapolis: University of
      Minnesota Press.
      Explores the varied and complex dimensions of African American culture including rap
      music, Toni Morrison, Michael Jackson, and Michael Jordan. Personal reflections, expository
      journalism, and scholarly investigation are included.

Wolf, N. (1992). *The beauty myth: How images of beauty are used against women.* New York: Anchor.
      The best-selling examination of how the media use stereotypical images of beauty in an
      attempt to control women's behavior. Wolf demonstrates how the beauty myth pervades all
      areas of women's lives including work, religion, culture, and violence. Strategies for overcom-
      ing this myth are suggested.

CHAPTER

9

Organizations

The world of work is one that most of us participate in or certainly will encounter someday. Organizational contexts present opportunities for communication that may reinforce or break down gender ideologies. If you work a 40-hour week outside the home (and many of you will work more hours than that) for the next 30 years, you will have spent at least 60,000 hours in various organizations. During these hours at work, gender is shaped and communicated.

Organizations in the United States and throughout the world are in transition, in part because of the changing nature of the workforce. The percentage of the workforce that is female doubled from 23 percent in 1970 to 46 percent in 1990. By 2010, it is estimated that white men will account for less than 40 percent of the total U.S. labor force (Loden & Rosener, 1991).

Nevertheless, the workplace still contains inequalities based on gender segregation and differences in earnings. Gender segregation is the "concentration of men and women in different occupations, jobs, and places of work" (Reskin & Padavic, 1994, p. 45). In other words, men and women may do different tasks at the same work site (female nurses work in hospitals with male surgeons) or the same tasks at different times or in different places (a convenience store may have a female manager during the day and a male manager at night). Gender segregation may inhibit a woman's opportunity for advancement or an increase in salary. The higher the proportion of women in an occupation, for example, the less that *both* men and women employees earn (Reskin & Padavic, 1994). Although some progress has been made in equalizing women and men's salaries, parity is still not the norm. In 1997, U.S. Department of Labor statistics indicated that women were paid approximately 25 percent less than men across all job categories (Equal pay, 1999). White women earned an average of $462 per week compared with $631 for white men, and minority women earned an average of $369 per week compared with $415 earned by minority men. The Institute for Women's Policy Research estimated that "if women were to receive wages equal to those of comparable men, working families across the United States would gain a staggering *$200 billion* in family income annually, with each working woman's family gaining more that $4,000 per year" (Equal pay, 1999, p. 1).

These difficulties, among others, have brought about increasing concern with diversity issues in the workplace. A number of excellent books have been written on this topic (see for example, Fernandez, 1991; Thiederman, 1991; Thomas, 1991).

This chapter will focus on one part of the diversity issue, gender. As noted earlier, however, other diversity issues such as ethnicity or sexual orientation are intertwined with gender at work. In this chapter, we will examine how women and men in organizations are perceived, how they communicate, and how their attitudes are shaped by their experiences. In addition, since many of you may plan to pursue managerial careers or are working in managerial-level jobs now, this chapter will focus specifically on gender issues in managerial communication.

Gendered Expectations

As discussed in Chapter 1, gender ideology includes the "belief that a set of traits and abilities is more likely to be found among one sex than the other" (Schein, 1978, p. 259). These beliefs include what is considered appropriate masculine or feminine behavior (Terborg, 1977). In the past, gender ideology may have influenced organizations to believe that women would not be able to balance both family life and the demands of a managerial-level job. Conversely, it was often assumed that men would devote the majority of their energies to their careers. These beliefs have changed considerably. In today's diverse organizations, both men and women are viewed as committed employees and a wide range of both traditionally masculine and feminine behaviors are viewed as necessary for success.

Early studies illustrated the ideology that men should be good leaders and women should be better followers. Since men were expected to be more competent than women in certain areas, they were perceived more negatively when they were not. In one study, when men and women performed with equal competence, the men were rated more positively than equally competent women (Nieva & Gutek, 1980). But when men and women performed incompetently, the incompetent men were rated even lower than the equally incompetent women. Since success at demanding jobs was expected of men but not of women, unsuccessful men were penalized more for doing a poor job than unsuccessful women were.

Cooper (1997) argues that "female leaders often face considerable bias in the way they are evaluated, in the way followers react and perform, and in their ultimate success as leaders" (p. 497). In addition, women may stereotype each other more and exhibit more jealousy with female leaders than with male leaders.

Leadership for women can also be influenced by gender ideology. For example, women who believe in nontraditional values are more likely to perceive themselves as assertive leaders and respond more positively to female leadership (Cooper, 1997). In addition, nontraditional women respond more positively to nontraditional women as leaders, whereas traditional women respond more positively to traditional women. In other words, women prefer leaders who are like themselves. Thus, it may be more productive to assign a traditional woman to be the leader of a group composed of other traditional women. More assertive women expect leaders to be assertive and respond less positively to leaders who do not exhibit this behavior.

Organizational leaders who are women tend to be rated as more democratic or participative, and organizational leaders who are men are rated as more autocratic or directive (Eagly & Johnson, 1990). More recent research, however, has focused on transformational and transactional leadership. Transformational leaders exhibit charisma, focus on developing their employees, encourage employees to question how they carry out their tasks, and treat employees equitably based on their needs (Bass & Avolio, 1993). Transactional leaders focus on how the current needs of employees can be met through an exchange of resources between the manager and employee (such as paying employees more to work overtime when there is a problem to be solved). In general, female managers are rated as more transformational than male managers by both male and female employees (Maher, 1997).

Early studies of leadership in organizations focused mainly on men. As women started to move up the corporate ladder, their communication began to be studied, too. Women have been very successful in managerial jobs. Recently, however, organizational analysts have identified a phenomenon called the *glass ceiling effect:* there seems to be a point in many organizations above which few women hold positions. For example, although the percentage of women in management increased from 6.3 percent in 1978 to 10.8 percent in 1988, only 2.6 percent of Fortune 500 corporate officers in 1988 were women (DiMona & Herndon, 1994). The U.S. government's Glass Ceiling Commission estimated that women held only 5 percent of senior executive positions in 1996 ("Women in American boardrooms," 1997).

According to a report by the Women's Research and Education Institute, the lack of women at the top of corporations cannot be explained solely by their recent entry into those professions. Women have failed to reach the top of organizations in part because of the gender ideology held by many corporate decision makers that women do not have the personality characteristics necessary for top leadership roles (Rich, 1990). *Fortune* magazine polled 1,000 CEOs to determine why women are not progressing into the highest levels of corporate management. Of the 241 respondents to the survey, 81 percent attribute the problem to stereotyping and preconceptions (Fierman, 1990). As one authority notes, "it's a little bit surprising that there hasn't been more breakthrough [for women and minorities]. There are barriers imposed if you don't share the same interests or follow the same football teams" (quoted in Silver, 1990). Buzzanell (1995) argues that the glass ceiling is, in part, a discursive phenomenon in which language creates and sustains gender divisions in organizations. In this way, talking about the existence of the glass ceiling reinforces its power to hold back women from positions of organizational authority.

Gender Ideology and Managers

Women have made progress in the managerial ranks in organizations. The percentage of women in managerial and executive positions has been steadily increasing from 18 percent in 1970, to 40 percent in 1990, to 48 percent in 1997 (Reskin & Padavic, 1994; "Women in American boardrooms," 1997). Nevertheless, African American women have fared particularly badly in terms of gaining access to managerial jobs. In 1988, only 2 percent of managers in the United States were African American women. A report by the Women's Research and Education Institute predicts that it

CONSIDER THIS!

Glass Ceilings

Many barriers prevent minorities and women from reaching positions where they can even see a glass ceiling:

- lack of management commitment to established systems, policies, and practices for achieving workplace diversity and upward mobility
- pay inequities for work of equal or comparable value
- gender-, race-, and ethnic-based stereotyping and harassment
- unfair recruitment practices
- lack of family-friendly workplace policies
- "parent-track" policies [more limited advancement opportunities for people with children]
- limited opportunities for advancement to decision-making positions

U.S. Department of Labor, 1991

---

may take 75 to 100 years to overcome inequities in hiring, promotion, and other aspects of employment (Rich, 1990).

Some of the difficulties faced by women in breaking the glass ceiling, or by men in balancing work and family activities, can be traced to the gender ideologies of managers. Although negative stereotypes were widely held in the past, they are changing in organizations that value diversity. A look back at some of the previous research will highlight the changes that have occurred.

In 1965, a *Harvard Business Review* study asked the question, "Are Women Executives People?" (Bowman, Worthy, & Greyser, 1965). This survey of 2,000 male and female executives indicated that female executives were considered people, but they were not particularly popular people. Attitudes toward female executives did differ by gender, though. Only 9 percent of the male respondents, but 48 percent of the female respondents, were "strongly favorable" toward women in management. Forty-one percent of the men and only 7 percent of the women were either "mildly" or "strongly unfavorable" to women in management. Male and female respondents (61 percent of the males, 47 percent of the females) agreed that the business community would never wholly accept female business executives. Male and female respondents agreed that "a woman has to be exceptional, indeed overqualified, to succeed in management today" (p. 15).

In 1971, managers felt other men *and* women would prefer a male supervisor and would be uncomfortable with a woman supervisor (Bass, Krusell, & Alexander, 1971). This supports Bowman, Worthy, and Greyser's (1965) earlier research in which relatively few men said they would be comfortable as a subordinate to a woman and the respondents believed men in general would not be comfortable. Bass and colleagues concluded in 1971 that "societal norms do not sanction the placement of women in dominant positions" in organizations (p. 223).

In 1973, Schein noted that management could be classified as a masculine occupation because of the high ratio of men to women and because of the belief that "this is how it should be." When asked to rate women in general, men in general, and successful middle managers on 92 descriptive terms, both men and women perceived that successful middle managers possesssed characteristics, attitudes, and temperaments more commonly ascribed to men than to women. Successful managers *and* men were thought to have leadership ability, competitiveness, objectivity, aggressiveness, forcefulness, ambitiousness, and to desire responsibility. A few managerial behaviors were applied to women: employee-centeredness, understanding, helpfulness, and intuition. Thus, as Schein concludes, "all else being equal, the perceived similarity between the characteristics of successful middle managers and men in general increases the likelihood of a male rather than a female being selected for or promoted to a managerial position" (p. 99).

The "masculine is best in management" ethic continued into the 1980s. Schein's research was replicated by Brenner, Tomkiewicz, and Schein in 1989. Once again, men indicated that successful middle managers were perceived to possess those characteristics, attitudes, and temperaments more commonly ascribed to men in general than to women in general. Women, however, viewed successful middle managers as possessing characteristics, attitudes, and temperaments that were ascribed to both men and women. Thus, women's attitudes toward effective management behaviors changed in the 1980s while men's attitudes tended to remain the same. Even recently, "good management" is still associated with more traditionally masculine behaviors such as competitiveness, aggressiveness, and independence (Berryman-Fink, 1997).

More workers are beginning to view management as a gender-neutral occupation. A 1998 survey found that 63 percent of adult workers responded "depends or doesn't matter" when asked their preference for a male or female boss ("Who's the boss?" 1998). Nevertheless, 23 percent still indicated that they preferred a male boss and only 12 percent preferred a female boss.

Helgesen (1990) examines "women's ways of leadership" and finds that women are more likely than men to view unscheduled tasks and encounters not as interruptions but as a natural part of the workday. Thus, informal communication (such as dropping by to ask a co-worker about a sick child) is seen as an important way to let employees know that a manager cares about them. Helgesen uses words such as "caring, being involved, helping, and being responsible" (p. 21) to describe the female managers she studied. Helgesen also points out that women managers preferred face-to-face communication over the telephone, but that the mail was seen as a valuable way to maintain relationships with others in the workforce.

As more people work with female managers, these attitudes are changing. For example, men who work for women managers generally have a higher acceptance of women in management roles than men who do not work with women managers (Wheeless & Berryman-Fink, 1985). In addition, the longer employees work for a woman manager, the more positive their attitudes toward their manager's communication behaviors are (Berryman-Fink, Heintz, Lowy, Sebohm, & Wheeless, 1986).

Young people are also less likely to have stereotyped attitudes. Students at a leading business school were surveyed after working on group projects to determine their attitudes toward their managers ("Men More Willingly Accept Women as Leaders," 1988). When a similar study was conducted in the 1970s, every man who worked on a team with more women than men claimed to be the group's leader. In 1988, only 70 percent of the male students in teams with more women than men claimed to be the leader. If a team had more male than female workers, males acknowledged that 56 percent of the women were leaders, although 61 percent of the women on male majority teams claimed to be the leader. Today women team leaders are even more common.

In addition, the type of organization may influence attitudes toward women in leadership positions. Companies that deal with high-technology products and small start-up companies are often more accommodating to female managers. Since new industries are less likely to be run by the old boys' network (Fierman, 1990), they allow women to maximize the benefits of their communication style.

Thus, as managerial roles in organizations change, women and men are beginning to share leadership responsibilities in organizations and to appreciate each other's talents.

Gendered Organizational Communication

The previous discussion examined how gender ideologies influence perceptions of men and women's communication in organizations. But how does gender influence communication in organizations? Studies of the actual communication behavior of organizational employees have found many similarities.

Birdsall (1980) notes that male and female managers use the same communication style in weekly staff meetings. Alderton and Jurma (1980) find that if male and female leaders do not differ in their task-oriented communication behavior, group members are equally satisfied with their leadership. Donnell and Hall (1980) report no differences in managerial style in a large group of male and female managers. These managers approach motivating their subordinates in the same way and employ participative practices in a similar manner. Donnell and Hall conclude that "women, in general, do not differ from men, in general, in the ways in which they administer the management process" (p. 76).

To find out how men and women in organizations actually communicate with each other, Statham (1987) surveyed a matched sample of women and men in management jobs and interviewed their secretaries. The managers worked for three diverse organizations: a financial institution, a manufacturing firm, and a technical institute. The female managers described themselves as both "people-" and "task-oriented." The male managers focused more on the importance of their jobs (called "image engrossment" by Statham). Statham concludes that the women used their people orientation to accomplish tasks while the men valued autonomy in their jobs. This difference in managerial style was most clear in the area of delegation. Women expressed a need to be involved with their subordinates while men believed that good management entailed not being involved in what their subordinates were doing. These styles were often resented by employees of the other sex. For example, women perceived male managers' autonomy as neglect, and men felt that women managers' need to be involved was an indication that the managers were not confident in their subordinates' abilities to carry out tasks. Statham differentiated between the male ethos of "give everybody space to do their jobs" and the female desire to "look over their shoulders" (p. 422). Although Statham acknowledges several exceptions in which women were concerned about autonomy and men were more involved, she concludes:

> Men managers leave women subordinates to struggle on their own because they believe this is the "best way to manage." Men subordinates resent women managers who "stand over their shoulders" because this signals to them a lack of confidence, while the woman believes she is demonstrating her "concern for the employee." And women resent men who "dump the work" onto others or who in other ways are perceived as not contributing as much as women. (p. 425)

Thus, as noted earlier, men and women in organizations may see the same behavior and perceive it differently.

In some instances, however, male and female interaction styles may differ. According to Putnam (1983), two males who are in conflict typically employ bargaining techniques, logical arguments, and anger to manage the interaction. Females, on the other hand, are more likely to focus on understanding each other's feelings. These differing strategies may cause problems between male and female supervisors and subordinates in conflict situations. The interactants may find it difficult to reach a compromise because of their differing interaction styles, not because they fundamentally disagree with one another.

Traditionally, organizations have emphasized productivity, competition, self-reliance, independence, and success (Grant, 1988). Thus, much of the formal communication in organizations is based on a traditionally masculine model of interaction. According to Devine & Markiewicz (1990), "organizations pride themselves on their creation of rational structures based primarily on a male perspective of interaction. Workers are expected to set aside interpersonal behaviors that do not directly contribute to task performance." Workers have been expected to focus on competition, strategy, and "bottom-line results" because

> organizations have traditionally been established and managed by men. Rational structures were consciously created where decision-making processes, communication patterns and norms of interaction were based on normative male experiences of relationships and approaches to work. . . . [Y]et as more women enter organizations at managerial levels, they bring with them their own norms of relationship, friendship and interaction. . . .
> The importance of relationships for women is reflected in such tendencies as (1) women's emphasis on assisting others to achieve the others' goals; (2) the emphasis on

establishing the security of intimate relationships prior to consideration of personal achievement; (3) women's tendency to define themselves in relation to others; (4) women's inclination towards self-disclosure and the development of close relationships with others.

[Related themes in men's lives include:] (1) relationships (e.g., mentor, spouse, friends) as instrumental to attaining one's career goals or "dream", (2) the emphasis on succeeding in one's career during early adulthood, (3) the importance of work and achievements in defining male identity, (4) men's tendency to avoid self-disclosure and to develop few, if any, close relationships with co-workers. (p. 333)

Grant (1988) believes that "women's greater ease with the relational world could help make organizations places in which affiliation, friendship, connection, and person-hood could also be valued in a more integrated manner" (p. 60). Female managers appear to be more open in terms of communication than men are. For example, Josephowitz (1980) reports that female managers are on the average twice as accessible to their subordinates as are male managers. Thus, women may be expressing their communication style by listening to subordinates more than other managers do.

As you can see from this discussion, there are many challenges facing employees in today's organizations. According to Colwill and Erhart (1985), "education, attitude change, the establishment of women's networks, and improved communication between men and women [are] catalysts for . . . change" in organizations (p. 30).

Researchers have examined various types of communication in organizations. Two of the most important of these are *informal communication networks* and *communication in task groups*. We will discuss each of these briefly in the next sections.

Informal Communication Networks

Conforming to traditional gender ideologies, in the past men were considered to be actively seeking promotions while women were more likely to be seen as waiting to be chosen for promotion. For example, in a classic study, Hennig and Jardim (1977) interviewed women at all levels of management: corporate vice-presidents and presidents, chief executive officers, middle managers, Harvard Business School M.B.A. students, and undergraduate business majors. They found an overwhelming sense of "waiting to be chosen." The women interviewed believed that if they were competent and performed their jobs well, they would be rewarded. Hennig and Jardim concluded that these women relied on the formal structure of the organization—its rules, policies, and procedures—to develop and sustain their careers. They felt uncomfortable using the "informal system of relationships and information sharing, ties of loyalty and of dependence, of favors granted and owed, of mutual benefit, or protection—which men unfailingly and invariably [took] into account" (p. 31).

This situation has changed to some extent in today's organizations. Many men have decided to get off the fast track and spend more time with their families. Many women are actively seeking promotions and have developed the skills necessary for a highly successful career. Many people of both sexes are striving for an appropriate balance between work and family.

Communication in Task Groups

Research indicates that there are no differences between women and men in task and positive socioemotional behaviors in same-sex task groups (Johnson, Clay-Warner & Funk, 1996). Nevertheless, women are more likely to agree with each other, while men have higher rates of counterarguments (i.e., refuting someone else's arguments) and are less likely to agree with each other. Thus, it appears that women are still expected to agree more often and to confront each other less often in groups than are men. Dominance in leader behaviors in groups may change depending on how a group is constituted. For example, men are more likely than women to exercise opinion leadership in mixed-gender groups that do not have an assigned leader. However, if a particular individual is assigned to be the leader of the group before the task begins, men and women participate equally in leader behaviors (Walker et al., 1996). Thus, women are as likely as men to serve as opinion leaders in groups that have a designated leader.

Research continues to support the double standard for judging competence in mixed-sex groups. Foschi (1996) found that even though males and females performed a task at the same level, the females were held to a higher standard for perceived competence. In this study, when men and women completed a perceptual task and the woman was better than the man, she was judged less competent than a man who performed at the same level.

Gender differences in group performance may disappear when the participants are undergraduate students. Meeker & Elliott (1996) found that undergraduates who were asked to imagine themselves the supervisor of a group of students who were conducting telephone surveys allocated "pay" based on whether they had a social orientation or a task orientation, not on gender. In other words, students who had a social orientation allocated the pay equally to the students they "supervised," while students with a task orientation allocated the pay based on perceived merit. There was no difference between women and men in terms of how they allocated rewards to their supervisees. Obviously, this study deals with a hypothetical situation, but it provides an interesting example of factors that may be more important in work settings than gender of supervisor.

Shackelford, Wood, and Worchel (1996) contend that women can increase their influence in groups in three ways. First, in mixed-sex groups, women can demonstrate their ability at the task before attempting to influence others. In other words, they can show the group that they can perform the task (e.g., showing a completed crossword puzzle) before the group begins a similar task (e.g., working as a group to complete a crossword puzzle). Second, women can adopt a group-oriented style that generates the perception that they are competent and enhances their ability to influence others. Third, in a more negative way, women can attract attention through disruptive, self-assertive behaviors. This strategy can lead the group to dislike the woman using it, but it does result in being able to influence a group. Thus, in order to have an effect on decision making in a group, it is more important for a woman to gain attention (even in a seemingly negative way) than to be ignored or isolated. Obviously, this advice is more useful in groups that are formed to accomplish a specific task and not to provide social support.

Implications and Consequences of Gender Ideology

Since 1964 in the United States, most companies have been required by the government to follow affirmative action and equal-employment guidelines that prohibit discrimination on the basis of race, color, religion, sex, and national origin. Subsequent additions to this legislation include age, physical disability, pregnancy, childbirth, or related medical conditions. Some communities have also included sexual orientation in their anti-discrimination laws. These laws are designed to give all members of the workforce equal access to opportunities for jobs and to protect employees from harassment. As we have seen from the previous discussion, however, these laws do not guarantee that all people progress through the organizational hierarchy at an equal rate or receive equal encouragement from the organization to participate in family activities.

Corporations are responding to the changing workforce, including gender issues, in a variety of ways. For example, in terms of structural changes, organizations are adding new functions such as cultural-diversity teams or women-in-sales task force groups. Human-resource specialists serve as counseling sources to reduce the stress and confusion that may result from dealing with a diversity of individual needs. Training programs have been changed to reflect the diverse populations in the workforce and to eliminate bias in content and presentation of programs. For example, it is no longer acceptable to use sexist language or all-male terminology in case-study materials (such as assuming that all machine operators are male or that all secretaries are female), or to use visual media that portray women and minorities only in support roles and men only in decision-making roles.

Some companies have expanded their employee services by adding child-care support, flexible work schedules, and special interest groups to address the needs of diverse employees. For example, one survey reports that 56 percent of 259 major employers offer some type of child-care aid and 56 percent allow flexible scheduling (Fierman, 1990). As we noted in Chapter 6, all large organizations must grant unpaid family leave to any employee who requests it.

Nevertheless, gender ideologies may affect employees at any stage of their careers. We will focus on three areas in this section. Getting a job is often the beginning of a lifetime in the work world. Thus, we will begin this section by describing the process of entering an organization and the role of gender stereotyping at the beginning stages of a career. Once you have a job, you may be interested in getting a promotion. We will discuss this area next. Finally, we turn our attention to a problem faced by many workers: sexual harassment.

Entering the Organization

Men and women may face different obstacles when entering organizations. For example, women are less likely to be offered interviews on the basis of their resumes than men. In one study, researchers sent unsolicited resumes and cover letters to various employers, applying for entry-level jobs (McIntyre, Moberg, & Posner, 1980). The resumes were equivalent except for the sex of the applicant. Female applicants were less likely to be offered interviews by the companies than male applicants. In addition, the companies took an average of 2.6 days longer to reply to the female applicants' letters.

Men and women are likely to be treated more equally once they get to an interview, however. In one study, 66 recruiters watched videotapes of male and female job applicants who behaved either passively or aggressively (Dipboye & Wiley, 1977). Gender of the applicant did not affect the recruiters' decision to invite the applicant for an interview. The researchers conclude that "a woman who clearly demonstrates . . . moderate aggressiveness, self-confidence, and ambition will be received no less favorably by raters than a man demonstrating the same traits" (p. 10).

Overall, the more an evaluator must infer about a job applicant, the more likely the evaluation will be biased (Nieva & Gutek, 1980). If there is a great deal of task-relevant information provided about the applicant, and the criteria to be used in the evaluation situation are explicit, less bias results. As one researcher notes, "Unless there are clear and valid predictors of performance potential, selection procedures may become particularistic" (Smith, 1979, p. 368). This situation is especially harmful to women because, when there is no background given on job applicants, evaluators may rely on gender stereotypes that assume that women do not have the appropriate educational background for managerial careers (Renwick & Tosi, 1978). Thus, evaluators may use gender stereotypes to fill in any missing information (Bartol, 1978).

As mentioned previously, employment interviewing is another area that is receiving increased attention in terms of preventing gender bias in organizations. Changes in interviewing practices include advertising, recruitment, interview structure, decision making, and record-keeping requirements. Companies often conduct outreach recruitment efforts to attract a more diverse group of applicants. The structure of the interview is carefully planned to include the job description, hiring criteria, and assessment of the applicant's qualifications. Decision making is based on multiple contacts and clear documentation. In addition, companies must keep accurate records that contain nondiscriminatory applicant profiles and clearly specify the results of the interviews.

Graves (1999) provides a comprehensive assessment of the research literature on employment interviewing and gender issues. She concludes that both the observational and experimental studies of gender bias in employment interviews yield mixed results. She notes: "The prevalence of complex interactions between applicant gender and other factors suggests that the critical issue is not whether gender bias occurs, but under what conditions it occurs" (p. 153). For example, women who are perceived as unattractive or obese are more likely to be victims of discrimination than men with the same characteristics.

If you are an applicant in an employment interview, the following questions may help you identify signs of gender bias:

1. Did you feel comfortable? Were you treated with courtesy and respect?
2. Did you experience any direct examples of discrimination (for example, questions, jokes, social references)?
3. Does the company have a public image of fair action? Look for a corporate mission statement or code of ethics.

4. What opportunities for training and advancement are available? Does your performance affect your consideration for these opportunities?
5. Are there special group activities, benefits, or projects that are of interest to you?
6. Check references and referrals. Some companies are recognized for their progress on gender issues. Review the annual report and product literature and talk to customers.
(Adapted from Stewart, 2001)

The more you understand about the company, the better you can evaluate the position as an opportunity for you.

Getting Promoted

Organizations are adapting their performance-appraisal process to reflect a diverse workforce and to avoid gender bias. Good appraisals are performance-based and results-oriented. They may be evenly distributed throughout the work year and routinely administered. Appraisers can be trained to eliminate bias in delivering feedback to employees. In addition, improvement programs based on weaknesses identified in performance appraisals encourage systematic, gradual change resulting in progressive action. It is important to remember, however, that assessment measures must be shown to predict job success for both female and male job candidates (Colwill, 1996). In other words, tests that have been validated with male samples must be tested with female workers as well.

A great deal of research has been conducted to identify various factors that could lead to bias in performance appraisals. Bartol (1999) has written a comprehensive review of this research and concludes that "studies to date suggest that neither males nor females give higher ratings to same gender ratees, nor do they consistently give higher or lower ratings to opposite-gender ratees" (p. 169).

Both men and women are concerned about opportunities to advance in their jobs. To make matters more complicated for women, promotion may not mean advancement. For example, in one study, older women who had received more promotions in an organization were at a lower level in the hierarchy than younger women with more education who had been in the organization for a shorter length of time (Stewart & Gudykunst, 1982). Older men were at higher levels in the organization than younger men regardless of their educational level.

Thus, women either may not be promoted or, if they are promoted, they still may not be moving up the organizational hierarchy at the same rate as men. One important reason for this phenomenon may be biased decisions based on gender stereotyping. An unbiased decision can be made when a candidate's qualifications for promotion are clearly acceptable or clearly unacceptable (Rosen & Jerdee, 1974). But this situation is rarely the case. Often, two or more candidates' qualifications are highly similar and there is no clear-cut, objective way of predicting who will be the most successful person on the next job. In this case, if information is missing or imprecise, a manager may tend to make promotion choices on the basis of personal values, and these values may not be work related. But there is likely to be increased conformity in organizations where only people of similar values are promoted and retained. An organization following such practices would have less creativity and energy than an organization where diversity is valued.

Sexual Harassment

Another consequence of the gender stereotyping within organizations is sexual harassment. Sexual harassment has been defined by the Equal Employment Opportunity Commission as:

> Unwelcome sexual advances, request for sexual favors, and other verbal and physical conduct of a sexual nature . . . when (1) submission to such conduct is made either explicitly or implicitly a term or condition of an individual's employment, (2) submission to or rejection of such conduct by an individual is used as the basis for employment decisions affecting such individuals, (3) or such conduct has the purpose or effect of unreasonably interfering with an individual's work performance or creating an intimidating, hostile, or offensive work environment. (Mastalli, 1981, p. 94)

Simon and Montgomery (1987) define sexual harassment, from a communication perspective, as an exchange between two people in which one exhibits sexual approach behaviors, the other counters with sexual avoidance behaviors, and the first subsequently exhibits additional sexual approach behavior. Sexual harassment includes any behavior of a sexual nature that adversely affects a person's job performance. These behaviors can range from off-color jokes to unwanted touching or even sexual assault. But as Booth-Butterfield (1986) notes, sexual harassment often appears in ascending

---

CONSIDER THIS!

Empirical Definitions of Sexual Harassment

SEXUAL HARASSMENT CONTINUUM	SPECIFIC EXAMPLE
gender harassment	generalized sexist remarks
seductive behavior	inappropriate and offensive, but essentially sanction-free, sexual advances
sexual bribery	solicitation of sexual activity or other sex-linked activity by promise of reward
sexual coercion	coercion of sexual activity by threat of punishment
sexual imposition	sexual crimes and misdemeanors

Paludi and Barickman, 1995

stages. In other words, the harasser may begin with more subtle behaviors that escalate to more dramatic ones. The box on the previous page lists behaviors that have been determined to be sexual harassment.

Sexual harassment often occurs without witnesses and, therefore, goes unreported. Nevertheless, some surveys have found startling results. In a survey conducted by *Redbook* magazine (Safran, 1981), nine out of ten of the female respondents said they had experienced some form of sexual harassment on the job; most, however, had experienced subtle forms of harassment such as sexual jokes. Forty-five percent of the respondents indicated that either they or a woman they knew had quit or been fired from a job because of sexual harassment. In a survey of more than 20,000 federal employees, 42 percent of the women and 15 percent of the men claimed they had been sexually harassed in the previous two years (U.S. Merit Systems Protection Board, 1981).

As discussed above, sexual harassment occurs in various forms. One survey based on a random sample of men and women (Loy & Stewart, 1984) found that approximately half the reported incidents of sexual harassment were verbal commentary, sexual messages delivered through innuendo, or off-color jokes. Thirty-six percent of the incidents involved physical contact such as unwanted touching or groping. Verbal negotiation (explicit requests to exchange sex for economic or career benefits) occurred 10 percent of the time. Three percent of the reported incidents involved actual physical assault.

Women are more likely to be the targets of harassment than men, and harassers are more likely to be male than female. Twenty percent of the male respondents in the U.S. Merit Systems Protection Board's survey reported that their harassers were male. Only 3 percent of the female respondents reported female harassers. Thus, while men may get harassed by both women and other men; women are much more likely to be harassed by men.

Forty percent of college women and almost 30 percent of college men report being harassed by a college professor or instructor (Kalof et al., 2001). Approximately one-third of students of color have experienced at least one incident of sexual harassment from a faculty member. The majority of this harassment is gender harassment, such as using sexist or inappropriate language, having a condescending attitude based on the student's gender, or displaying suggestive materials in class. Students report relatively little unwanted sexual attention or coercion from faculty. Professors who do not engage in harassing behaviors are rated more positively by students (especially by female students) than professors who engage in harassing behaviors such as unexpected touching—for example, touching a student's thigh (Lannutti, Laliker & Hale, 2001).

The perception of sexual harassment often differs depending on whether the harasser is a man or woman. Katz, Hannon, and Whitten (1996) found that college students were more likely to perceive a behavior such as sneaking up on someone and tickling his or her ribs as harassment when the perpetrator was male and the victim was female than vice versa. Men and women have similar views about harassment as long as the harasser is male and the victim is female. When the harasser is a woman and the victim is a man, men rate the interactions as less harassing than women. Thus, women may be focusing more on the behavior, not on the gender of the initiator of the behavior.

Women in nontraditional jobs are often the targets of sexual harassment. A report issued by the National Council for Research on Women (Sexual Harassment, 1995) points out that many occupations, ranging from construction worker to neurosurgeon, have been historically dominated by men, with 25 percent or less of the job holders being women. Women working in these professions are often the targets of harassment both from co-workers and supervisors.

Women of color may suffer a particularly negative impact of sexual harassment. As Crenshaw (1991) notes: "Pervasive stereotypes about black women not only shape the kinds of harassment that black women experience but they also influence whether black women's stories are likely to be believed, and even when they are believed, whether their insult or violation matters" (cited in Sexual Harassment, 1995, p. 30). African American women may be harassed because of both race and sex (Sexual Harassment, 1995).

Sexual harassment has profoundly negative consequences for its victims. People who have experienced sexual harassment on the job report both personal and professional consequences (Loy & Stewart, 1984). On a personal level, people who have been harassed report symptoms such as nervousness, irritability, loss of motivation, sleeplessness, and weight loss. On a professional level, the targets of sexual harassment may be ignored by their harasser (who is often their supervisor and, therefore, can negatively influence their career), transferred to a different department, or even fired.

Numerous suggestions have been offered on ways to respond to sexual harassment, from joking or bluntly asking the harasser to stop, to taking legal action (Backhouse & Cohen, 1978). Although ignoring sexual harassment is the most prevalent response, it is ineffective in getting the harassment to stop. In a Working Women United survey, for the 76 percent of the respondents who used this strategy, the harassment continued in the same form or worsened (Collins & Blodgett, 1981).

No one knows what causes a particular person in an organization to harass another person. There is some evidence, however, that power or the need to exercise power is one cause of harassment (Buzza, 1982). Low self-esteem may also be a cause. Individuals who do not value their own worth may not be able to value or respect other people. Nevertheless, companies are responsible for their employees' behavior and can be held legally liable for the negative consequences suffered as a result of this behavior (Sandroff, 1988).

Most employers have established sexual harassment policies with clear guidelines for reporting problems at work. To respond to sexual harassment when there is no organizational grievance policy, Jacobs (1992) suggests going to someone at the top of the organization who cares about the business. She suggests that the employee make it clear that he or she wants to work things out, is keeping a journal of the times, dates and descriptions of harassment incidents, and expects the problem to be corrected.

Strategies for Change

In the previous sections of this chapter we have discussed gender ideologies of men and women in organizations and some of the consequences of these stereotypes. It is important to remember that gender stereotypes negatively affect both men and women. Some women may be hindered in their career advancement while some men find it difficult to spend as much time with their families as they would like. Women in today's organizations may have reached a "glass ceiling." In other words, there are many women in entry-level positions and few in top management. Thus, some women do not seem to be developing their full potential in organizations. In contrast, many men would like to devote more time to their families but feel pressured to pursue a profitable career. (Read Consider This: "Men Whose Wives Work Earn Less," for one view of the problems faced by these men.) In this section, we will discuss some communicative strategies that have been suggested to overcome these negative consequences.

Mentors

One of the many communication strategies both men and women can use to overcome gender stereotypes in organizations is by acquiring a **mentor,** *someone who gives advice on appropriate career strategies and who may even help you gain a desired promotion by influencing decisions affecting your future in an organization.* Mentorship appears to be related to success and mobility for both men and women (Hunt & Michael, 1983). Mentors are especially useful at two points in a career: (1) in the early phase when the idea to move up in an organization crystallizes and (2) when it is time for the final push to the top rungs of the organizational ladder (Halcomb, 1980).

There are four stages in a mentor relationship: initiation, cultivation, separation, and redefinition (Kram, 1983). In the *initiation* stage, the relationship is started. The mentor is admired and respected for his or her competence or ability to provide guidance. The protégé feels cared for and admired by the mentor who has more status in the organization. Studies have found that, on average, this stage lasts approximately a year. In the second stage, *cultivation*, the relationship between the mentor and protégé develops further. The mentor coaches or challenges the protégé. The protégé develops a growing self-confidence. This stage typically may last two to five years. In the *separation* stage, the protégé experiences more independence and autonomy, causing both participants to reassess their relationship. The protégé may be physically separated from the mentor by a promotion to a new location or psychologically separated by a growing feeling of independence. As the separation increases, the participants redefine their relationship. If the *redefinition* stage is successful, the mentor and protégé become friends. They may continue to see each other and support each other's careers, but the mentor is no longer involved in the day-to-day guidance of the protégé's career.

Interestingly, even though we might expect the most mentoring to occur between female supervisors and female subordinates, male subordinates are more likely to perceive that they are being mentored by female supervisors than female subordinates are (Locke & Williams, 2000). This situation may occur because female managers tend to be younger and may be more focused on their own careers than in assisting other women or may be distancing themselves from other women in order to succeed in a workplace that values more masculine behaviors. In addition, male subordinates may recognize the value of mentoring and thus may be more willing to admit that they are being mentored.

In fact, men who are in a formal mentor program are more likely to have higher career commitment and to report that their mentor is more effective than women are (Ragins, Cotton, & Miller, 2000). Thus, formal mentoring programs that have often been put in place specifically to ensure that all members of the workforce are receiving guidance from organizational leaders may not be accomplishing their goals since women are less satisfied with this type of mentoring than men are.

Casbolt and DeWine (1982) identified the communication behaviors associated with mentors. Mentors have effective interpersonal skills and are good listeners who are reflective and nonjudgmental. Mentors are trusting and take their protégés into their confidence. They exhibit openness by not being dogmatic and by allowing their protégés to argue without fear of losing trust in the relationship. Mentors share valuable organizational information that their protégés would not hear otherwise. They give verbal recognition and rewards for their protégés' achievements. They serve as a sounding board for new or controversial ideas and give counsel, not opinions. Mentors link protégés with other influential members of the organization or profession. Finally, mentors verbally encourage their protégés to continue the relationship. Through this process, mentors can serve as upward communication channels for both women and men in organizations to overcome traditional gender ideologies.

Networking

Having a mentor allows you access to a useful *internal* organizational communication system. Networking gives you an *external* organizational communication system that may help you gain valuable information throughout your career.

Networking is "*the process of developing and using your contacts for information, advice, and moral support as you pursue your career*" (Welch, 1980, p. 15). Men have traditionally had their "old boys' networks" that helped them find jobs, make stock deals, or get the best seats at sporting events. Helgesen (1990) found that the successful women managers she studied maintained a complex network of relationships with people outside the office as did their male counterparts. Although women's networking may include contacts with groups that include men, the number of business networks solely for women is increasing (Northcraft & Gutek, 1993).

Thus, one of the best communication strategies for women to use to overcome gender bias in the workplace is networking. As we have seen previously, although women are entering management in increasing numbers, their progress in organizations may be blocked by barriers such as the glass ceiling that limits the advancement and compensation of female executives. Colwill & Erhart (1985) found that women who used networks (such as membership in private clubs or on corporate boards) were more successful than women who did not have these contacts. Networking can be done through formal information channels such as head-hunting firms or through informal channels such as family and friends (Bartlett & Miller, 1985). These networks are often successful because more than 40 percent of managerial jobs are discovered by word of mouth (Corcoran, Datcher, & Duncan, 1980).

Networks may be developed for specific purposes or they may result from casual friendships. For example, a group of photographers may decide to meet once a month to share ideas and discuss potential opportunities for jobs. In some cities, people in prominent positions in organizations are invited to meet each other. Some networks are formally run. There may be membership requirements and dues. Meetings may be scheduled in advance.

If you cannot find a formal network that supports people in your particular field, you can still find valuable career-related information by establishing a networking pattern of your own. Think about people you know and what they know. Do you know someone who knows someone who works for a company that interests you? Ask that person to put you in contact with their contact. You will be surprised at how helpful people are if you explain your desire for information and are able to demonstrate your qualifications for a particular career.

Welch (1980) offers the following do's and don'ts for successful networking:

- Do try to give as much as you get *from your network. The more people you can be useful to, the more will be useful to you.*
- Don't be afraid to ask *for what you need. . . . Trust the other person to decide . . . whether [he or] she wants to do what you ask; don't decide for her [or him] by not asking.*
- Do report back *to anyone who ever gives you a lead, telling what happened and repeating your thanks.*
- Do follow up *on any leads and names you're given.*
- Do be businesslike *in your approach to your network. Keep your conversation on track and your phone calls [or e-mails] short.*
- Don't pass up any opportunities *to network. (pp. 98–99)*

Organizational Policies

As discussed earlier, gender ideology may negatively affect both men and women in organizations. Some individuals may be prevented from advancing while others may be working so hard that they miss out on family activities. One way that everyone can become a better participant in an organization and in family life is by changing organizational policies that block full participation in all aspects of employees' lives. Many companies are experimenting with flextime policies that allow employees to set their own hours. Some companies provide on-site day care for employees' children. Others subsidize off-site facilities. The Family Leave Act gives most organizational employees the opportunity to stay at home to take care of children. Some companies encourage their employees to job share so that individuals balance part-time work with family responsibilities.

Telecommuting is an organizational phenomenon that is increasingly available to workers today. Experts expect that this work option will help women in particular by allowing them to work from home while caring for small children. Companies are beginning to offer employees training in telecommuting, including advice on setting up appropriately designed home offices as well as assistance in coping with the isolation from co-workers (Johnson, 1997). Some theorists even speculate that the availability

CONSIDER THIS!
Men Whose Wives Work Earn Less

Working mothers often worry about the "mommy track," fearing that they will be consigned to lower-paid, less prestigious jobs. But their husbands, at least those who are managers or professionals, may face a penalty, too.

According to several recent studies, men from traditional families, in which the wives stay home to care for their children, earn more and get higher raises than men from two-career families.

Just why a gap exists is a topic of considerable debate. Some experts attribute it to individual choices, with men who are the sole breadwinners working longer, producing more and pushing harder for raises and promotions . . . others suggest corporate prejudice is to blame. . . .

The studies ruled out some possible explanations: they found no significant differences between the two groups of men in age, experience, or number of children. . . .

Lewin, 1994

of telecommuting will encourage men to become more involved in their family's day-to-day activities. Northcraft and Gutek (1993) note that "flextime scheduling and telecommuting provide ways for men to retain career involvement while becoming primary caregivers for their children" (p. 223).

These policies and other creative solutions to the problems faced by employees who play multiple roles can help all employees overcome gender bias and to participate fully in the important worlds of work and home if they choose.

Summary

As we have seen in this chapter, the work environment may be quite different for men and for women and may have a differential effect on their behavior. In terms of gender stereotypes, management was formerly perceived as a stereotypically male occupation, but this stereotype is changing. The acceptance of women in leadership roles is growing. Evidence suggests that men are more willing to support women in managerial roles once they have had experience working with women supervisors.

Nevertheless, perceptions of male and female managerial styles differ. A rewarding communication style is rated as more effective for male managers and a friendly, dependent style is rated more effective for female managers if the subordinate is of the other sex. In addition, perceptions of a leader's effectiveness may be affected by the sex composition of the group of employees, as well as by employees' general attitudes toward women in management roles.

Men who seek promotion are generally rewarded for effective performance by rapid advancement while women may not be. This phenomenon, called the *glass ceiling effect*, may be due to gender stereotypes. If a supervisor believes a woman is less likely than a man to be aggressive, competitive, or ambitious, the supervisor may be less likely to give the woman assignments calling for these skills.

Gender stereotyping in organizations may be overcome through a variety of communicative strategies including assertive communication, development of mentors, networking, and changing organizational policies.

FINDING YOUR VOICE

1. List as many gender ideologies that occur in the workplace as you can. What is the effect of each of these ideologies on men and women at work? Which ideologies have negative consequences for men? Which ideologies have negative consequences for women? What can be done to overcome each of these gender stereotypes?

2. Find two student groups on campus or in your community, one with a female leader and one with a male leader. Interview each leader. Try to determine the leaders' communication style. Ask them how they conduct meetings, how they deal with particular problems in their groups, how they make decisions. In addition, attend a meeting conducted by each leader. Did you find any differences in communication style between the two leaders? Compare and contrast their communication styles. Do these styles reflect a gender ideology? Which style was more effective? Why? What advice would you give the leaders for improving their leadership behavior?

3. Imagine yourself in the following situation: You are a personnel analyst in a large insurance company. Your company is considering starting a flextime program in which employees could work during different hours of the day depending on their preference. For example, instead of working from 9:00 A.M. until 5:00 P.M., a person could work from 6:00 A.M. until 2:00 P.M. or from noon to 8:00 P.M. Your boss, Pat Simmons, is opposed to the idea. Pat thinks everyone should work from 9 to 5. You think, however, that Pat's boss, Chris Carpenter, likes the idea. You are asked to write a report on flextime and give your recommendation on whether it should be implemented. How are you going to present your report? List several strategies you could use when you write your recommendations. Compare your strategies with your classmates' strategies. Are there any gender ideologies apparent in the strategies chosen? If you assumed that Pat and Chris were men, were your strategies different from the strategies chosen by people who assumed Pat and Chris were women? How do your responses compare with the material in this chapter on upward communication?

4. Locate a group devoted to networking (for example, a chapter of a Business and Professional Women's Club, the Jaycees, Women in Communications, or similar organizations). Attend several meetings. (You may have to get permission from the group's leader to attend meetings. Make sure that you tell the leader that you want to observe the meeting and describe it to your class.) Answer the following questions:

    ■ What is the purpose of the network?
    ■ How old are the members?

- What other personal characteristics of members seem to be significant (for example, all members are bankers, all members are business owners)?
- How are the meetings conducted?
- What kinds of things do participants discuss at meetings?

During a class discussion, compare networks that are primarily male, primarily female, or mixed. How are they similar? How do they differ? In your opinion, which of the networks are most effective in overcoming barriers to effective organizational communication? Why?

FURTHER READING

Dziech, B. W., & Weiner, L. (1990). *The lecherous professor: Sexual harassment on campus*, 2d ed. Urbana, IL: University of Illinois Press.
This book describes the problems of sexual harassment on college campuses and how some universities have instituted policies to counter this negative behavior. Harassment against both students and faculty is described and suggestions are offered for responding to harassment incidents.

Hochschild, A. R. (1997). *The time bind: When work becomes home and home becomes work.* New York: Henry Holt.
Through a series of interviews with employees at a Fortune 500 company, Hochschild demonstrates how people are deriving satisfaction from their jobs at the expense of their families, how family-friendly companies' policies are not taken advantage of, and how the workplace is becoming a surrogate home.

Karsten, M. F. (1994). *Management and gender: Issues and attitudes.* Westport, CT: Praeger.
This is a comprehensive work on the development of a more diverse workforce. Included are discussions of attitudes toward managerial women, networking, mentors, sexual and racial harassment, and balancing career and work life.

Powell, G. N. (Ed.). (1999). *Handbook of gender and work.* Thousand Oaks, CA: Sage.
This comprehensive overview includes articles on a variety of topics, including the changing nature of work, interviewer biases, work group relations, women as global leaders, sexual harassment, and diversity initiatives.

REFERENCES

Aiex, N. (1988). Literature-based reading instruction. *The Reading Teacher, 41*, 458–461.

Alderton, S. M., & Jurma, W. F. (1980). Genderless/gender related task leader communication and group satisfaction: A test of two hypotheses. *Southern Speech Communication Journal, 46*, 48–60.

Aleguire, D. G. (1978). *Interruptions as turn-taking*. Paper presented at the International Sociological Association Ninth World Congress of Sociology, Uppsala University, Sweden.

Alexander, R. (1988, August 3). Metropolitan diary. *The New York Times*, p. C2.

Allan, K., & Coltrane, S. (1997). Gender displaying television commercials: A comparative study of television commercials in the 1950s and 1980s. *Sex Roles, 35*, 185–203.

Almquist, E. M., & Freudiger, P. (1978). Male and female roles in the lyrics of three genres of contemporary music. *Sex Roles, 4*, 51–65.

American Association of University Women. (1991). *Shortchanging girls, shortchanging America*. Washington, DC: Greenberg-Lake Analysis Group.

American Association of University Women. (1993). *Hostile hallways: The AAUW survey on sexual harassment in America's schools*. Washington, DC: AAUW.

American Association of University Women. (1998). *Gender gaps: Where schools fail our children*. Washington, DC: AAUW.

Anderson, C. M., Raptis, P. R., Lin, Y., & Clark, F. R. (2000). Motives as predictors of argumentativeness and verbal aggressiveness of black and white adolescents. *Communication Research Reports, 17*, 115–126.

Apple, M., & Jungck, L. (1990). "You don't have to be a teacher to teach this unit": Teaching, technology, and gender in the classroom. *American Educational Research Journal, 27*, 227–251.

Argyle, M., & Furnham, A. (1983). Sources of satisfaction and conflict in long-term relationships. *Journal of Marriage and the Family, 45*, 481–493.

Aria, M. (1993, November/December). The risky business of raising sons. *Ms.*, p. 41.

Aries, E. (1987). Gender and communication. In P. Shaver & C. Hendrick (Eds.), *Sex and gender* (pp.149–176). Newbury Park, CA: Sage.

Aries, E. J. (1976). Interaction patterns and themes of male, female, and mixed groups. *Small Group Behavior, 7*, 7–18.

Aries, E. J. (1982). Verbal and nonverbal behavior in single-sex and mixed-sex groups: Are traditional sex roles changing? *Psychological Reports, 51*, 127–134.

Aries, E. J., & Johnson, F. L. (1983). Close friendship in adulthood: Conversational content between same-sex friends. *Sex Roles, 9*, 1183–1196.

Arlow, P., & Froschel, M. (1976). Women in the high school curriculum: A review of U.S. history and English literature texts. In C. Ahlum, J. Fralley & F. Howe (Eds.), *High school feminist studies* (pp. xi–xxviii). Old Westbury, NY: Feminist Press.

Arntson, P., & Turner, L. (1987). Sex role socialization: Children's enactments of their parents' behaviors in regulative and interpersonal context. *Western Journal of Speech Communication, 51*, 304–316.

Ashby, M. S., & Wittmaier, B. C. (1978). Attitude changes in children after exposure to stories about women in traditional and nontraditional occupations. *Journal of Educational Psychology, 70*, 945–949.

Atkin, C., & Miller, M. (1975). *The effects of television advertising on children: Experimental evidence*. Paper presented at the meeting of the International Communication Association, Chicago.

Aukett, R., Richie, J., & Mill, K. (1988). Gender differences in friendship patterns. *Sex Roles, 19*, 57–66.

Ayim, M. (1993). Issues in gender and language: An annotated bibliography. *Resources for feminist research, 22*(1/2), 1–35.

Bachen, C., McLoughlin, M., & Garcia, S. (1999). Assessing the role of gender in college students' evaluations of faculty. *Communication Education, 48*, 193–210.

Backhouse, C., & Cohen, L. (1978). *Sexual harassment on the job.* Englewood Cliffs, NJ: Prentice-Hall.

Baenninger, M. A., & Newcombe, N. (2000). Environmental input to the development of sex-related differences in spatial and mathematical ability. In E. L. Paul (Ed.), *Taking sides: Clashing views on controversial issues in sex and gender* (pp. 76–85). Guilford, CT: Dushkin/McGraw-Hill.

Bailey, M. (1986, November 23). Professor sees need for more "Cathys" in comics. *The Home News,* p. D5.

Baker, D., & Leary, R. (1995). Let girls speak out. *Journal of Research in Science Teaching, 32,* 3–28.

Bandura, A. (1969). Social-learning theory and identification processes. In D. A. Goslin (Ed.), *Handbook of socialization theory and research* (pp. 213–262). Chicago: Rand McNally.

Barner, M. R. (1999). Gender stereotyping and intended audience age: An analysis of children's educational/informational TV programming. *Communication Research Reports, 16,* 193–202.

Baron, A. S., & Abrahamsen, K. (1981, November). Will he—or won't he—work with a female manager? *Management Review,* pp. 48–53.

Baron, D. (1989). *Declining grammar and other essays on the English vocabulary.* Urbana, IL: National Council of Teachers of English.

Barth, R. J., & Kinder, B. N. (1988). A theoretical analysis of sex differences in same-sex friendships. *Sex Roles, 19,* 349–363.

Bartlett, R. L., & Miller, T. I. (1985). Executive compensation: Female executives and networking. *AEA Papers and Proceedings, 75,* 267–270.

Bartol, K. M. (1978). The sex structuring of organizations: A search for possible causes. *Academy of Management Review, 3,* 805–815.

Bartol, K. M. (1999). Gender influences on performance evaluations. In G. N. Powell (Ed.), *Handbook of gender and work* (pp. 165–178). Thousand Oaks, CA: Sage.

Barton, L. (1984). What are boys like in books these days? *Learning, 13,* 130–131.

Bass, B., & Avolio, B. (1993). Transformational leadership: A response to critiques. In M. Chemers & R. Ayman (Eds.), *Leadership theory and research: Perspectives and directions.* San Diego, CA: Academic Press.

Bass, B. M., Krusell, J., & Alexander, R. A. (1971). Male managers' attitudes toward working women. *American Behavioral Scientist, 15,* 221–236.

Bate, B., & Memmott, J. (1984). Three principles for dual-career marriages. Unpublished manuscript, Northern Illinois University, DeKalb, IL.

Baxter, L. A. (1985). Accomplishing relationship disengagement. In S. Duck & D. Perlman (Eds.), *Understanding personal relationships: An interdisciplinary approach* (pp. 243–265). Beverly Hills, CA: Sage.

Baxter, L. A. (1986). Gender differences in the heterosexual relationship rules embedded in breakup accounts. *Journal of Social and Personal Relationships, 3,* 289–306.

Baxter, L. A., & Wilmot, W. W. (1984). "Secret tests": Social strategies for acquiring information about the state of the relationship. *Human Communication Research, 11,* 171–201.

Bazler, J. (1989, November). Chem text photos discourage women. *NEA Today,* p. 33.

Bazler, J. A., & Simonis, D. A. (1991). Are high school chemistry books gender free? *Journal of Research in Science Teaching, 28,* 353–362.

Beach, D. R., & Sokoloff, M. J. (1974). Spatially dominated nonverbal communication of children: A methodological study. *Perceptual and Motor Skills, 38,* 1303–1310.

Beauchamp, B., & Wheeler, B. (1988). From Achilles to the hell: Teaching masculinity. *Women's Studies Quarterly, 14,* 100–111.

Becker, B. (1990). Item characteristics and gender differences on the SAT-M for mathematically able youths. *American Educational Research Journal, 27,* 68–87.

Beckwith, L. (1972). Relationships between infants' social behavior and their mothers' behavior. *Child Development, 43,* 397–411.

Beebe, S. T., & Masterson, J. T. (1986). *Family talk: Interpersonal communication in the family.* New York: Random House.

Bell, R. (1981). *Worlds of friendship.* Beverly Hills, CA: Sage.

Bell, R., & Buerkel-Rothfuss, N. L. (1990). S(he) loves me, s(he) loves me not: Predictors of relational information-seeking in courtship and beyond. *Communication Quarterly, 38,* 64–82.

Bell, R. A., Buerkel-Rothfuss, N. L., & Gore, K. E. (1987). "Did you bring the yarmulke for the cabbage patch kid?" The idiomatic communication of young lovers. *Human Communication Research, 14,* 47–67.

Bell, R. Q., Weller, G. M., & Waldrop, M. F. (1971). Newborn and preschooler: Organization of behavior and relations between periods. *Monographs of the Society for Research in Child Development, 36*(1–2), Serial No. 142.

Bellinger, D. C., & Gleason, J. B. (1982). Sex differences in parental directives to young children. *Sex Roles, 8,* 1123–1139.

Bem, S. L. (1974). The measurement of psychological androgyny. *Journal of Counseling and Clinical Psychology, 42,* 155–162.

Bennetts, L. (1979, October 14). Women: New opportunity, old reality. *New York Times,* Sec. 12, p. 58.

Benz, C. R., Pfeiffer, I., & Newman, I. (1981). Sex role expectations of classroom teachers, grades 1–12. *American Educational Research Journal, 18,* 289–302.

Benzel, J. (1995, January 19). Close to home: Of Dr. Seuss and preening princesses. *The New York Times,* p. C11.

Berg, J. H., & McQuinn, R. D. (1986). Attraction and exchange in continuing and noncontinuing dating relationships. *Journal of Personality and Social Psychology, 50,* 942–952.

Berger, J., Rosenholtz, S. J., & Zelditch, M., Jr. (1980). Status organizing processes. In A. Inkeles et al. (Eds.), *Annual review of sociology* (pp. 479–508). Palo Alto, CA: Annual Reviews.

Berryman-Fink, C. (1997). Gender issues: Management style, mobility and harassment. In P. Y. Byers (Eds.), *Organizational communication: Theory and behavior* (pp. 259–283). Boston: Allyn and Bacon.

Berryman-Fink, C., Heintz, M. A., Lowy, M. S., Sebohm, M. L., & Wheeless, V. E. (1986, November). *Perceptions of women as managers: Implications for organizational success.* Paper presented at the meeting of the Speech Communication Association, Chicago, IL.

Berscheid, E., Walster, E., & Bohrnstedt, G. (1973, November). Body image. *Psychology Today,* p. 119.

Binion, V. J. (1990). Psychological androgyny: A black female perspective. *Sex Roles, 22,* 487–507.

Birdsall, P. (1980). A comparative analysis of male and female managerial communication style in two organizations. *Journal of Vocational Behavior, 16,* 183–196.

Birdwhistell, R. (1970). *Kinesics and context.* Philadelphia: University of Pennsylvania Press.

Bjorklund, E. (1986). Women and Star Trek fandom: From sf to sisterhood. *Minerva: Quarterly Report on Women and the Military, 4*(1), 16–65.

Blair, S. (1993). Employment, family, and perceptions of marital quality among husbands and wives. *Journal of Family Issues, 14,* 189–212.

Bleakley, M., Westerberg, V., & Hopkins, K. (1988). The effect of character sex on story interest and comprehension in children. *American Educational Research Journal, 25,* 145–155.

Blieszner, R., & Adams, R. (1992). *Adult friendships.* Newbury Park, CA: Sage.

Block, J. H. (1983). Differential premises arising from differential socialization of the sexes: Some conjectures. *Child Development, 54,* 1335–1354.

Block, J. H. (1984). *Sex role identity and ego development.* San Francisco: Jossey-Bass.

Blumer, H. (1969). *Symbolic interactionism: Perspective and method.* Englewood Cliffs, NJ: Prentice-Hall.

Bochner, A. P. (1983). The function of human communication in interpersonal bonding. In C. C. Arnold & J. W. Bowers, *Handbook of rhetorical and communication theory* (pp. 544–621). Boston, MA: Allyn & Bacon.

Bohan, J. S. (1973). Age and sex differences in self-concept. *Adolescence, 8,* 379–384.

Bonnelli, L. (1988). Sex-role stereotyping in fragrance advertisements. In C. M. Lont & S. A. Friedley (Eds.), *Beyond boundaries: Sex and gender diversity in communication* (pp. 265–282). Fairfax, VA: George Mason University Press.

Booth-Butterfield, M. (1986). Recognizing and communicating in harassment-prone organizational climates. *Communication Quarterly, 9,* 42–51.

Botta, R. A. (1999). Television images of adolescent girls' body image disturbance. *Journal of Communication, 49*(2), 22–41.

"Bound to be muscular." (1997, December 30). *The Buffalo News*, p. D3.

Bowen, S. P., & Wyatt, N. J. (Eds.). (1993). *Transforming visions: Feminist critiques of speech communication.* Cresskill, NJ: Hampton Press.

Bowman, G. W., Worthy, N. B., & Greyser, S. A. (1965). Are women executives people? *Harvard Business Review, 43*(4), 14–28, 164–178.

Bozzi, V. (1988, June). Mellowing dads. *Psychology Today*, p. 15.

Brabant, S., & Mooney, L. (1986). Sex-role stereotyping in the Sunday comics: 10 years later. *Sex Roles, 14,* 141–148.

Bradley, P. H. (1981). The folk-linguistics of women's speech: An empirical examination. *Communication Monographs, 48,* 73–90.

Brandon, P., Newton, B., & Hammond, O. (1987). Children's mathematics achievement in Hawaii: Sex differences favoring girls. *American Educational Research Journal, 24,* 437–461.

Bray, J. H., & Howard, G. S. (1980). Interaction of teacher and student sex and sex role orientations and student evaluations of college instruction. *Contemporary Educational Psychology, 5,* 241–248.

"Breaking the airwaves." (2000, June/July). *Ms.*, p. 41.

Brems, C., & Johnson, M. E. (1989). Problem-solving appraisal and coping style: The influence of sex-role orientation and gender. *Journal of Psychology, 123,* 187–194.

Brenner, O. C., Tomkiewicz, J., & Schein, V. A. (1989). The relationships between sex role stereotypes and requisite management characteristics revisited. *Academy of Management Journal, 32,* 662–669.

Bretl, D. J., & Cantor, J. (1987, November). *The portrayal of men and women in U.S. television commercials: A recent content analysis and trends over fifteen years.* Paper presented at the meeting of the Speech Communication Association, Boston, MA.

Bright, M. C., & Stockdale, D. E. (1984). Mothers', fathers', and preschool children's interactive behavior in a play setting. *Journal of Genetic Psychology, 144,* 219–232.

Brooks, J., & Lewis, M. (1974). Attachment behavior in thirteen-month-old opposite sex twins. *Child Development, 45,* 243–247.

Brooks-Gunn, J., & Matthews, W. S. (1979). *He and she: How children develop their sex role identity.* Englewood Cliffs, NJ: Prentice-Hall.

Brophy, J. (1985). Interactions of male and female students with male and female teachers. In L. C. Wilkinson & C. B. Marrett (Eds.), *Gender influence in classroom interaction* (pp. 115–142). Orlando, FL: Academic Press.

Brown, L. M., & Gilligan, C. (1992). *Meeting at the crossroads: Women's psychology and girls' development.* Cambridge, MA: Harvard University Press.

Browne, B. A. (1998). Gender stereotypes in advertising on children's television in the 1990s: A cross-national analysis. *Journal of Advertising, 27,* 83–96.

Bruess, C. J. S., & Pearson, J. C. (1997). Interpersonal rituals in marriage and adult friendships. *Communication Monographs, 64,* 25–46.

Buck, R. (1976). A test of nonverbal receiving ability: Preliminary studies. *Human Communication Research, 2,* 162–171.

Buerkel-Rothfuss, N. L., Covert, A. M., Keith, J., & Nelson, C. (1986). *Early adolescent and parental communication patterns.* Paper presented at the annual meeting of the Speech Communication Association, Chicago.

Buhrke, R. A., & Fuqua, D. R. (1987). Sex differences in same- and cross-sex supportive relationships. *Sex Roles, 17,* 339–351.

Bumpass, L. L. (1990). What's happening to the family? Interactions between demographic and institutional change. *Demography, 27,* 483–498.

Burke, R., Weir, T., & Harrison, D. (1976). Disclosure of problems and tensions experienced by marital partners. *Psychological Reports, 38,* 531–542.

Burleson, B. R., Kunkel, A. W., Samter, W., & Werking, K. J. (1996). Men's and women's evaluations of communication skills in personal relationships: When sex differences make a difference—and when they don't. *Journal of Social and Personal Relationships, 13,* 201–224.

Burr, E., Dunn, S., & Farquhar, N. (1972). Women and the language of inequality. *Social Education, 36,* 841–845.

Butruille, S. G., & Taylor, A. (1987). Women in American popular song. In L. P. Stewart & S. Ting-Toomey (Eds.), *Communication, gender, and sex roles in diverse interaction contexts* (pp. 179–188). Norwood, NJ: Ablex.

Buzza, B. W. (1982, November). *Three communication responsibilities concerning sexual harassment.* Paper presented at the meeting of the Speech Communication Association, Louisville, KY.

Buzzanell, P. M. (1995). Reframing the glass ceiling as a socially constructed process: Implications for understanding and change. *Communication Monographs, 62,* 327–354.

Byrne, B., & Shavelson, R. (1987). Adolescent self-concept: Testing the assumption of equivalent structures across gender. *American Education Research Journal, 24,* 365–385.

Caldera, Y. M., Huston, A. C., & O'Brien, M. (1989). Social interactions and play patterns of parents and toddlers with feminine, masculine, and neutral toys. *Child Development, 60,* 70–76.

Caldwell, M. A., & Peplau, L. A. (1982). Sex differences in same-sex friendships. *Sex Roles, 8,* 721–732.

Cameron, D., McAlinden, F., & O'Leary, K. (1988). Lakoff in context: The social and linguistic functions of tag questions. In J. Coates & D. Cameron (Eds.), *Women in their speech communities: New perspectives on language and sex* (pp. 74–93). New York: Longman.

Campbell, K. (1991). Hearing women's voices. *Communication Education, 40,* 33–48.

Campbell, P., & Wirtenberg, J. (1980). How books influence children: What the research shows. *Interracial Books for Children Bulletin, 11,* 3–6.

Campion, K. L. (1983, February). Intimate strangers: The readers, the writers, and the experts. *Ms.,* pp. 98–99.

Canary, D. J., & Hause, K. S. (1993). Is there any reason to research sex differences in communication? *Communication Quarterly, 41,* 129–144.

Capsuto, S. (2000). *Alternate channels: The uncensored story of gay and lesbian images on radio and television.* New York: Ballantine.

Carli, L. L. (1990). Gender, language, and influence. *Journal of Personality and Social Psychology, 59,* 941–951.

Carlson, M. (1989). Guidelines for a gender-based curriculum in English, grades 7–12. *English Journal, 36,* 30–33.

Carmody, D. (1987, April 17). SAT's are biased against girls, report by advocacy group says. *The New York Times,* p. B2.

Carnegie Commission on Higher Education. (1973). *Opportunity for women in higher education.* New York: McGraw-Hill.

Carter, K., & Spitzack, C. (Eds.). (1989). *Doing research on women's communication: Perspectives on theory and method.* Norwood, NJ: Ablex.

Casbolt, D., & DeWine, S. (1982). *How do women use mentors? A field research study.* Paper presented at the Fifth Annual Communication, Language and Gender Conference, Athens, OH.

Cash, T. F., & Henry, P. E. (1995). Women's body images: The results of a national survey in the U.S.A. *Sex Roles, 33,* 19–28.

Cate, R. M., & Lloyd, S. A. (1992). *Courtship.* Newbury Park, CA: Sage.

Chandler, Z. (1990). Beyond the veil: An interview with Toni Cade Bambara and Sonia Sanchez. In J. Braxton & A. N. McLaughlin (Eds.), *Wild women in the whirlwind: Afra-America culture and the contemporary literary renaissance.* New Brunswick, NJ: Rutgers University Press.

Chavez, D. (1985). Perpetuation of gender inequality: A content-analysis of comic strips. *Sex Roles, 13,* 93–102.

Cherry, L., & Lewis, M. (1978). Differential socialization of girls and boys: Implications for sex differences in language development. In N. Waterson & C. Snow (Eds.), *The development of communication* (pp. 189–197). New York: John Wiley & Sons.

Chethik, N. (1994, August 28). Boys, too, shortchanged in classroom. *The Plain Dealer,* p. 5.

Cheyne, J. A. (1976). Development of forms and functions of smiling in preschoolers. *Child Development, 47,* 820–823.

Chodorow, N. (1974). Family structure and feminine personality. In M. Z. Rosaldo & L. Lamphere (Eds.), *Women, culture and society* (pp. 43–66). Stanford, CA: Stanford University Press.

Chodorow, N. (1978). *The reproduction of mothering: Psychoanalysis and the sociology of gender.* Berkeley, CA: University of California Press.

Christian-Smith, L. K. (1988). Girls' romance novel reading and what to do about it. *The New Advocate, 1,* 177–185.

Clarke-Stewart, K. A. (1973). Interactions between mothers and their young children: Characteristics and consequences. *Monographs of the Society for Research in Child Development, 38*(6–7), Serial No. 153.

Clarke-Stewart, A., Friedman, S., & Koch, J. (1985). *Child development: A topical approach.* New York: John Wiley and Sons.

Coates, J. (1986). *Women, men and language.* New York: Longman.

Coates, J. (1988). Introduction. In J. Coates & D. Cameron (Eds.), *Women in their speech communities: New perspectives on language and sex* (pp. 63–73). New York: Longman.

Cohen, L. J., & Campos, J. J. (1974). Father, mother, and stranger as elicitors of attachment behaviors in infancy. *Development Psychology, 10,* 146–154.

Colleary, K. (1999, June 22). Tarzan bulks up. *The New York Times,* p. A27.

Collins, E. G. C., & Blodgett, T. B. (1981). Sexual harassment . . . Some see it . . . Some won't. *Harvard Business Review, 59*(2), 76–94.

Collis, B., & Ollila, L. (1990). The effect of computer use on Grade 1 children's gender stereotypes about reading, writing, and computer use. *Journal of Research and Development in Education, 24,* 14–20.

Colwill, N. (1993). Sexist language revisited (and revisited and revisited . . .). *Women in Management, 3*(4), 4.

Colwill, N. (1996). As I see it: Assessing managerial assessment. *Women in Management, 6*(4), 6.

Colwill, N. L., & Erhart, M. (1985, Spring). Have women changed the workplace? *Business Quarterly,* pp. 27–31.

Comstock, J. (1994). Parent–adolescent conflict: A developmental approach. *Western Journal of Communication, 58,* 263–282.

Condry, J., & Condry, S. (1976). Sex differences: A study of the eye of the beholder. *Child Development, 47,* 812–819.

Cooney, T. (1993). Recent demographic change: Implications for families planning for the future. In B. Settles, R. Hanks, & M. Sussman (Eds.), *American families and the future: Analysis of possible destinies* (pp. 37–55). New York: Haworth Press.

Cooper, P. (1987). Sex role stereotypes of stepparents in children's literature. In L. P. Stewart and S. Ting-Toomey (Eds.), *Communication, gender, and sex roles in diverse interaction contexts* (pp. 61–82). Norwood, NJ: Ablex.

Cooper, P. (1989). Children's literature: The extent of sexism. In C. Lont & S. Friedley (Eds.), *Beyond boundaries: Sex and gender diversity in education* (pp. 233–250). Fairfax, VA: George Mason University Press.

Cooper, P. (1993a). Communication and gender in the classroom. In D. Borisoff and L. Arliss (Eds.), *Women and men communicating: Challenges and changes* (pp. 122–141). New York: Harcourt Brace.

Cooper, P. (1993b). Women and power in the Caldecott and Newbery winners, 1980–90. In C. Berryman-Fink, D. Ballard-Reisch, and L. Newman (Eds.), *Communication and sex-role socialization* (pp. 7–27). New York: Garland.

Cooper, P. (1994). The image of stepmothers in children's literature 1980–1991. In L. Turner & H. Sterk (Eds.), *Differences that make a difference.* Westport, CT: Bergin & Garvey.

Cooper, P., & Simonds, C. (1999). *Communication for the classroom teacher,* 6th ed. Boston: Allyn and Bacon.

Cooper, P., Stewart, L. P., & Friedley, S. A. (1989). Twenty years of research by and about women in major communication journals: 1967–1986. *ACA Bulletin, 67,* 46–61.

Cooper, P., Stewart, L. P., & Gudykunst, W. B. (1982). Relationship with instructor and other variables influencing student evaluations of instruction. *Communication Quarterly, 30,* 308–315.

Cooper, V. W. (1985). Women in popular music: A quantitative analysis of feminine images over time. *Sex Roles, 13,* 499–506.

Cooper, V. W. (1997). Homophily or the Queen Bee Syndrome: Female evaluation of female leadership. *Small Group Research, 28,* 483–499.

Corcoran, M., & Datcher, L., & Duncan, G. J. (1980). Most workers find jobs through word of mouth. *Monthly Labor Review, 103,* 33–35.

Cowan, G., & Koziej, J. (1979). The perception of sex-inconsistent behavior. *Sex Roles, 5,* 1–10.

Cox, T., Jr. (1993). *Cultural diversity in organizations: Theory, research and practice.* San Francisco: Berrett-Koehler.

Craig, R. S. (1992). The effect of television day part on gender portrayals in television commercials: A content analysis. *Sex Roles, 26,* 197–211.

Crawford, M. (2000). Two sexes, two cultures. In E. L. Paul (Ed.), *Taking sides: Clashing views on controversial issues in sex and gender* (pp. 96–102). Guilford, CT: Dushkin/McGraw-Hill.

Crenshaw, K. (1991, November). Presentation at the Center for the American Woman in Politics Forum for Women State Legislators, San Diego, CA.

Croyle, K. (1987). Sex-role messages in the themes and lyrics of contemporary music: A 25-year perspective. *Ohio Journal of Science, 87*(2), 28.

Dads change diapers, too. (1989, May 2). *New York Times,* p. 11.

Dainton, M., Stafford, L., & McNeilis, K. S. (1992). *The maintenance of relationships through the use of routine behaviors.* Paper presented at the annual meeting of the Speech Communication Association, Chicago.

Daly, B. (1980). Laughing with or at the young-adult romance. *English Journal, 27,* 50–60.

Davidson, L. R., & Duberman, L. (1982). Friendship: Communication and interactional patterns in same-sex dyads. *Sex Roles, 8,* 809–822.

Davis, B., & Gilbert, L. (1989). Effect of dispositional and situational influences on women's dominance expression in mixed-sex dyads. *Journal of Personality and Social Psychology, 57,* 294–300.

Daviss, B. (1988, Winter). The gender gap: Does it still exist? *Television and Families, 10,* 2–9.

Dehler, K. (1989). Diaries: Where women reveal themselves. *English Journal, 34,* 53–54.

Denisoff, R. S., & Bridges, J. (1982). Popular music: Who are the recording artists? *Journal of Communication, 32*(1), 132–142.

Deveny, K. (1994, December 5). Chart of kindergarten awards. *Wall Street Journal,* p. B1.

Devine, I., & Markiewicz, D. (1990). Cross-sex relationships at work and the impact of gender stereotypes. *Journal of Business Ethics, 9,* 333 338.

DiMona, L., & Herndon, C. (1994). *Women's sourcebook: Resources and information for everyday use.* Boston, MA: Houghton Mifflin.

Dindia, K. (1987). The effects of sex of subject and sex of partner on interruptions. *Human Communication Research, 13,* 345–371.

Dindia, K., & Allen, M. (1992). Sex differences in disclosure: A meta-analysis. *Psychological Bulletin, 112,* 106–124.

Dion, K. L. (1987). What's in a title? The Ms. stereotype and images of women's titles of address. *Psychology of Women Quarterly, 11,* 21–36.

Dipboye, R. L., & Wiley, J. W. (1977). Reactions of college recruiters to interviewee sex and self-presentation style. *Journal of Vocational Behavior, 10,* 1–12.

Dolin, D. J., & Booth-Butterfield, M. (1993). Reach out and touch someone: Analysis of nonverbal comforting responses. *Communication Quarterly, 41,* 383–393.

Donahue, T. J. (1976). *Discrimination against young women in career selection by high school counselors.* Unpublished doctoral dissertation, Michigan State University.

Donlan, D. (1972). The negative image of women in children's literature. *Elementary English, 49,* 604–611.

Donnell, S. M., & Hall, J. (1980). Men and women as managers: A significant case of no significant difference. *Organizational Dynamics, 8*(4), 60–77.

Dorman, S. M. (1998). Technology and the gender gap. *Journal of School Health, 68,* 165–166.

Dougherty, W., & Engel, R. (1987). An 80s look for sex equality in Caldecott winners and honor books. *The Reading Teacher, 40,* 394–398.

Downs, A. C., & Harrison, S. K. (1985). Embarrassing age spots or just plain ugly: Physical attractiveness stereotyping as an instrument of sexism on American television commercials. *Sex Roles, 13,* 9–19.

Downs, V. C., & Downs, T. M. (1993, May). *An exploratory and descriptive study identifying communicative behaviors associated with effective college teaching.* Paper presented at the International Communication Association annual meeting, Washington, DC.

Drewnowski, A., & Yee, D. (1987). Men and body image: Are males satisfied with their body weight? *Psychosomatic Medicine, 49,* 626–634.

Dubois, B. L., & Crouch, I. (1975). The question of tag questions in women's speech: They don't really use more of them, do they? *Language in Society, 4,* 289–294.

Duck, S., Rutt, D., Hurst, M., & Strejc, H. (1991). Some evident truths about conversations in everyday relationships: All communications are not created equal. *Human Communication Research, 18,* 228–267.

Dumlao, R., & Botta, R. A. (2000). Family communication patterns and the conflict styles young adults use with their fathers. *Communication Quarterly, 48,* 174–189.

Duran, R. L., & Kelly, L. (1985). An investigation into the cognitive domain of communicative competence. *Communication Research Reports, 2,* 112–119.

Durkin, K., & Nugent, B. (1998). Kindergarten children's gender-role expectations for television actors. *Sex Roles, 38,* 387–402.

Eagly, A. H. (2000). The science and politics of comparing women and men. In E. L. Paul (Eds.), *Taking sides: Clashing views on controversial issues in sex and gender* (pp. 106–111). Guilford, CT: Dushkin/McGraw-Hill.

Eagly, A., & Johnson, B. (1990). Gender and leadership style: A meta-analysis. *Psychological Bulletin, 108,* 233–256.

Eakins, B. W., & Eakins, R. G. (1978). *Sex differences in human communication.* Boston: Houghton Mifflin.

Eaky, K. (1991, Jan. 9). Girls' low self-esteem slows their progress, study finds. *San Francisco Examiner.*

Earle, J., Roach, V., & Fraser, K. (1987). *Female dropouts: A new perspective.* Alexandria, VA: National Association of State Boards of Education.

Eberts, E. H., & Lepper, M. R. (1975). Individual consistency in the proxemic behavior of preschool children. *Journal of Personality and Social Psychology, 32,* 841–848.

Eccles, J. S., & Hoffman, L. W. (1984). Sex roles, socialization, and occupational behavior. In H. W. Stevenson & A. E. Siegel (Eds.), *Child development research and social policy* (Vol. 1, pp. 367–420). Chicago: University of Chicago Press.

Edelsky, C. (1976). The acquisition of communicative competence: Recognition of linguistic correlates of sex roles. *Merrill-Palmer Quarterly, 22,* 47–59.

Eisenberg, A. (2000, October 12). Mars and Venus, online: As the net finds its voices, old stereotypes prevail. *New York Times,* pp. G1, G11.

Eisenstock, B. (1984). Sex role differences in children's identification with counterstereotypical televised portrayals. *Sex Roles, 10,* 417–430.

Eman, V. A., Dierks-Stewart, K., & Tucker, R. K. (1978). *Implications of sexual identity and sexually identified situations on nonverbal touch.* Paper presented at the meeting of the Speech Communication Association, Minneapolis, MN.

Emihovich, C. A., Gaier, E. L., & Cronin, N. C. (1984). Sex-role expectation changes by fathers for their sons. *Sex Roles, 11,* 861–868.

Endres, K. L. (1984). Sex role standards in popular music. *Journal of Popular Culture, 18,* 9–18.

Engelhard, P. A., Jones, K. O., & Stiggins, R. J. (1976). Trends in counselor attitude about women's roles. *Journal of Counseling Psychology, 23,* 365–372.

Epstein, C. F. (1988). *Deceptive distinctions: Sex, gender, and the social order.* New Haven, CT: Yale University Press.

Equal pay for working families: A national overview. (1999). *Institute for Women's Policy Research Research-in-Brief,* 1–4.

Erens, P. (1979). *Sexual strategems: The world of women in film.* New York: Horizon Press.

Etaugh, C., & Liss, M. B. (1992). Home, school, and playroom: Training groups for adult gender roles. *Sex Roles, 26,* 129–147.

Ethington, C., & Wolfe, L. (1988). Women's selection of quantitative undergraduate fields of study: Direct and indirect influences. *American Educational Research Journal, 25,* 157–175.

Evans, G. W., & Howard, R. B. (1973). Personal space. *Psychological Bulletin, 80,* 334–344.

Fagot, B. I. (1978). The influence of sex of child on parental reactions to toddler children. *Child Development, 49,* 459–465.

Fagot, B., Leinbach, M., & O'Boyle, C. (1992). Gender labeling, gender stereotyping, and parenting behaviors. *Developmental Psychology, 28,* 225–230.

Falbo, T. (1977). Relationships between sex, sex role, and social influence. *Psychology of Women Quarterly, 2,* 62–72.

Feather, N. T. (1984). Masculinity, femininity, psychological androgyny, and the structure of values. *Journal of Personality and Social Psychology, 47,* 604–620.

Feiner, S., & Morgan, B. (1987). Women and minorities in introductory economics textbooks: 1974 to 1984. *Journal of Economic Education, 18,* 376–92.

Feiner, S., & Roberts, B. (1990). Hidden by the invisible hand: Neoclassical economic theory and the textbook treatment of race and gender. *Gender and Society, 4,* 159–181.

Feldman, S. S., Nash, S. C., & Aschenbrenner, B. G. (1983). Antecedents of fathering. *Child Development, 54,* 1628–1636.

Feldman, R. S., & White, J. B. (1980). Detecting deception in children. *Journal of Communication, 30*(2), 121–128.

Ferguson, A. (1989). A feminist aspect theory of the self. In A. Garry & M. Pearsall (Eds.), *Women, knowledge, and reality: Explorations in feminist philosophy* (pp. 93–107). Boston, MA: Unwin Hyman.

Fernandez, J. P. (1991). *Managing a diverse work force: Regaining the competitive edge.* Lexington, MA: Lexington Books.

Ferree, M. M., & Hall, E. J. (1990). Visual images of American society: Gender and race in introductory sociology textbooks. *Gender and Society, 4,* 500–533.

Fierman, J. (1990, July 30). Why women still don't hit the top. *Fortune,* pp. 40–62.

Fillmer, H. T., & Haswell, L. (1977). Sex-role stereotyping in English usage. *Sex Roles, 3,* 257–263.

Firester, L., & Firester, J. (1974). Wanted: A new deal for boys. *Elementary School Journal, 75,* 28–36.

Fishman, P. M. (1978). Interaction: The work women do. *Social Problems, 25,* 397–406.

Fitzpatrick, M. A. (1983). Effective interpersonal communication for women of the corporation: Think like a man, talk like a lady. In J. J. Pilotta (Ed.), *Women in organizations: Barriers and breakthroughs* (pp. 73–84). Prospect Heights, IL: Waveland.

Fitzpatrick, M. A. (1988). *Between husbands & wives: Communication in marriage.* Newbury Park, CA: Sage.

Fitzpatrick, M. A., & Indvik, J. (1982). The instrumental and expressive domains of marital communication. *Human Communication Research, 8,* 195–213.

Flannery-Schroeder, E. C., & Chrisler, J. C. (1996). Body esteem, eating attitudes, and gender-role orientation in three age groups of children. *Current Psychology, 15,* 235–248.

Flerx, V. C., Fidler, D. S., & Rogers, R. W. (1976). Sex role stereotypes: Developmental aspects and early intervention. *Child Development, 47,* 998–1007.

Floyd, K., & Morman, M. T. (1999, May). *Affectionate same-sex touch: Understanding the influence of homophobia on observer's perceptions.* Paper presented at the International Communication Association annual meeting, San Francisco, CA.

Foschi, M. (1996). Double standards in the evaluation of men and women. *Social Psychology Quarterly, 59,* 237–254.

Fox, M. F., Gibbs, M., & Auerbach, D. (1985). Age and gender dimensions of friendship. *Psychology of Women Quarterly, 9,* 489–502.

Foxley, C. H. (1982). Sex equity in education: Some gains, problems, and future needs. *Journal of Teacher Education, 33,* 6–9.

Frazier, P., Aridian, N., Benson, S., Losoff, A., & Maurer, S. (1996). Desire for marriage and life satisfaction among unmarried heterosexual adults. *Journal of Social and Personal Relationships, 13,* 225–239.

Freedman, N., O'Hanlon, J., Oltman, P., & Witkin, H. A. (1972). The imprint of psychological differentiation on kinetic behavior in varying communicative contexts. *Journal of Abnormal Psychology, 79,* 239–258.

Friedman, L. (1989). Mathematics and the gender gap: A meta-analysis of recent studies on sex differences in mathematical tasks. *Review of Educational Research, 59*, 185–213.

Frieze, I. H., Parsons, J. E., Johnson, P. B., Ruble, D. N., & Zellman, G. L. (1978). *Women and sex roles: A social psychological perspective*. New York: W. W. Norton.

Frueh, T., & McGhee, P. E. (1975). Traditional sex role development and amount of time spent watching television. *Developmental Psychology, 11*, 109.

Furman, W., & Buhrmester, D. (1985). Children's perceptions of their personal relationships in their social networks. *Developmental Psychology, 21*, 1016–1024.

Gallo, M. (1987). *Sex bias in counseling materials: A follow-up study*. Unpublished paper, Rutgers University, Department of Communication, New Brunswick, NJ.

Galvin, K. M., & Brommel, B. J. (1999). *Family communication: Cohesion and change*, 5th ed. Reading, MA: Addison-Wesley.

Ganong, L. H., & Coleman, M. (1992). Gender differences in expectations of self and future partner. *Journal of Family Issues, 13*, 55–64.

Garner, T. (1989). *Black male images as portrayed in the songs of Black females*. Paper presented at the Speech Communication Association, San Francisco, CA.

Gartner, M. (1995, November 21). So much for traditional families. *USA Today*, p. 11A.

Gelb, S. A. (1989). Language and problem of male salience in early childhood classroom environments. *Early Childhood Research Quarterly, 4*, 205–215.

Gill, S., Stockard, J., Johnson, J., & Williams, S. (1987). Measuring gender differences: The expressive dimension and a critique of androgyny scales. *Sex Roles, 17*, 375–400.

Gilligan, C. (1982). *In a different voice: Psychological theory and women's development*. Cambridge, MA: Harvard University Press.

Gilligan, C., Lyons, W., & Hanmer, T. (1990). *Making connections*. Cambridge, MA: Harvard University Press.

Gillikin, J. (1989). Rooms of one's own: Nontraditional literature in the classroom. *Women's Studies Quarterly, 17*, 89–94.

Gold, D., Crombie, G., & Noble, S. (1987). Relations between teachers' judgments of girls' and boys' compliance and intellectual competence. *Sex Roles, 16*, 351–358.

Goldsmith, D. (1990). A dialectic perspective on the expression of autonomy and connection in romantic relationships. *Western Journal of Speech Communication, 54*, 537–556.

Goldsmith, D., & Dun, S. (1997). Sex differences and similarities in the communication of social support. *Journal of Social and Personal Relationships, 14*, 317–337.

Goleman, D. (1987, August 2). Girls and math: Is biology really destiny? *New York Times Educational Life*, pp. 42–46.

Golinkoff, R. M., & Ames, G. J. (1979). A comparison of fathers' and mothers' speech with their young children. *Child Development, 50*, 28–32.

Good, T., & Slavings, R. (1988). Male and female student question-asking behavior in elementary and secondary mathematical and language arts classes. *Journal of Research in Childhood Education, 3*, 5–23.

Goodwin, M. H. (1988). Cooperation and competition across girls' play activities. In S. Fisher & A. D. Todd (Eds.), *Gender and discourse: The power of talk* (pp. 55–94). Norwood, NJ: Ablex.

Gould, K. H. (1988, September–October). Old wine in new bottles: A feminist perspective on Gilligan's theory. *Social Work*, pp. 411–415.

Graham, G. H., Unruh, J., & Jennings, P. (1991, Winter). The impact of nonverbal communication in organizations: A survey of perceptions. *Journal of Business Communication, 28*, 45–62.

Grant, J. (1988). Women as managers: What they can offer to organizations. *Organizational Dynamics, 16*(3), 56–63.

Grauerholz, E., & Pescosolido, B. (1989). Gender presentation in children's literature: 1900–1984. *Gender and Society, 3*, 113–125.

Graves, L. M. (1999). Gender bias in interviewers' evaluations of applicants: When and how does it occur? In G. N. Powell (Ed.), *Handbook of gender and work* (pp. 145–164). Thousand Oaks, CA: Sage.

Graziano, W., Brothen, T., & Berscheid, E. (1978). Height and attraction: Do men and women see eye to eye? *Journal of Personality, 46*, 128–145.

Greenblatt, L., Hasenauer, J. E., & Freimuth, V. S. (1980). Psychological sex type and androgyny in the study of communication variables: Self-disclosure and communication apprehension. *Human Communication Research, 6*, 117–129.

Guardo, C. J. (1976). Personal space, sex differences, and interpersonal attraction. *Journal of Psychology, 92*, 9–14.

Guerrero, L. K. (1994). "I'm so mad I could scream": The effects of anger expression on relational satisfaction and communication competence. *Southern Communication Journal, 59*, 124–141.

Gunnar, M. R., & Donahue, M. (1980). Sex differences in social responsiveness between six months and twelve months. *Child Development, 51*, 262–265.

Gunnar-Von Gnechten, M. R. (1978). Changing a frightening toy into a pleasant toy by allowing the infant to control its actions. *Developmental Psychology, 14*, 157–162.

Guttman, J., & Bar-Tal, D. (1982) Stereotypic perceptions of teachers. *American Educational Research Journal, 19*, 519–528.

Haas, A. (1978). *Sex-associated features of spoken language by four-, eight-, and twelve-year-old boys and girls.* Paper presented at the 9th World Congress of Sociology, Uppsala, Sweden. (Cited in Coates, 1986).

Hacker, H. M. (1981). Blabbermouths and clams: Sex differences in self-disclosure in same-sex and cross-sex friendship dyads. *Psychology of Women Quarterly, 5*, 385–401.

Halcomb, R. (1980, February). Mentors and the successful woman. *Across the Board*, pp. 13–18.

Hall, E. (1987, November). All in the family. *Psychology Today*, pp. 54–60.

Hall, J. A. (1978). Gender effects in decoding nonverbal cues. *Psychological Bulletin, 85*, 845–857.

Hall, J. A. (1979). Gender, gender-roles, and nonverbal communication skills. In R. Rosenthal (Ed.), *Skill in nonverbal communication: Individual differences* (pp. 32–67). Cambridge, MA: Oelgeschlager, Gunn & Hain.

Hall, R., & Sandler, B. (1982). *The classroom climate: A chilly one for women?* Washington, D.C.: Association of American Colleges Project on the Status and Education of Women.

Hallingby, L. (1988, February). *Sesame Street*'s old boy network. *Ms.*, p. 12.

Hanice, C. (1987). Teaching about women in the visual arts: The art history survey transfigured. *Women's Studies Quarterly, 15*, 17–20.

Harper, L., & Sanders, K. M. (1975). Preschool children's use of space: Sex differences in outdoor play. *Developmental Psychology, 11*, 119.

Harriman, A. (1985). *Women/men management.* New York: Praeger.

Harway, M. (1977). Sex bias in counseling materials. *Journal of College Student Personnel, 18*, 57–64.

Harwood, N. (1992). Writing women into textbooks. *Feminist Teacher, 6*(3), 16–17, 31.

Haskell, M. (1987). *From reverence to rape: The treatment of women in the movies,* 2d ed. Chicago: University of Chicago Press.

Haslett, B. J. (1983). Communicative functions and strategies in children's conversations. *Human Communication Research, 9*, 114–129.

Haviland, J. M. (1977). Sex-related pragmatics in infants' nonverbal communication. *Journal of Communication, 27*(2), 80–84.

Hays, R. B. (1989). The day-to-day functioning of close versus casual friendships. *Journal of Social and Personal Relationships, 7*, 21–37.

Healey, J. G., & Bell, R. A. (1990). Effects of social networks on individuals' responses to conflicts in friendship. In D. D. Cahn (Ed.), *Intimates in conflict* (pp. 121–150). Hillsdale, NJ: Lawrence Erlbaum.

Heinz, K. (1987). An examination of sex and occupational role presentations of female characters in children's picture books. *Women's Studies in Communication, 11*, 67–78.

Helgesen, S. (1990). *The female advantage: Women's ways of leadership.* New York: Doubleday.

Hellinger, M. (1984). Effecting social change through group action: Feminine occupational titles in transition. In C. Kramarae, M. Schultz, & W. O'Barr (Eds.), *Language and power* (pp. 136–153). Beverly Hills, CA: Sage.

"Help the Guerrilla Girls send a message to those body-obsessed guys in Hollywood." (2001, February/March). *Ms.*, p. 96.

Hendrick, S. S., & Hendrick, C. (1992). *Romantic love.* Newbury Park, CA: Sage.

Henley, N. M. (1977). *Body politics: Power, sex, and nonverbal communication.* Englewood Cliffs, NJ: Prentice-Hall.

Hennig, M., & Jardim, A. (1977). *The managerial woman.* New York: Pocket Books.

Henry, T. (2001, January 25). Study: Latinas shortchanged by U.S. schools. *USA Today*, p. 8D.

Henton, J. M., Cate, R. M., Koval, J. E., Lloyd, S. A., & Christopher, F. S. (1983). Romance and violence in dating relationships. *Journal of Family Issues, 4*, 467–582.

Herek, G. (1987). On heterosexual masculinity: Some psychical consequences of the social construction of gender and sexuality. In M. Kimmel (Ed.), *Changing men: New directions in research on men and masculinity* (pp. 68–82). Newbury Park, CA: Sage.

Hewitt, N. (1988). Sisterhood in international perspective: Thoughts on teaching comparative women's history. *Women's Studies Quarterly, 16*, 22–32.

Higginbotham, E. (1990). Designing an inclusive curriculum: Bringing all women into the core. *Women's Studies Quarterly, 18*, 7–23.

Hill, S. (1991, July 21). Teachers give thought to subtle sex, race bias. *The Home News*, p. C2.

Hochschild, A. (1989). *The second shift: Working parents and the revolution at home.* New York: Viking.

Hoffman, M. L. (1977). Sex differences in empathy and related behaviors. *Psychological Bulletin, 84*, 712–722.

Holmes, B., & Ammon, R. (1985). Teaching content with trade books: A strategy. *Childhood Education, 61*, 366–370.

Holmes, J. (1984). Hedging your bets and sitting on the fence: Some evidence for hedges as support structures. *Te Reo, 27*, 47–62.

Honeycutt, J. M., Cantrill, J. G., & Greene, R. W. (1989). Memory structures for relational escalation: A cognitive test of the sequencing of relational actions and stages. *Human Communication Research, 16*, 62–90.

Hopper, R., Knapp, M. L., & Scott, L. (1981). Couples' personal idioms: Exploring intimate talk. *Journal of Communication, 31*(1), 23–33.

Houston Stanback, M. (1985). Language and black woman's place: Evidence from the black middle class. In P. A. Treichler, C. Kramarae & B. Stafford (Eds.), *For alma mater: Theory and practice in feminist scholarship* (pp. 177–193). Urbana: University of Illinois Press.

Howell, W. S. (1981). *The empathic communicator.* Belmont, CA: Wadsworth.

Hughes, J. O., & Sandler, B. R. (1988). *Peer harassment: Hassles for women on campus.* Washington, DC: Project on the Status and Education of Women, Association of American Colleges.

Hunt, D. M., & Michael, C. (1983). Mentorship: A career training and development tool. *Academy of Management Review, 8*, 475–485.

Illfelder, J. K. (1980). Fear of success, sex role attitudes, and career salience and anxiety levels of college women. *Journal of Vocational Behavior, 16*, 7–17.

Infante, D. A. (1985). Inducing women to be more argumentative: Source credibility effects. *Journal of Applied Communication Research, 13*, 33–44.

Infante, D. A. (1989). Response to high argumentatives: Message and sex differences. *Southern Communication Journal, 54*, 159–170.

Infante, D. A., & Rancer, A. S. (1982). A conceptualization and measure of argumentativeness. *Journal of Personality Assessment, 46*, 72–80.

Infante, D. A., Wall, C. H., Leap, C. J., & Danielson, K. (1984). Verbal aggression as a function of the receiver's argumentativeness. *Communication Research Reports, 1*, 33–37.

Infante, D. A., & Wigley, C. J. (1986). Verbal aggressiveness: An interpersonal model and measure. *Communication Monographs, 53*, 61–69.

Insdorf, A. (1988, April 24). Women film directors make a strong comeback. *The New York Times*, pp. H19–20.

Isenhart, M. W. (1980). An investigation of the relationship of sex and sex role to the ability to decode nonverbal cues. *Human Communication Research, 6*, 309–318.

Ivy, D., & Backlund, P. (1994). *Exploring gender speak: Personal effectiveness in gender communication.* New York: McGraw-Hill.

Jacklin, C. N., & Maccoby, E. E. (1978). Social behavior at 33 months in same-sex and mixed sex dyads. *Child Development, 49,* 557–569.

Jacko, C. M., Karmos, A. H., & Karmos, J. S. (1980). Classroom teachers and sex-role stereotyping: Awareness, attitudes, and behaviors. *Journal of Instructional Psychology, 7*(2), 43–49.

Jackson, L. A. (1983). The perception of androgyny and physical attractiveness: Two is better than one. *Personality and Social Psychology Bulletin, 9,* 405–430.

Jackson, L. A. (1992). *Physical appearance and gender: Sociobiological and sociocultural perspectives.* Albany: State University of New York Press.

Jacobs, D. L. (1992, January 10–16). How to respond to sexual harassment. *National Business Employment Weekly,* pp. 4–6.

Jacobson, M. B., & Insko, W. R. (1985). Use of nonsexist pronouns as a function of one's feminist orientation. *Sex Roles, 13,* 1–7.

James, D., & Clarke, S. (1993). Women, men, and interruptions: A critical review. In D. Tannen (Ed.), *Gender and conversational interaction* (pp. 231–280). New York: Oxford University Press.

James, D., & Drakich, J. (1993). Understanding gender differences in amount of talk: A critical review of research. In D. Tannen (Ed.), *Gender and conversational interaction* (pp. 281–312). New York: Oxford University Press.

Jenkins, M. M., Gappa, J. M., & Pearce, J. (1983). *Removing bias: Guidelines for student–faculty communication.* Annandale, VA: Speech Communication Association.

Jensen, A., & Carlin, D. (1991). Communication and gender. *Communication Education, 40,* 99–104.

Johnson, C., Clay-Warner, J., & Funk, S. J. (1996). Effects of authority structures and gender on interaction in same-sex task groups. *Social Psychology Quarterly, 59,* 221–236.

Johnson, K. (1997, December 17). Limits on the work-at-home life. *The New York Times,* pp. B1, B4.

Johnson, K. L., & Edwards, R. (1991, Spring). The effects of gender and type of romantic touch on perceptions of relational commitment. *Journal of Nonverbal Behavior, 15,* 43–55.

Johnson, L. (1988). Women's history in cross-cultural perspective. *Women's Studies Quarterly, 16,* 74–86.

Jones, M. (1989). Gender issues in teacher education. *Journal of Teacher Education, 40,* 33–44.

Jones, M. G. (1987). Gender differences in student-teacher interactions in physical science and chemistry classes. Doctoral Dissertation, North Carolina State University, Raleigh, NC.

Jones, S. E. (1986). Sex differences in touch communication. *Western Journal of Speech Communication, 50,* 227–241.

Jones, T. S., & Brunner, C. C. (1984). The effects of self-disclosure and sex on perceptions of interpersonal communication competence. *Women's Studies in Communication, 7,* 23–37.

Jordan, F. F., McGreal, E. A., & Wheeless, V. E. (1990). Student perceptions of teacher sex-role orientation and use of power strategies and teacher sex as determinants of student attitudes toward learning. *Communication Quarterly, 38,* 43–53.

Jordan, K. (1987, April 26). Pumping irony: Tender loving dads muscle their way into the ads. *Chicago Tribune,* Sec. 6, p. 7.

Josephowitz, N. (1980). Management of men and women: Closed vs. open doors. *Harvard Business Review, 58*(5), 56–62.

Kalof, L., Eby, K. K., Matheson, J. L., & Kroska, R. J. (2001). The influence of race and gender on student self-reports of sexual harassment by college professors. *Gender & Society, 15,* 282–302.

Kaplan, D., & Keys, Ch. (1997). Sex and relationship variables as predictors of sexual attraction in cross-sex platonic friendships between young heterosexual adults. *Journal of Social and Personal Relationships, 14,* 191–206.

Kaplan, S., & Tinsley, A. (1989, Jan.–Feb.). The unfinished agenda: Women in higher education administration. *Academe,* pp. 18–22.

Karen, D. (1991). The politics of class, race, and gender: Access to higher education in the United States, 1960–1986. *American Journal of Education, 99,* 208–225.

Karp, D. A., & Yoels, W. C. (1976). The college classroom: Some observations on the meanings of student participation. *Sociology and Social Research, 60,* 421–439.

Katz, R. C., Hannon, R., & Whitten, L. (1996). Effects of gender and situation on the perception of sexual harassment. *Sex Roles, 34,* 35–42.

Keegan, P. (1989, August 6). Playing favorites. *New York Times,* Section 4A, p. 26.

Kelck, R. E., Richardson, S. A., & Ronald, L. (1974). Physical appearance cues and interpersonal attraction in children. *Child Development, 45,* 305–310.

Kessler, S. J., & McKenna, W. (1978). *Gender: An ethnomethodological approach.* Chicago, IL: University of Chicago Press.

Khosroshahi, F. (1989). Penguins don't care, but women do: A social identity analysis of a Whorfian problem. *Language in Society, 18,* 505–525.

Kilbourne, W. E. (1990). Female stereotyping in advertisements: An experience on male–female perceptions of leadership. *Journalism Quarterly, 67,* 25–31.

Kimlicka, T., Cross, H., & Tarnai, J. (1983). A comparison of androgynous, feminine, masculine, and undifferentiated women on self-esteem, body satisfaction, and sexual satisfaction. *Psychology of Women Quarterly, 7,* 291–294.

Kimmel, M. (1987). *Changing men: New directions in research on men and masculinity.* Newbury Park, CA: Sage.

Kimmel, M. S., & Messner, M. A. (1998). *Men's lives,* 4th ed. Boston: Allyn and Bacon.

Kimura, D. (2000). Sex differences in the brain. In E. L. Paul (Ed.), *Taking sides: Clashing views on controversial issues in sex and gender* (pp. 66–75). Guilford, CT: Dushkin/McGraw-Hill.

Kingsolver, P. S., & Cordry, H. V. (1987). Gender and the press: An update. In L. B. Nadler, M. K. Nadler, & W. R. Todd-Mancillas (Eds.), *Advances in gender and communication research* (pp. 307–315). Lanham, MD: University Press of America.

Kirchmeyer, C., & Bullin, C. (1997). Gender roles in a traditionally female occupation: A study of emergency, operating, intensive care, and psychiatric nurses. *Journal of Vocational Behavior, 50,* 78–95.

Kitto, J. (1989). Gender reference terms: Separating the women from the girls. *British Journal of Social Psychology, 28,* 185–187.

Klein, E. (1984). *Gender politics.* Cambridge, MA: Harvard University Press.

Klein, R. P., & Durfee, J. T. (1978). Effects of sex and birth order on infant social behavior. *Infant Behavior and Development, 1,* 106–117.

Kleinke, C. L., Desautels, M., & Knapp, B. (1977). Adult gaze and affective and visual responses of preschool children. *Journal of Genetic Psychology, 131,* 321–322.

Knapp, M. L., & Hall, J. A. (1996). *Nonverbal communication in human interaction,* 4th ed. Fort Worth, TX: Harcourt Brace Jovanovich.

Koblinsky, S. G., & Sugawara, A. I. (1984). Nonsexist curricula, sex of teacher, and children's sex role learning. *Sex Roles, 10,* 357–367.

Koblinsky, S. G., Cruse, D. F., & Sugawara, A. I. (1978). Sex role stereotypes and children's memory for story content. *Child Development, 49,* 452–458.

Kohlberg, L. (1981). *The philosophy of moral development.* San Francisco: Harper and Row.

Kolbe, R., & LaVoie, J. C. (1981). Sex-role stereotyping in preschool children's picture books. *Social Psychology Quarterly, 44,* 369–374.

Kon, I. (1975). Women at work: Equality with a difference. *International Social Science Journal, 27,* 655–665.

Korabik, K. (1990). Androgyny and leadership style. *Journal of Business Ethics, 9,* 283–292.

Kram, K. E. (1983). Phases of the mentor relationship. *Academy of Management Journal, 26,* 608–625.

Kramarae, C., Schultz, M., & O'Barr, W. (Eds). (1984). *Language and power.* Beverley Hills, CA: Sage.

Kramer, C. (1974). Stereotypes of women's speech: The word from the cartoons. *Journal of Popular Culture, 8,* 624–630.

Kramer, C. (1978). Male and female perceptions of male and female speech. *Language and Speech, 20,* 151–161.

Kropp, J., & Halverson, C. (1983). Preschool children's preferences and recall for stereotyped versus nonstereotyped stories. *Sex Roles, 9,* 261–273.

Kumin, L., & Lazar, M. (1974). Gestural communication and preschool children. *Perceptual and Motor Skills, 38*, 708–710.

Lafky, S., Duffy, M., Steinmaus, & Berkowitz, D. (1996). Looking through gendered lenses: Female stereotyping in advertisements and gender role expectations. *Journalism & Mass Communication Quarterly, 73*, 379–388.

LaFrance, M. (1991). School for scandal: Different educational experiences for females and males. *Gender and Education, 3*, 3–13.

LaFrance, M., & Carmen, C. (1980). The nonverbal display of psychological androgyny. *Journal of Personality and Social Psychology, 38*, 36–49.

Lakoff, R. (1975). *Language and woman's place*. New York: Harper & Row.

Lamb, M. E., & Roopnarine, J. L. (1979). Peer influences on sex-role development in preschoolers. *Child Development, 50*, 1219–1222.

Lamke, L. K. (1982). The impact of sexual orientation on self-esteem in early adolescence. *Child Development, 53*, 1530–1535.

Langlois, J. H., & Downs, A. C. (1979). Peer relations as a function of physical attractiveness: The eye of the beholder or behavioral reality? *Child Development, 50*, 409–418.

Langlois, J. H., Gottfried, N. W., Barnes, B. M., & Hendricks, D. E. (1978). The effect of peer age on the social behavior of preschool children. *Journal of Genetic Psychology, 132*, 11–19.

Lannutti, P. J., Laliker, M., & Hale, J. L. (2001). Violations of expectations and social-sexual communication in student/professor interactions. *Communication Education, 50*, 69–82.

Lau, S. (1982). The effect of smiling as person perception. *Journal of Social Psychology, 117*, 63–67.

Lawrenz, F. P., & Welch, W. W. (1983). Student perceptions of science classes taught by males and females. *Journal of Research in Science Teaching, 20*, 655–662.

Leach, M. (1990). Toward writing feminist scholarship into history education. *Educational Theory, 40*, 453–461.

Leach, M., & Davies, B. (1990). Crossing the boundaries: Educational thought and gender equity. *Educational Theory, 40*, 321–332.

Lehne, G. (1989). Homophobia among men: Supporting and defining the male role. In M. Kimmel & M. Messner (Eds.), *Men's lives* (pp. 416–429). New York: Macmillan.

Levine, T. R., McCornack, S. A., & Avery, P. B. (1992). Sex differences in emotional reactions to discovered deception. *Communication Quarterly, 40*, 289–296.

Lewin, T. (1994, October 12). Men whose wives work earn less, studies show. *The New York Times*, pp. A1, A21.

Lewin, T. (1998, April 15). Men assuming bigger share at home, new survey shows. *The New York Times*, p. A18.

Lewis, M. (1972, May). Culture and gender roles—there's no unisex in the nursery. *Psychology Today*, pp. 54–57.

Licht, B., Stader, S., & Swenson, C. C. (1989). Children's achievement related beliefs: Effects of academic area, sex and achievement level. *Journal of Educational Research, 82*, 253–260.

Lin, C. A. (1998). Uses of sex appeals in prime-time television commercials. *Sex Roles, 38*, 461–473.

Liska, J., Mechling, E. W., & Stathas, S. (1981). Differences in subjects' perceptions of gender and believability between users of deferential and nondeferential language. *Communication Quarterly, 29*, 40–48.

Lister, L. (1997, Fall). Among schoolgirls. *Independent School*, pp. 42–45.

Lloyd, S. A. (1987). Conflict in premarital relationships: Differential perceptions of males and females. *Family Relations, 36*, 290–294.

Lloyd, S. A. (1991). The dark side of courtship. *Family Relations, 40*, 14–20.

Locke, V. N., & Williams, M. L. (2000). Supervisor mentoring: Does a female manager make a difference? *Communication Research Reports, 17*, 49–57.

Loden, M., & Rosener, J. B. (1991). *Workforce America! Managing employee diversity as a vital resource*. Homewood, IL: Business One Irwin.

Lombardo, J. P., & Berzonsky, J. D. (1979). Sex differences in self-disclosure: Topic intimacy makes the difference. *Journal of Social Psychology, 107*, 281–282.

Lombardo, W. K., Cretser, G. A., Lombardo, B., & Mathis, S. L. (1983). Fer cryin' out loud—there is a sex difference. *Sex Roles, 9,* 987–1003.

Longstreth, L. E. (1970). Birth order and avoidance of dangerous activities. *Developmental Psychology, 2,* 154.

Lont, C. M. (1988, October). *It's not what they play, it's what they say: A content analysis of DJ chatter.* Paper presented at the Eleventh Annual Communication, Language and Gender Conference, San Diego, CA.

Lont, C. M. (1990). The roles assigned to females and males in non-music radio programming. *Sex Roles, 22,* 661–669.

Lorber, J., & Farrell, S. A. (1991). *The social construction of gender.* Newbury Park, CA: Sage.

Lott, B. (2000). The personal and social correlates of a gender difference ideology. In E. L. Paul (Ed.), *Taking sides: Clashing views on controversial issues in sex and gender* (pp. 112–121). Guilford, CT: Dushkin/McGraw-Hill.

Loy, P. H., & Stewart, L. P. (1984). The extent and effects of the sexual harassment of working women. *Sociological Focus, 17,* 31–43.

Lugones, M. C., & Spelman, E. V. (1983). Have we got a theory for you! Feminist theory, cultural imperialism and the demand for the "woman's voice." *Women's Studies International Forum, 6,* 573–581.

Lutes-Dunckley, C. J. (1978). Sex role preferences as a function of sex of storyteller and story context. *Journal of Psychology, 100,* 151–158.

Lye, D., & Biblarz, T. (1993). The effects of attitudes toward family life and gender roles on marital satisfaction. *Journal of Family Issues, 14,* 157–188.

Lytton, H., & Romney, D. M. (1991). Parents' differential socialization of boys and girls: A meta-analysis. *Psychological Bulletin, 109,* 267–296.

Maccoby, E. E., & Jacklin, C. N. (1974). *The psychology of sex differences.* Stanford, CA: Stanford University Press.

Maccoby, E. E., & Jacklin, C. N. (1980). Sex differences in aggression: A rejoinder and reprise. *Child Development, 51,* 964–980.

Mack, R. N. (1989). Spouse abuse—A dyadic approach. In G. R. Weeds (Eds.), *Treating couples: The intersystem model of the Marriage Council of Philadelphia* (pp. 191–214). New York: Brunner/Mazel.

Macke, A. S., & Richardson, L. W. (1980). *Sex-typed teaching styles of university professors and student reactions.* Columbus: Ohio State University Research Foundation.

Maher, F., & Rathbone, C. (1986). Teacher education and feminist theory: Some implications for practice. *American Journal of Education, 44,* 214–235.

Maher, K. J. (1997). Gender-related stereotypes of transformational and transactional leadership. *Sex Roles, 37,* 209–225.

Mahony, P. (1983). How Alice's chin really came to be pressed against her foot: Sexist processes of interaction in mixed-sex classrooms. *Women's Studies International Forum, 6,* 107–115.

Major, B., Carnevale, P. J., & Deaux, K. (1981). A different perspective on androgyny: Evaluation of masculine and feminine characteristics. *Journal of Personality and Social Psychology, 41,* 988–1001.

Major, B., Schmidlin, A. M., & Williams, L. (1990). Gender patterns in social touch: The impact of setting and age. *Journal of Personality and Social Psychology, 58,* 634–643.

Maltz, D. N., & Borker, R. A. (1982). A cultural approach to male–female miscommunication. In J. J. Gumperz (Ed.), *Language and social identity* (pp. 196–216). New York: Cambridge University Press.

Maple, S., & Stage, F. (1991). Influences on the choice of math/science major by gender and ethnicity. *American Educational Research Journal, 28,* 37–60.

Marche, T. A., & Peterson, C. (1993). The developmental and sex-related use of interruption behavior. *Human Communication Research, 19,* 388–408.

Mark, E. W., & Alper, T. G. (1985). Women, men and intimacy motivation. *Psychology of Women Quarterly, 9,* 81–88.

Marsh, H., & Myers, M. (1986). Masculinity, femininity, and androgyny: A methodological and theoretical critique. *Sex Roles, 14,* 397–430.

Marshall, M. M. S. (1985). Marital power, role expectations and marital satisfaction. *International Journal of Women's Studies, 8*, 40–46.

Martin, C. L. (1990). Attitudes and expectations about children with nontraditional and traditional gender roles. *Sex Roles, 22*, 151–166.

Martin, C. L., Wood, C. H., & Little, J. K. (1990). The development of gender stereotype components. *Child Development, 61*, 1891–1904.

Martin, J. N., & Craig, R. T. (1983). Selected linguistic sex differences during initial social interactions of same-sex and mixed sex student dyads. *Western Journal of Speech Communication, 47*, 16–28.

Martin, V., & Nivens, M. K. (1987). The attributional response of males and females to noncontingent feedback. *Sex Roles, 16*, 453–462.

Maslin, J. (1988a, February 14). Sexism on film: The sequel. *The New York Times*, pp. H1, 17.

Maslin, J. (1988b, May 15). Dizzy dames on a new whirl. *The New York Times*, p. 27.

Mastalli, G. L. (1981). Appendix: The legal context. *Harvard Business Review, 59*(2), 94–95.

McArthur, L. Z., & Eisen, S. V. (1976). Achievements of male and female storybook characters as determinants of achievement behavior by boys and girls. *Journal of Personality and Social Psychology, 33*, 467–473.

McClain, D. L. (2001, March 7). Computer programmers needed. Women please apply. *The New York Times*, p. G1.

McCorkle, S. (1982). An analysis of verbal language in Saturday morning children's programs. *Communication Quarterly, 30*, 210–216.

McGhee, P., & Frueh, T. (1980). Television viewing and the learning of sex role stereotypes. *Sex Roles, 6*, 179–188.

McIntyre, S., Moberg, D. J., & Posner, B. Z. (1980). Preferential treatment in preselection decisions according to sex and race. *Academy of Management Journal, 23*, 738–749.

McMinn, M. R., Troyer, P. K., Hannum, L. E., & Foster, J. D. (1991). Teaching nonsexist language to college students. *Journal of Experimental Education, 59*, 153–161.

Mead, G. H. (1934). *Mind, self and society*. Chicago: University of Chicago Press.

Media Report to Women. (1983, August–September). (Available from 3306 Ross Place NW, Washington, DC).

Meeker, B., F., & Elliott, G. C. (1996). Reward allocations, gender, and task performance. *Social Psychology Quarterly, 59*, 294–302.

Mehrabian, A. (1972). *Nonverbal communication*. Chicago: Aldine-Atherton.

Mehrabian, A. (1981). *Silent messages: Implicit communication of emotion and attitudes*, 2d ed. Belmont, CA: Wadsworth.

Mellen, J. (1974). *Women and their sexuality in the new film*, 2d ed. New York: Horizon Press.

Mellen, J. (1977). *Big bad wolves: Masculinity in the American film*. New York: Pantheon Books.

Melson, G. F. (1976). Determinants of personal space in young children: Perception of distance cues. *Perceptual and Motor Skills, 43*, 107–114.

Melton, G. W., & Fowler, G. L. (1987). Female roles in radio advertising. *Journalism Quarterly, 64*, 145–149.

Men more willingly accept women leaders. (1988, March 4). *The Wall Street Journal*, p. 31.

Menzel, K. E., & Carrell, L. J. (1999). The impact of gender and immediacy on willingness to talk and perceived learning. *Communication Education, 48*, 31–41.

Michaud, S. L., & Warner, R. M. (1997). Gender differences in self-reported response to troubles talk. *Sex Roles, 37*, 527–540.

Miller, C., & Swift, K. (1988). *The handbook of nonsexist writing*, 2d ed. New York: Harper & Row.

Milroy, L. (1980). *Language and social networks*. Oxford, England: Basil Blackwell.

Mliner, J. (1977). *Sex stereotypes in mathematics and science textbooks for elementary and junior high schools: Report of sex bias in the public schools*. New York: National Organization for Women.

Moely, B. E., & Kriecker, K. (1984). Ladies and gentlemen, women and men: A study of the connotations of words indicating gender. *Psychology of Women Quarterly, 8*, 348–353.

Montgomery, B. M., & Norton, R. W. (1981). Sex differences and similarities in communicator style. *Communication Monographs, 48*, 121–132.

Montgomery, C. L., & Burgoon, M. (1980). The effects of androgyny and message expectations on resistance to persuasive communication. *Communication Monographs, 47,* 56–67.

Mooney, L., & Brabant, S. (1987). 2 martinis and a rested woman: Liberation in the Sunday comics. *Sex Roles, 17,* 409–420.

Morse, B. W., & Eman, V. A. (1980). The construct of androgyny: An overview and implications for research. In C. L. Berryman & V. A. Eman (Eds.), *Communication, language and sex* (pp. 76–90). Rowley, MA: Newbury House.

Morse, S. (1995, Winter). Why girls don't like computer games. *AAUW Outlook,* pp. 16–19.

Morton, T. L. (1978). Intimacy and reciprocity of exchange: A comparison of spouses and strangers. *Journal of Personality and Social Psychology, 36,* 72–81.

Moses, Y. T. (1989). *Black women in academe: Issues and strategies.* Washington, DC: Project on the Status and Education of Women, Association of American Colleges.

Mulac, A., Studley, L. B., Wiemann, J. M., & Bradac, J. J. (1987). Male/female gaze in same-sex and mixed-sex dyads. *Human Communication Research, 13,* 323–343.

Mulac, A., Wiemann, J. M., Widenmann, S. J., & Gibson, T. W. (1988). Male/female language differences and effects in same-sex and mixed-sex dyads: The gender-linked language effect. *Communication Monographs, 55,* 315–335.

Mulvaney, B. M. (1989). *Images of men in women's reggae music: Vision and revision.* Paper presented at the Speech Communication Association, San Francisco, CA.

Murdock, N., & Forsyth, D. R. (1985). Is gender-biased language sexist? A perceptual approach. *Psychology of Women Quarterly, 9,* 39–49.

Nadler, L., & Nadler, M. (1990). Perceptions of sex differences in classroom communication. *Women's Studies in Communication, 13,* 46–65.

Nardi, P. (1992). Seamless "souls": An introduction to men's friendships. In P. Nardi (Ed.), *Men's friendships* (pp. 1–14). Newbury Park, CA: Sage.

National Commission on Working Women. (1982). *What's wrong with this picture? A look at working women on television.* Washington, DC: National Commission on Working Women.

National Forum Gallery of Cartoons. (1992, November 27). Washington, DC: National Forum. [Available from The National Forum, Inc., PO Box 7099, Fairfax Station, VA 22039.]

Nezlek, J. B. (1995). Social construction, gender/sex similarity and social interaction in close personal relationships. *Journal of Social and Personal Relationships, 12,* 503–520.

Nicotera, A. M., & Rancer, A. S. (1994). The influence of sex on self-perceptions and social stereotyping of aggressive communication predispositions. *Western Journal of Communication, 58,* 283–307.

Nieva, V. F., & Gutek, B. A. (1980). Sex effects on evaluation. *Academy of Management Review, 5,* 267–276.

Nieves-Squires, S. (1990). *Hispanic women in academe: Issues and strategies.* Washington, DC: Project on the Status and Education of Women, Association of American Colleges.

Nilsen, A. P. (1979). You'll never be the man your mother was, and other truisms. *Et cetera, 36,* 365–370.

Nilsen, A. P. (1987). Three decades of sexism in school science materials. *School Library Journal, 33,* 117–122.

Noble, H. B. (1999, June 1). Steroid use by teen-age girls is rising. *The New York Times,* p. F8.

Noller, P. (1986). Sex differences in nonverbal communication: Advantage lost or supremacy regained? *Australian Journal of Psychology, 38*(1), 23–32.

Northcraft, G. B., & Gutek, B. A. (1993). Point–counterpoint: Discrimination against women in management—Going, going, gone or going but never gone? In E. A. Fagenson (Ed.), *Women in management: Trends, issues and challenges in managerial diversity* (pp. 219–245). Newbury Park, CA: Sage.

Norton, R. W. (1978). Foundation of a communicator style construct. *Human Communication Research, 4,* 99–112.

Notarius, C., & Johnson, J. (1982). Emotional expression in husbands and wives. *Journal of Marriage and the Family, 44,* 483–490.

O'Barr, W. M., & Atkins, B. K. (1980). "Women's language" or "powerless language"? In S. McConnell-Ginet, R. Borker & N. Furman (Eds.), *Women and language in literature and society* (pp. 93–110). New York: Praeger.

Oliker, S. J. (1989). *Best friends and marriage: Exchange among women.* Berkeley, CA: University of Berkeley Press.

Olson, B., & Douglas, W. (1997). The family on television: Evaluation of gender roles in situation comedy. *Sex Roles, 36,* 409–427.

Orbe, M. P. (1994). "Remember, it's always whites' ball": Descriptions of African American male communication. *Communication Quarterly, 42,* 287–300.

Orenstein, P. (1994). *School Girls.* New York: Doubleday.

Otto, H. (1988). America's youth: A changing profile. *Family Relations,* 37, 385–391.

Owen, W. F. (1987). The verbal expression of love by women and men as a critical communication event in personal relationships. *Women's Studies in Communication, 10,* 15–24.

Paff, J. L., & Lakner, H. B. (1997). Dress and the female gender role in magazine advertisements of 1950–1994: A content analysis. *Family and Consumer Sciences Research Journal, 26,* 29–58.

Pallas, A. M., & Alexander, K. L. (1983). Sex differences in quantitative SAT performance: New evidence on the differential coursework hypothesis. *American Educational Research Journal, 20,* 165–182.

Paludi, M. A., & Barickman, R. B. (1995). Sexual harassment definitions apply to academia. In K. Swisher (ed.), *What is sexual harassment?* (pp. 32–45). San Diego, CA: Greenhaven Press.

Parlee, M. B. (1979a, March). Women smile less for success. *Psychology Today,* p. 16.

Parlee, M. B. (1979b, May). Conversational politics. *Psychology Today,* pp. 48–56.

Parsons, J. E., Heller, K. A., & Kaczala, C. (1980). The effects of teachers' expectancies and attributions on students' expectancies for success in mathematics. In D. McGuigan (Ed.), *Women's lives: New theory, research and policy* (pp. 373–380). Ann Arbor: University of Michigan Center for Continuing Education of Women.

Parsons, T. (1964). *Social structure and personality.* New York: Free Press.

Patton, B. R., Jasnoski, M., & Skerchock, L. (1977). *Communication implications of androgyny.* Paper presented at the meeting of the Speech Communication Association, Washington, DC.

Paulsen, K., & Johnson, M. (1983). Sex role attitudes and mathematical ability in 4th, 8th, and 11th grade students from a high socioeconomic area. *Developmental Psychology, 19,* 210–214.

Pearce, W. B., & Sharp, S. M. (1973). Self-disclosing communication. *Journal of Communication, 23*(4), 409–425.

Pearson, J. (1985). *Innovations in teaching gender and communication: Excluding and including women and men.* Paper presented at the annual meeting of the Organization for the Study of Communication, Language, and Gender, Lincoln, NE.

Pearson, J., & Davilla, R. (1993). The gender construct: Understanding why men and women communicate differently. In L. Arliss & D. Borisoff (Eds.), *Women and men communicating* (pp. 1–13). Fort Worth, TX: Harcourt Brace Jovanovich.

Pearson, J., & Spitzberg, B. (1990). *Interpersonal communication: Concepts, components, and contexts,* 2d ed. Dubuque, IA: Wm. C. Brown.

Pearson, J., & West, R. (1991). An initial investigation of the effects of gender on student questions in the classroom: Developing a descriptive base. *Communication Education, 40,* 22–32.

Peng, S. S., & Jaffe, J. (1979). Women who enter male-dominated fields of study in higher education. *American Educational Research Journal, 16,* 285–293.

Peplau, L. A. (1983). Roles and gender. In H. H. Kelley (Ed.), *Close relationships.* San Francisco: W. H. Freeman.

Peterson, E. (1991). Moving toward a gender balanced curriculum in basic speech communication courses. *Communication Education, 40,* 60–72.

Peterson, K. (1994, September 7). Teens' tales from the classroom. *USA Today,* pp. 1–2D.

Peterson, K. S. (2001, March 4). Adult children prefer stepdads to stepmoms. *Home News Tribune,* p. D3.

Peterson, P. (1976). An investigation of sex differences in regard to nonverbal body gestures. In B. Eakins, G. Eakins, & B. Lieb-Brilhart (Eds.), *Siscom '75: Women's (and men's) communication* (pp. 20–27). Falls Church, VA: Speech Communication Association.

Peterson, S., & Lach, M. (1990). Gender stereotypes in children's books: Their prevalence and influence on cognitive and affective development. *Gender and Education, 2,* 185–197.

Peterson, S. B., & Kroner, T. (1992). Gender biases in textbooks for introductory psychology and human development. *Psychology of Women Quarterly, 16,* 17–36.

Petronio, S. S. (1982). The effect of interpersonal communication on women's family role satisfaction. *Western Journal of Speech Communication, 46,* 208–222.

Phillips, B. S. (1990). Nicknames and sex-role stereotypes. *Sex Roles, 23,* 281–289.

Pincus, A. R. H., & Pincus, R. E. (1980). Linguistic sexism and career education. *Language Arts, 57,* 70–76.

Pleck, J. H. (1977). The psychology of sex roles: Traditional and new views. In L. A. Cater, A. F. Scott, & W. Martyna, *Women and men: Changing roles, relationships, and perceptions* (pp. 181–199). New York: Praeger.

"Poll: Parents see pink for girls." (1995, September 22). *Daily Targum,* p. 3.

Political pix: Cartoons for thoughtful people. (1988, May 23). (Available from Ambience, Inc., P.O. Box 804, Main Street, Norwich, VT 05055-0804)

Political pix: Cartoons for thoughtful people. (1988, June 27). (Available from Ambience, Inc., P.O. Box 804, Main Street, Norwich, VT 05055-0804)

Pollitt, K. (1990, April 7). The Smurfette principle. *New York Times Magazine,* p. 22.

Powell, A. D., & Kahn, A. S. (1995). Racial differences in women's desires to be thin. *International Journal of Eating Disorders, 17,* 191–195.

Powers, W. (1993). The effects of gender and consequence upon perceptions of deceivers. *Communication Quarterly, 41,* 328–337.

Pritchard, M. (1991). *On becoming responsible.* Lawrence: University of Kansas Press.

Pruett, K. D. (1987). *The nurturing father.* New York: Warner Books.

Pruett, K. D. (1993). The paternal parent. *Families in Society, 12,* 46–51.

Pruett, K. D., & Litzenberger, B. (1992). Latency development in children of primary nurturing fathers: Eight-year follow-up. *Psychoanalytic Study of the Child, 47,* 85–101.

Prusank, D. T., Duran, R. L., & DeLillo, D. A. (1991). *Interpersonal relationships in women's magazines in the 1970s and 1980s.* Paper presented at the International Network Conference on Personal Relationships, Normal, IL.

Purcell, P., & Stewart, L. (1990). Dick and Jane in 1989. *Sex Roles, 22,* 177–185.

Putnam, L. L. (1983). Lady you're trapped: Breaking out of conflict cycles. In J. J. Pilotta (Ed.), *Women in organizations: Barriers and breakthroughs* (pp. 39–53). Prospect Heights, IL: Waveland.

Putnam, L. L., & McCallister, L. (1980). Situational effects of task gender on nonverbal display. In D. Nimmo (Ed.), *Communication Yearbook 4,* (pp. 679–697). New Brunswick, NJ: Transaction.

Ragins, B. R., Cotton, J. L., & Miller, J. S. (2000). Marginal mentoring: The effects of type of mentor, quality of relationship, and program design on work and career attitudes. *Academy of Management of Journal, 43,* 1177–1194.

Raines, R. S., Hechtman, S. B., & Rosenthal, R. (1990). Nonverbal behavior and gender as determinants of physical attractiveness. *Journal of Nonverbal Behavior, 14,* 253–267.

Rakow, L. F. (1986). Rethinking gender research in communication. *Journal of Communication, 36*(4), 11–26.

Rand, M., & Levinger, N. J. (1979). Implicit theories of relationship: An intergenerational student. *Journal of Personality and Social Psychology, 37,* 645–661.

Randall, P. R. (1985). Sexist language and speech communication texts: Another case of benign neglect. *Communication Education, 34,* 128–134.

Rawlins, W. K. (1992). *Friendship matters: Communication, dialectics, and the life course.* Hawthorne, NY: Aldine de Gruyter.

Rawlins, W. K. (1993). Communication in cross-sex friendships. In L. P. Arliss & D. J. Borisoff (Eds.), *Women and men communicating: Challenges and changes* (pp. 51–70). Fort Worth, TX: Harcourt Brace Jovanovich.

Reiser, C., & Troost, K. (1986). Gender and gender role influences upon self and other-reports of communication competence. *Sex Roles, 14,* 431–443.

Rekers, G. A., Amoro-Plotkin, H. D., & Low, B. P. (1977). Sex-typed mannerisms in normal boys and girls as a function of sex and age. *Child Development, 48,* 275–278.

Rekers, G. A., & Rudy, J. P. (1978). Differentiation of childhood body gestures. *Perceptual and Motor Skills, 46,* 839–845.

Renwick, P. A., & Tosi, H. (1978). The effects of sex, marital status, and educational background on selection decisions. *Academy of Management Journal, 21,* 93–103.

Reskin, B., & Padavic, I. (1994). *Women and men at work.* Thousand Oaks, CA: Pine Forge Press.

Rice, F. P. (1990). *Intimate relationships, marriage, and families.* Mountain View, CA: Mayfield.

Rich, S. (1990, April 26). Women's pay still far behind men's, group reports. *Washington Post,* p. A9.

Richmond, V. P., & Gorham, J. (1988). Language patterns and gender role orientation among students in grades 3–12. *Communication Education, 37,* 142–149.

Richmond-Abbott, M. (1992). *Masculine and feminine: Gender roles over the life cycle.* New York: McGraw Hill.

Riddell, L. (1989). Pupils, resistance and gender codes: A study of classroom encounters. *Gender and Education, 1,* 183–197.

Roberts, M. (1987, March). Baby love. *Psychology Today,* p. 22.

Robinson, J. D., & Skill, T. (1995). The invisible generation: Portrayals of the elderly on prime-time television. *Communication Reports, 8,* 111–119.

Roese, N. J., Olson, J. M., Borenstein, M. N., Martin, A., & Shores, A. L. (1992). Same-sex touching behavior: The moderating role of homophobic attitudes. *Journal of Nonverbal Behavior, 16,* 249–59.

Roloff, M. E., & Greenberg, B. S. (1979). Resolving conflict: Methods used by T.V. characters and teenage viewers. *Journal of Broadcasting, 23,* 285–300.

Roop, L. (1989). The English teacher as midwife: Gender sensitivity in teaching methods. *English Journal, 34,* 90–91.

Rose, S. M. (1985). Same- and cross-sex friendships and the psychology of homosociality. *Sex Roles, 12,* 63–74.

Rosen, B., & Jerdee, T. H. (1974). Sex stereotyping in the executive suite. *Harvard Business Review, 52*(2), 45–58.

Rosen, L. W., Shafer, C. L., Dummer, G. M., Cross, L. K., Deuman, G. W., & Malmberg, S. R. (1988). Prevalence of pathogenic weight-control behaviors among Native American women and girls. *International Journal of Eating Disorders, 7,* 807–811.

Rosenfeld, L. B. (1979). Self-disclosure avoidance: Why am I afraid to tell you who I am? *Communication Monographs, 46,* 63–74.

Rosenfeld, L. B., & Jarrard, M. W. (1985). The effects of perceived sexism in female and male college professors on students' descriptions of classroom climate. *Communication Education, 34,* 205–213.

Rosenfeld, L. B., & Jarrard, M. W. (1986). Student coping mechanisms in sexist and nonsexist professors' classes. *Communication Education, 35,* 157–162.

Rosenfeld, L. B., Kartus, S., & Ray, C. (1976). Body accessibility revisited. *Journal of Communication, 26*(3), 27–30.

Rosenthal, R., Hall, J. A., DiMatteo, R., Rogers, L., & Archer, D. (1979). *Sensitivity to nonverbal communication: The PONS test.* Baltimore: Johns Hopkins University Press.

Rosenthal, R., & Jacobson, L. (1968). *Pygmalion in the classroom.* New York: Holt, Rinehart & Winston.

Rotenberg, K. J. (1986). Same-sex patterns and sex differences in the trust-value basis of children's friendship. *Sex Roles, 15,* 613–626.

Roth, M. (1987). Teaching modern art history from a feminist perspective: Challenging conventions, my own and others. *Women's Studies Quarterly, 15,* 21–24.

Rotter, N. G., & Rotter, G. S. (1988). Sex differences in the encoding and decoding of negative facial emotions. *Journal of Nonverbal Behavior, 12,* 139–147.

Rubin, J. (1986). How does the way women are referred to and described affect their participation in development and democracy? In J. A. Fishman et al. (Eds.), *The Fergusonian impact. II: Sociolinguistics and the sociology of language* (pp. 315–323). Berlin: Mouton de Gruyter.

Rubin, L. B. (1983). *Intimate strangers: Men and women together.* New York: Harper & Row.

Rubin, N. (1988, June). Math stinks! *Parents,* pp. 132–136, 207–208, 210.

Rubin, R. B., Perse, E. M., & Barbato, C. S. (1988). Conceptualization and measurement of interpersonal communication motives. *Human Communication Research, 14,* 602–627.

Rubin, Z., Hill, C. T., Peplau, L. A., & Dunkel-Schettes, C. (1980). Self-disclosure in dating couples: Sex roles and the ethic of openness. *Journal of Marriage and the Family, 42,* 305–316.

Ruble, D. N., Balaban, T., & Cooper, J. (1981). Gender constancy and the effects of sex-typed televised toy commercials. *Child Development, 52,* 667–673.

Ruvolo, A., & Veroff, J. (1997). For better or for worse: Real-ideal discrepancies and the marital well-being of newlyweds. *Journal of Social and Personal Relationship, 14,* 223–242.

Sadker, M., & Sadker, D. (1981). The development and field trial of a non-sexist teacher education curriculum. *The High School Journal, 64,* 331–336.

Sadker, M., & Sadker, D. (1985, March). Sexism in the schoolroom of the eighties. *Psychology Today,* pp. 54–57.

Sadker, M., & Sadker, D. (1994). *Failing at fairness: How our schools cheat girls.* New York: Simon & Schuster.

Sadker, M., Sadker, D., & Steindam, S. (1989). Gender equity and educational reform. *Educational Leadership, 47,* 44–47.

Safran, C. (1981, March). Sexual harassment: A view from the top. *Redbook,* pp. 1–7.

St. Peter, S. (1979). Jack went up the hill . . . but where was Jill? *Psychology of Women Quarterly, 4,* 256–260.

Sandler, B. (1991). Women faculty at work in the classroom, or Why it still hurts to be a woman in labor. *Communication Education, 40,* 6–15.

Sandler, B., & Hall, R. (1986). *The campus climate revisited: Chilly for women faculty, administrators, and graduate students.* Washington, DC: Project on the Status and Education of Women, Association of American Colleges.

Sandroff, R. (1988, December). Sexual harassment in the Fortune 500. *Working Woman,* pp. 69–73.

Sapadin, L. A. (1988). Friendship and gender: Perspectives of professional men and women. *Journal of Social and Personal Relationships, 5,* 387–403.

Satir, V. (1988). *The new peoplemaking.* Mountain View, CA: Science & Behavior Books.

Saucier, K. A. (1986). Healers and heartbreakers: Images of women and men in country music. *Journal of Popular Culture, 20,* 147–166.

Saucier, K. A. (1989). *"After all he's just a man": The outlaw and hero image in country music.* Paper presented at the Speech Communication Association, San Francisco, CA.

Sayers, F., & Sherblom, J. (1987). Qualification in male language as influenced by age and gender of conversational partner. *Communication Research Reports, 4,* 88–92.

Schau, C. G., & Scott, K. P. (1984). Impact of gender characteristics of instructional materials: An integration of the research literature. *Journal of Educational Psychology, 76,* 183–193.

Schein, V. E. (1973). The relationship between sex role stereotypes and requisite management characteristics. *Journal of Applied Psychology, 57,* 95–100.

Schein, V. E. (1978). Sex role stereotyping, ability and performance: Prior research and new directions. *Personnel Psychology, 31,* 259–268.

Scott, K. (1986). Effects of sex-fair reading materials on pupils' attitudes, comprehension and interest. *American Educational Research Journal, 23,* 105–115.

Scott, K. D. (1995). Identity and ideology in Black women's talk about their talk: A report of research in progress. *Women and Language, 28*(1), 8–9.

Seidler, V. (1992). Rejection, vulnerability, and friendship. In P. Nardi (Ed.), *Men's friendships* (pp. 15–34). Newbury Park, CA: Sage.

Seiter, E. (1986). Stereotypes and the media: A reevaluation. *Journal of Communication, 36*(2), 14–26.

Severy, L. J., Forsyth, D. R., & Wagner, P. J. (1980). A multimethod assessment of personal space development in female and male, black and white children. *Journal of Nonverbal Behavior, 4,* 68–86.

Sexual harassment: Research & resources. (1995). New York: National Council for Research on Women.

Sgan, M. L., & Pickert, S. M. (1980). Cross-sex and same-sex assertive bids in a cooperative group task. *Child Development, 51,* 928–931.

Shackelford, S., Wood, W., & Worchel, S. (1996). Behavioral styles and the influence of women in mixed-sex groups. *Social Psychology Quarterly, 59,* 284–293.

Sharps, M. J., Price, J. L., & Williams, J. K. (1994). Spatial cognition and gender: Instructional and stimulus influences on mental image rotation performance. *Psychology of Women Quarterly, 18,* 413–425.

Shear, M. (1985, October). Solving the great pronoun debate: 14 ways to avoid the sexist singular. *Ms. Magazine,* pp. 106–109.

Sherman, M. A., & Haas, A. (1984, June). Man to man, woman to woman. *Psychology Today,* pp. 72–73.

Sherrod, D. (1989). The influence of gender on same-sex friendships. In C. Hendrick (Ed.), *Close relationships* (pp. 164–187). Newbury Park, CA: Sage.

Shimanoff, S. B. (1985). Rules governing the verbal expression of emotions between married couples. *Western Journal of Speech Communication, 49,* 85–100.

Silberstein, L. R., Striegel-Moore, R. H., Timko, C., & Rodin, J. (1988). Behavioral and psychological implications of body dissatisfaction: Do men and women differ? *Sex Roles, 19,* 219–232.

Sillars, A. L., Weisberg, J., Burggraf, C. S., & Wilson, E. A. (1987). Content themes in marital conversations. *Human Communication Research, 13,* 495–528.

Silver, L. (1990, August 14). Few women, minorities at the top. *Washington Post,* pp. A1, A5.

Silverstein, B., Perdue, L., Peterson, B., & Kelly, E. (1986). The role of the mass media in promoting a thin standard of bodily attractiveness for women. *Sex Roles, 14,* 519–532.

Simmons, B., & Whitfield, E. (1979). Are boys victims of sex-role stereotyping? *Childhood Education, 56,*(2) 75–79.

Simon, S., & Montgomery, B. M. (1987, May). *Sexual harassment: Applying a communication perspective.* Paper presented at the meeting of the Eastern Communication Association, Syracuse, NY.

Skelly, G. U., & Lundstrom, W. (1981). Male sex roles in magazine advertising, 1959–1979. *Journal of Communication, 31,*(4) 52–57.

Slama, K. M., & Slowey, B. J. (1988). Gender-specific common nouns: Sex differences in self-use. *Sex Roles, 18,* 205–213.

Smith, C. B. (1979). Influence of internal opportunity structure and sex of worker on turnover patterns. *Administrative Science Quarterly, 24,* 362–381.

Smith, N. R. (1994). From the hearts of the handmaidens. *Images—Women in transition, 5(6),* 1. (Available from P.O. Box 303, Carlsbad, CA 92018).

Smith, P. M. (1985). *Language, the sexes and society.* Oxford, England: Basil Blackwell.

Smith, P. K., & Daglish, L. (1977). Sex differences in parent and infant behavior in the home. *Child Development, 48,* 1250–1254.

Sommer, R. (1959). Studies in personal space. *Sociometry, 22,* 247–260.

Sorrels, B. D. (1983). *The nonsexist communicator: Solving the problems of gender and awkwardness in modern English.* Englewood Cliffs, NJ: Prentice-Hall.

Spence, J. T., & Helmreich, R. L. (1978). *Masculinity and femininity: Their psychological dimensions, correlates and antecedents.* Austin: University of Texas Press.

Spender, D. (1985). *Man made language* (2d ed). London: Routledge & Kegan Paul.

Spender, D. (1989). *Invisible women: The schooling scandal.* London: Women's Press.

Spender, D. (1995). *Nattering on the net: Women, power and cyberspace.* Melbourne, Australia: Spiniflex.

Sprafkin, J. N., & Liebert, R. M. (1978). Sex-typing and children's television preferences. In G. Tuchman, A. K. Daniels, & J. Benet (Eds.), *Hearth and home: Images of women in the mass media* (pp. 228–239). New York: Oxford University Press.

Sprecher, S. (1987). The effects of self-disclosure given and received on affection for an intimate partner and stability of the relationship. *Journal of Social and Personal Relationships, 4,* 115–127.

Staffieri, J. R. (1967). A study of social stereotype of body image in children. *Journal of Personality and Social Psychology, 7,* 101–104.

Staffieri, J. R. (1972). Body build and behavioral expectancies in young females. *Developmental Psychology, 6,* 125–127.

Stake, J. E., & Katz, J. F. (1982). Teacher–pupil relationships in the elementary school classroom: Teacher-gender and pupil-gender differences. *American Educational Research Journal, 19,* 465–471.

Staley, C. C., & Cohen, J. L. (1988). Communicator style and social style: Similarities and differences between the sexes. *Communication Quarterly, 36,* 192–202.

Stanley, A. (1991, April 6). Militants back "queer," shoving "gay" the way of "Negro." *The New York Times,* pp. 23–24.

Stanworth, M. (1981). *Gender and schooling: A study of sexual divisions in the classroom.* London: Women's Research and Resources Centre.

Statham, A. (1987). The gender model revisited: Differences in the management styles of men and women. *Sex Roles, 16,* 409–429.

Statham, A., Richardson, L., & Cook, J. A. (1991). *Gender and university teaching: A negotiated difference.* Albany, NY: State University of New York Press.

Stattin, H., & Klackenberg-Larsson, I. (1991). The short- and long-term implications for parent–child relations of parents' prenatal preferences for their child's gender. *Developmental Psychology, 27,* 141–147.

Stein, P. (1986). Men and their friendships. In R. Lewis & R. Salt (Eds.), *Men in families* (pp. 261–270). Beverly Hills, CA: Sage.

Stephen, T. (2000). Concept analysis of gender, feminist, and women's studies research in the communication literature. *Communication Monographs, 67,* 193–214.

Stephen, T. D., & Harrison, T. M. (1985). Gender, sex-role identity, and communication style: A Q-sort analysis of behavioral differences. *Communication Research Reports, 2,* 53–61.

Sternglanz, S. H., & Serbin, L. A. (1974). Sex role stereotyping in children's television programs. *Developmental Psychology, 10,* 710–715.

Stewart, A. D. (1989a). Declarations of independence: The female rock and roller comes of age. In C. M. Lont & S. A. Friedley (Eds.), *Beyond boundaries: Sex and gender diversity in communication* (pp. 283–298). Fairfax, VA: George Mason University Press.

Stewart, A. D. (1989b). *Sweethearts, babies, unfaithful lovers, and tattooed love boys: Male roles in the work of female performers.* Paper presented at the Speech Communication Association, San Francisco, CA.

Stewart, J. (1999, April 7). Go figure: A closer look at equal pay. *Chicago Tribune,* Section 8, p. 1.

Stewart, L. P. (2001). Gender issues in corporate communication. In L. P. Arliss & D. J. Borisoff (Eds.), *Women and men communicating: Challenges and changes,* 2nd ed. (pp. 137–150). Prospect Heights, IL: Waveland.

Stewart, L. P., & Gudykunst, W. B. (1982). Differential factors influencing the hierarchical level and number of promotions of males and females within an organization. *Academy of Management Journal, 25,* 586–597.

Strips. (1993, January 10). Washington, DC: National Forum. [Available from The National Forum, Inc., PO Box 7099, Fairfax Station, VA 22039.]

Stoddard, K. M. (1981). Bewitched and bewildered: The effect of syndication on sex roles. *Journal of Popular Film and Television, 8,* 50–52.

Straus, M. A. (1991). Physical violence in American families: Incidence rates, causes, and trends. In D. D. Knudsen & J. L. Miller (Eds.), *Abused and battered: Social and legal responses to family violence* (pp. 17–34). New York: Aldine de Gruyter.

Surrey, J. L. (1991). The self-in-relation: A theory of women's development. In J. Jordan, A. Kaplan, J. Miller, I. Stiver, & J. Surrey (Eds.), *Women's growth in connection* (pp. 51–68). New York: Guilford.

Swain, S. (1992). Men's friendships with women: Intimacy, sexual boundaries, and the informant role. In P. Nardi (Ed.), *Men's friendships* (pp. 153–172). Newbury Park, CA: Sage.

Tan, A. S. (1982). Television use and social stereotypes. *Journalism Quarterly, 59*, 119–122.

Tannen, D. (1990a). Gender differences in topical coherence: Creating involvement in best friend talk. *Discourse Processes, 13*, 73–90.

Tannen, D. (1990b). *You just don't understand: Men and women in conversation.* New York: William Morrow.

Tannen, D. (1991, June 19). Teachers' classroom strategies should recognize that men and women use language differently. *The Chronicle of Higher Education*, pp. B1, B3.

Tauber, M. A. (1979). Sex differences in parent–child interaction styles during a free-play session. *Child Development, 50*, 981–988.

Tavris, C. (1992). *The mismeasure of woman.* New York: Simon and Schuster.

Tedesco, N. S. (1974). Patterns in prime time. *Journal of Communication, 24*, 119–124.

Terborg, J. R. (1977). Women in management: A research review. *Journal of Applied Psychology, 62*, 647–664.

Tetenbaum, T. J., & Pearson, J. (1989). The voices in children's literature: The impact of gender on the moral decisions of storybook characters. *Sex Roles, 20*, 381–395.

Teven, J. J., & Gorham, J. (1999). A qualitative analysis of low-inference student perceptions of teacher caring and non-caring behaviors within the college classroom. *Communication Research Reports, 15*, 288–298.

Teven, J. J., & McCroskey, J. C. (1997). The relationship of perceived teacher caring with student learning and teacher evaluation. *Communication Education, 46*, 1–9.

Thaler, B. (1987). Gender stereotyping in the comic strips. In L. P. Stewart & S. Ting-Toomey (Eds.), *Communication, gender, and sex roles in diverse interaction contexts* (pp. 189–199). Norwood, NJ: Ablex.

Thiederman, S. (1991). *Bridging cultural barriers for corporate success: How to manage the multicultural work force.* New York: Lexington Books.

Thomas, A. H., & Stewart, N. R. (1971). Counselor response to female clients with deviate and conforming career goals. *Journal of Counseling Psychology, 18*, 352–357.

Thomas, B. (1989). Body-image satisfaction among Black women. *Journal of Social Psychology, 129*, 107–112.

Thomas, B. G., & James, M. D. (1988). Body image, dieting tendencies, and sex-role traits in urban black-women. *Sex Roles, 24*, 261–278.

Thomas, R. R., Jr. (1991). *Beyond race and gender: Unleashing the power of your total work force by managing diversity.* New York: Amacom.

Thompson, E. G., Hatchett, P., & Phillips, J. L. (1981). Sex differences in the judgment of interpersonal verbs. *Psychology of Women Quarterly, 5*, 523–531.

Thompson, S. K. (1975). Gender labels and early sex role development. *Child Development, 46*, 339–347.

Thompson, L., & Walker, H. (1989). Gender in families: Women and men in marriage, work, and parenthood. *Journal of Marriage and the Family, 51*, 845–871.

Thompson, T. L., & Zerbinos, E. (1997). Television cartoons: Do children notice it's a boy's world? *Sex Roles, 37*, 415–432.

Thorne, B. (1979). *Claiming verbal space: Women, speech and language in college classrooms.* Paper presented at the Research Conference on Educational Environments and the Undergraduate Woman, Wellesley College, Wellesley, MA.

Thorne, B. (1993). *Gender play: Girls and boys in school.* New Brunswick, NJ: Rutgers University Press.

Thornton, A., & Freedman, D. (1983). The changing American family. *Population Bulletin, 38*, 1–44.

Tibbetts, S. L. (1976). Elementary schools: Do they stereotype or feminize? *Journal of National Association for Women Deans, Administrators and Counselors, 40*, 27–33.

Till, F. (1980). *Sexual harassment: A report on the sexual harassment of students.* Washington, DC: National Advisory Council on Women's Educational Programs.

Timmer, S. G., Veroff, J., & Hatchett, S. (1996). Family ties and marital happiness: The different marital experiences of black and white newlywed couples. *Journal of Social and Personal Relationships, 13,* 335–359.

Ting-Toomey, S. (1984). Perceived decision-making power and marital adjustment. *Communication Research Reports, 1,* 15–20.

Todd-Mancillas, W. R. (1981). Masculine generics = sexist language: A review of literature and implications for speech communication professionals. *Communication Quarterly, 29,* 107–115.

Treichler, P. A., & Kramarae, C. (1983). Women's talk in the ivory tower. *Communication Quarterly, 31,* 118–132.

Trepanier-Street, M., Romatowski, J., & McNair, S. (1990a). Children's written responses to stereotypical and nonstereotypical story characters. *Journal of Research in Childhood Education, 5,* 60–68.

Trepanier-Street, M., Romatowski, J., & McNair, S. (1990b). Development of story characters in gender-stereotypic and nonstereotypic occupational roles. *Journal of Early Adolescence, 10,* 496–510.

Trotter, R. J. (1983, August). Baby face. *Psychology Today,* pp. 14–20.

Tucker, J. S., & Friedman, H. S. (1993, Summer). Sex differences in nonverbal expressiveness: Emotional expression, personality, and impressions. *Journal of Nonverbal Behavior, 17,* 103–117.

Turner, L. H. (1992). An analysis of words coined by women and men: Reflections on the muted group theory and Gilligan's model. *Women and Language, 15*(1), 21–26.

Turner, L. H., Dindia, K., & Pearson, J. C. (1995). An investigation of female-male verbal behaviors in same-sex and mixed-sex conversations. *Communication Reports, 8,* 86–96.

Unger, R., & Crawford, M. (1992). *Women and gender: A feminist psychology.* New York: McGraw-Hill.

U.S. Commission on Civil Rights. (1979). *Window dressing on the set: Women and minorities in television.* Washington, DC: U.S. Government Printing Office.

U.S. Department of Labor. (1987). *Jobs for the future.* Washington, DC: U.S. Government Printing Office.

U.S. Department of Labor (1991). *A report on the glass ceiling initiative.* Washington, DC. U.S. Government Printing Office.

U.S. Merit Systems Protection Board. (1981). *Sexual harassment in the federal workplace: Is it a problem?* Washington, DC: Office of Merit Systems Review and Studies.

Vaughan-Roberson, C., Tompkins, G., Hitchcock, M., & Oldham, M. (1989). Sexism in basal readers: An analysis of male main characters. *Journal of Research in Childhood Education, 4*(1), 62–68.

Vuchinich, S. (1987). Starting and stopping spontaneous family conflicts. *Journal of Marriage and the Family, 49,* 591–601.

Wagner, H. L., Buck, R., & Winterbotham, M. (1993). Communication of specific emotions: Gender differences in sending accuracy and communication measures. *Journal of Nonverbal Behavior, 17,* 29–53.

Walker, H. A., Ilardi, B. C., McMahon, A. M., & Fennell, M. L. (1996). Gender, interactions, and leadership. *Social Psychology Quarterly, 59,* 255–272.

Ware, N., & Lee, V. (1988). Sex differences in choice of college science majors. *American Educational Research Journal, 25,* 593–614.

Waterman, A. S., & Whitbourne, S. K. (1982). Androgyny and psychological development among college students and adults. *Journal of Personality, 50,* 121–133.

Webb, L. (1986). Eliminating sexist language in the classroom. *Women's Studies in Communication, 9,* 21–29.

Weatherall, A (1998b). Re-visioning gender and language research. *Women and Language, 21*(1), 1–9.

Weatherall, A. (1998b). Women and men in language: An analysis of seminaturalistic person descriptions. *Human Communication Research, 25,* 275–292.

Weiller, K., & Higgs, C. (1989). Female learned helplessness in sport: An analysis of children's literature. *Journal of Physical Education, Recreation and Dance, 60*(6), 65–67.

Weitzman, L. J., Eifler, D., Hokada, E., & Ross, C. (1972). Sex role socialization in picture books for preschool children. *American Journal of Sociology, 77,* 1125–1150.

Weitzman, L. J., & Rizzo, D. (1975). Sex bias in textbooks. *Today's Education, 64*(1), 49–52.

Welch, M. S. (1980). *Networking: The great new way for women to get ahead.* New York: Harcourt Brace Jovanovich.

Welch, R. L., Huston-Stein, A., Wright, J. C., & Plenhal, R. (1979). Subtle sex-role cues in children's commercials. *Journal of Communication, 29*(3), 202–209.

West, C. (1984). When the doctor is a lady. *Symbolic Interaction, 7,* 87–106.

West, C., & Fenstermaker, S. (1995). Doing difference. *Gender & Society, 9,* 8–37.

Whalen, C. K., Flowers, J. V., Fuller, M. J., & Jernigan, T. (1975). Behavioral studies of personal space during early adolescence. *Man Environment Systems, 5,* 289–297.

Wheeless, L. R., & Wheeless, V. E. (1982). Attribution, gender orientation, and adaptability: Reconceptualization, measurement, and research results. *Communication Quarterly, 30,* 56–66.

Wheeless, V. E. (1984). A test of the theory of speech accommodation using language and gender orientation. *Women's Studies in Communication, 7,* 13–22.

Wheeless, V. E., & Berryman-Fink, C. (1985). Perceptions of women managers and their communicator competencies. *Communication Quarterly, 33,* 137–148.

Wheeless, V. E., Berryman-Fink, C., & Serafini, D. (1982). The use of gender-specific pronouns in the 1980s. *The Encoder, 9*(3–4), 35–46.

Wheeless, V. E., & Dierks-Stewart, K. (1981). The psychometric properties of the Bem sex-role inventory: Questions concerning reliability and validity. *Communication Quarterly, 29,* 173–186.

Wheeless, V. E., & Duran, R. (1982). *Sexual identity and flexibility as correlates to interpersonal competency.* Paper presented at the meeting of the International Communication Association, Acapulco, Mexico.

Wheeless, V. E., & Potorti, P. (1987). *Student assessment of teacher masculinity and femininity: A test of the sex role congruency hypothesis on student learning.* Paper presented at the Tenth Annual Communication, Language and Gender Conference, Milwaukee, WI.

White, B. (1989). Gender differences in marital communication patterns. *Family Process, 28,* 89–106.

Who's the boss? (1998, Dec 27). *Home New Tribune,* p. E1.

Wigutoff, S. (1982). Junior fiction: A feminist critique. *Top of the News, 38,* 113–124.

Wilcoxon, S. A. (1989). He/she/they/it?: Implied sexism in speech and print. *Journal of Counseling and Development, 68,* 114–116.

Wilder, G., Mackie, D., & Cooper, J. (1985). Gender and computers: Two surveys of computer-related attitudes. *Sex Roles, 13,* 215–223.

Wilford, J. N. (1994, March 29). Sexes equal on South Sea island. *The New York Times,* pp. C1, C11.

Will, J. A., Self, P., & Datan, N. (1976). Maternal behavior and perceived sex of infant. *American Journal of Orthopsychiatry, 46,* 135–139.

Willis, F. N., Jr., & Briggs, L. F. F. (1992, Spring). Relationship and touch in public settings. *Journal of Nonverbal Behavior, 16*(1), 55–63.

Willis, F. N., & Dodds, R. A. (1998). Age, relationship, and touch initiation. *Journal of Social Psychology, 138,* 115–123.

Willis, F. N., & Hofmann, G. E. (1975). Development of tactile patterns in relation to age, sex and race. *Developmental Psychology, 11,* 866.

Wilmot, W. W. (1987). *Dyadic communication,* 3d ed. New York: Random House.

Wolfe, L., & Rosser, P. (1997, March 30). It's time to close the SAT gap. *Chicago Tribune,* Section 13, p. 2.

"Women in American boardrooms: Through a glass, darkly." (1997, March/April). *Women in Management, 7*(3), 3.

Women on words and images. (1972). *Dick and Jane as victims.* Princeton, NJ: Author.

Wood, J. (1989). *Feminist pedagogy in interpersonal communication courses.* Paper presented at the Speech Communication Association, San Francisco, CA.

Wood, J. (1999). *Gendered lives: Communication, gender and culture,* 3rd ed. Belmont, CA: Wadsworth.

Wood, J., & Inman, C. (1993). In a different mode: Masculine styles of communicating closeness. *Journal of Applied Communication Research, 21,* 279–296.

Wood, J. T., & Lenze, L. F. (1991). Gender and the development of self: Inclusive pedagogy in interpersonal communication. *Women's Studies in Communication, 14*(1), 1–23.

Wood, W., Rhodes, N., & Whelan, M. (1989). Sex differences in positive well-being: A consideration of emotional style and marital status. *Psychological Bulletin, 106,* 245–254.

Woods, N. (1988). Talking shop: Sex and status as determinants of floor apportionment in a work setting. In J. Coates & D. Cameron (Eds.), *Women in their speech communities: New perspectives on language and sex* (pp. 141–157). New York: Longman.

Worell, J. (1980). New directions in counseling women. *Personnel and Guidance Journal, 58,* 477–484.

Yelsma, P., & Brown, C. T. (1985). Gender roles, biological sex, and predisposition to conflict management. *Sex Roles, 12,* 731–747.

Yaeger-Dror, M. (1998). Factors influencing the contrast between men's and women's speech. *Women and Language, 21*(1), 40–46.

Yogev, S., & Brett, J. M. (1985). Patterns of work and family involvement among single and dual earner couples. *Journal of Applied Psychology, 70,* 754–768.

Youniss, J., & Smollar, J. (1985). Adolescent relations with mothers, fathers, and friends. Chicago: University of Chicago Press.

Zucker, K. J., & Corter, C. M. (1980). Sex-stereotyping in adult–infant interaction: Some negative evidence. *American Journal of Orthopsychiatry, 50,* 160–164.

CREDITS

INDEX